FOREWORD
CARMELO EZPELETA

The 2015 FIM MotoGP™ World Championship was one that truly brought us almost every type of race and emotion imaginable as Jorge Lorenzo stormed to his fifth title in a sensational final race in Valencia.

When the red lights went out for the first race in Qatar, it looked like many of the 25 riders on the grid could challenge for the World Championship. We were kept on our toes all the way with four riders sharing the wins throughout, and many more gracing the podiums across the 18 rounds. In the end it came down to Valentino Rossi and Jorge Lorenzo to provide us with a final almost never seen before, with both keeping us on the edge of our seats until the chequered flag.

Repsol Honda's Marc Marquez had his first difficult season in MotoGP™, having to overcome numerous obstacles on his path to finishing third in the championship, as did his team-mate Dani Pedrosa, who finished the season in the kind of form we've come to expect from him in the past.

In recent years I have often spoken about a Ducati revival, yet this time it can truly be called a comeback, as both Andrea Iannone and Andrea Dovizioso put in some stunning performances on the GP15, only missing out on victory by a fraction on occasion. On that note I must praise the returning factories and riders of both Suzuki and Aprilia, both of which put their heart and soul into taking ever-greater strides.

Britain's Bradley Smith had his best-ever year on a MotoGP™ bike, scoring a podium alongside compatriot Scott Redding at the San Marino GP, whilst Cal Crutchlow's first year on a Honda was marked by his hard-fought podium in Argentina. His Australian team-mate Jack Miller also deserves a mention after a string of exceptional performances on his Honda, which saw him win the Open Class twice, including at his home GP in Phillip Island. With one young talent emerging on the Open Class Honda, another one parts, and I must give a big thank you to our long-serving 2006 World Champion, American Nicky Hayden, who will be plying his trade in the World Superbike Championship from next year. However, the Open Class title this year went to Hector Barbera with an excellent season on his Avintia Ducati.

Departing talent makes way for new talent, of which I'm pleased to say there is an abundance in the support classes. The intermediate Moto2™ category saw Frenchman Johann Zarco show his full potential in a record-braking season, where he took his first ever World Championship title in dominant style. His calmness under pressure in what is an extremely talented field has firmly established him as a rider to watch in the future. Alongside him on numerous championship podiums we have had the outstanding rookie Alex Rins and the title defender Tito Rabat, who will be stepping up to the top class next season.

The lightweight Moto3™ class had looked like it would be wrapped up early this year, though its unpredictability struck again. Miguel Oliveira took it down to the wire in Valencia, yet in the end it was Danny Kent who secured his first-ever title, and the first for Britain in 38 years. This, among the season-long onslaught by the likes of emerging talents like Enea Bastianini, Niccolò Antonelli, Jorge Navarro, Romano Fenati and many more, is an achievement to behold.

I also want to address the fact that the season did end amid controversy that showed a side of MotoGP™ that riders, fans and teams alike don't want repeated. All has now been dealt with, lessons have been learned, and in the future we don't expect to see a recurrence.

So I urge you to relive the season through the admiring eyes of fans who love the characters and the racing that has made this season one of the best championships in the world.

CARMELO EZPELETA
DORNA SPORTS CEO
NOVEMBER 2015

Published in November 2015

A catalogue record for this book is available from the British Library

ISBN 978-1-910505-09-0

Published by Evro Publishing, Westrow House, Holwell, Sherborne, Dorset DT9 5LF

Printed and bound in the UK by Gomer Press, Llandysul Enterprise Park, Llandysul, Ceredigion SA44 4JL

This product is officially licensed by Dorna SL, owners of the MotoGP trademark (© Dorna 2015)

Editorial Director Mark Hughes
Design Richard Parsons
Special Sales & Advertising Manager
David Dew (david@motocom.co.uk)
Photography Front cover, race action and portraits by Andrew Northcott/AJRN Sports Photography; side-on studio technical images of bikes (pp13–29) by Dorna; other technical images (pp13–29) by Neil Spalding

Author's acknowledgements
My thanks to all contributors for their hard work: Mat Oxley, Neil Spalding, Peter Clifford and photographer Andrew Northcott.
    At BT Sport: Keith Huewen, Gavin Emmett, Neil Hodgson and James Toseland
    In the paddock: Matt Birt, Nick Harris, Dean Adams, Mike and Irene Trimby and the staff of IRTA

www.evropublishing.com

CONTENTS
MotoGP™ 2015

It's time for
a challenge.

TISSOT PRS 516 AUTOMATIC.
A VERY SPECIAL PIECE WITH A VINTAGE
TOUCH THAT PAYS HOMAGE TO
RACING CARS. THE HOLES IN THE
STRAP INVENTED BY TISSOT
ILLUSTRATE THOSE OF
A STEERING WHEEL.
AUTOMATIC MOVEMENT
WITH UP TO 60 HOURS
OF POWER RESERVE.

T+ TISSOT THIS IS YOUR TIME

THE SEASON
MAT OXLEY

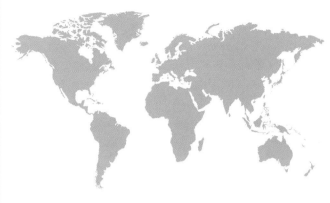

REVENGE OF THE SHARK

Rossi led nearly all season, but Lorenzo caught him at the last round amid conspiracy theories and oceans of bad blood

This introduction might have run under the headline 'The King of Circumstances defeats the Prince of Speed' if Valentino Rossi had won the 2015 MotoGP world title or 'The Prince of Speed beats the King of Circumstances' if Jorge Lorenzo had won it.

But either headline ceased to make perfect sense at the penultimate round of the championship at Sepang when Rossi unleashed his verbal attack on Marc Marquez, accusing him of assisting Lorenzo in the previous week's unforgettable Phillip Island encounter. The master of mind games had unravelled so many earlier rivals that perhaps this latest might help him win another world title. Surely it had to be some kind of ingenius double bluff, worthy of the most devious KGB agent.

It wasn't. And it had the opposite of the desired effect. A man like Marquez doesn't back down if you ask him to; instead he comes back at you harder. In the Sepang race his message was clear: if you think I was messing with you at Phillip Island, this is what it's like when I mess with you.

Rossi's reaction during the race was perhaps understandable but it was also unforgivable and it destroyed his championship chances. In effect he lost his chance to win a tenth world championship at 5pm on Thursday 22 October.

The reverberations from that press conference continued to be felt even after the season had ended. Many got dragged into the argument: the riders, their teams, Honda and Yamaha. At Sepang, security had to be called to prevent Rossi's fan club management from invading Marquez's pit. MotoGP may be one of the toughest sports on the planet but it has mercifully been spared such ugly scenes – until now.

At the final round at Valencia, even Bridgestone got sucked into the mire. Rossi needed the Repsol Hondas to take a 1–2 ahead of Lorenzo to have any chance of winning the

ABOVE Ducati Corse's new general manager Gigi Dall'Igna's redesign of the Desmosedici produced eight rostrums and two pole positions. Andrea Dovizioso finished second in the first three races

title. So when warmer-than-expected track conditions caused the Hondas front-tyre problems, the conspiracy theorists shifted into top gear. Social media had a lot to answer for in all of this, but it's an aspect of modern life to which MotoGP must get accustomed.

In the past, Rossi successfully played mind games with Max Biaggi, Sete Gibernau and others, his grinning persona always getting the upper hand. But of course there is another side to Rossi; you don't get to win nine world titles and more than a 100 GP wins by being a giggling clown. Former Ducati MotoGP rider Troy Bayliss once called Rossi 'a maniac' and former team-mate Colin Edwards said he was 'a sly fox'. Rossi is possibly the most intelligent rider of all time, but playing games with Marquez was a different proposition. MotoGP's most ruthless assassin finally met his match.

Rossi should have known what was coming after the pair collided at the final corner at Assen, where the Italian took the win ahead of the incandescent Spaniard.

The first mind games were played out during the post-race press conference and the subsequent pre-event conference at the Sachsenring. After smiling and shaking hands for the cameras, the pair never made eye contact. However, whenever Rossi spoke, Marquez was anxious to hear every word, then when the reigning champ spoke Rossi leaned back in his chair, eyes forward, ignoring his rival. Perhaps Rossi had got the upper hand. But then Marquez said this, 'Valentino is really smart and he taught us something. We must learn from it…'

Little did he know it at the time, but Rossi's stunning Assen move on Marquez laid the foundations of his own destruction. Sometime, somewhere, Marquez was coming to get him.

But let's not bury the enormity of the man's achievements

in the rubble of the final months of the 2015 season. Rossi may not have won the title but his campaign surely confirms his status as MotoGP's 'Greatest of all Time', ahead of Mike Hailwood, Giacomo Agostini, King Kenny Roberts and the rest. This was his 20th season as a GP winner, which places him way ahead of his fellow bike racers – and also ahead of pretty much everyone else in any sport. What really marks Rossi out as unique is his comeback from what seemed like terminal decline at Ducati to once again becoming a challenger for the title, and without any technical advantage over his greatest rival, Lorenzo.

There are particular stresses and strains in any contest within a team, just as there are with arguments within a family. There's even a word for it: internecine, meaning deadly, internal conflict. And that's what 2015 turned out to be: a year of dramatic twists and turns, on the track and off it, like never before.

After the first month of racing, Lorenzo seemed already out of the fight. Myriad problems kept him off the podium at the first three races: his leathers were too tight, his helmet lining came apart, he chose the wrong front tyre, and so on.

Before Jerez he sat down for a heart-to-heart with crew chief Ramon Forcada. 'Jorge prepared his pre-season very well, but then he was a bit confused – too many things to control,' Forcada explained. 'To get good results he needs everything to be in the right place.'

At Jerez Lorenzo began a unique reign at the front, leading each and every lap of the Spanish, French, Italian and Catalan GPs. It was some comeback and it bore testament to the Majorcan's warrior-like strength of will.

During the winter Yamaha had made various subtle improvements, most significantly a fully seamless gearbox, a mere five years after Honda had introduced the same technology to its RCV. Previously Yamaha riders had only had seamless upshifts, which kept the bike more stable exiting corners, but they lacked stability during braking, which is where Honda had dominated in earlier seasons.

The new gearbox changed everything. Rossi and Lorenzo were able to match Marquez on the brakes for the first time in years. At the same time Honda took a step back. The 2015 RC213V was lively and tricky to control, locking the rear into corners and spinning up on the exits. The fact that Honda was unable to fix the problem suggests it was an engine issue, most likely too little crankshaft flywheel mass. In the old days HRC would have had that sorted within a race or two, but current MotoGP regulations require all engines to be sealed at the first race – so there's no way to fix problems.

Marquez suffered most because his riding technique was already right on the very edge, squirming the front tyre to make the bike turn. Whenever the rear wheel locked and the tyre skidded, it overstressed the front tyre, either pushing him wide or throwing him off. It must have been a frustrating few months for the youngster, who was working towards an historic title hat-trick.

So the balance of power shifted from Honda to Yamaha, and after Marquez crashed at Termas de Rio Hondo, Mugello and Catalunya, the title duel changed, from Rossi versus Marquez to Rossi versus his team-mate.

The pendulum swung this way and that for the rest of the season, at times gently, at others ferociously.

Lorenzo was nearly always faster than Rossi but only nearly always. At Assen the Italian produced his first pole/victory double since Misano 2009, when he was on the verge of a fifth MotoGP crown. Two weeks later at the Sachsenring he again beat Lorenzo, who was off the

pace because the German track is so tough on tyres that Bridgestone didn't include his preferred 'soft-edge' tyre treatment in their rear slicks.

As the paddock went its separate ways for the summer break, Rossi had widened his advantage to 13 points, after Lorenzo had closed to within a single point at Catalunya. Two races later, after Lorenzo's Brno win, his first since June, they were dead level.

Lorenzo had the momentum and even Rossi admitted that he simply wasn't fast enough. 'We need to take another step,' he said.

And then came the weather. Rossi's victory in rain-lashed Britain was one of the greatest of his career, resisting Marquez lap after lap as they battled Silverstone's bumps and puddles. He was so fast in these conditions that Marquez crashed trying to keep up. Meanwhile Lorenzo struggled to fourth, partially blinded by a fogged visor.

A quarter of a century earlier Randy Mamola had lost the 500cc world title for the same reason, and he still remembers it. 'Trying to hold your breath at 170 miles an hour with your heart doing 150 beats a minute… I was furious.'

The weather would intervene twice at the next three races and each time Rossi bettered his rival, still the King of Circumstances.

And then the world championship went weird in Malaysia. The title fight changed complexion once again at Phillip Island, where Rossi accused Marquez of aiding Lorenzo in the race of the year. At Sepang Rossi continued on this theme, enraging his former fan and paying the price in the race. It wasn't Rossi's finest hour, even if you could see his point. However, while there are rules against riding dangerously, there are no rules against racing a championship contender.

BELOW LEFT, UPPER Maverick Viñales was a brilliant Rookie of the Year on the Suzuki, which was new for 2015

BELOW LEFT, LOWER Dani Pedrosa returned from career-threatening surgery to remind everyone that he still enjoys Alien status

BELOW RIGHT Danilo Petrucci finished in the top ten in his first season on the Pramac Ducati and his Silverstone rostrum was one of the feelgood stories of the year

Dani Pedrosa's win at Sepang, his second of the year, went largely unnoticed amid all the shouting and screaming, which for many fans soured the final two weeks of the championship. Pedrosa had another injury-blighted season, this time recurring arm pump that forced him to miss three races for surgery. On his return he was 15th in the championship but by season's end he was fourth. It was another impressive performance by MotoGP's unluckiest rider.

Pedrosa found the 2015 RCV a handful – 'It moves around a lot' – just as did Marquez and satellite Honda riders Cal Crutchlow and Scott Redding, who both mostly under-performed on the bike.

Crutchlow scored his only podium of the year in Argentina, with a brave, final-corner move on Andrea Iannone, who was undoubtedly the surprise of the year. Promotion to the factory team and a brace of GP15s transformed this wild young man into Ducati's strongest contender, well ahead of Andrea Dovizioso, riding his third season with the factory squad.

Iannone is possibly best known with many fans for the words on the back of his leathers – 'The Maniac Joe'. But fans have been confused, according to his manager Carlo Pernat.

'Andrea is not a maniac in riding,' says Pernat. 'He is a maniac of precision.' So it's all been a big misunderstanding? 'Yes,' adds Iannone. 'Always in my life I've wanted everything to be perfect – I'm that kind of maniac.'

Iannone's riding on the GP15 seemed to confirm that. He was smooth, fast and devastatingly aggressive; everything he hadn't been on the GP14. The difference was front-end feel; the GP14 had none, so Iannone crashed 14 times in 2014.

In 2015 he fell on just five occasions and may have beaten Pedrosa to fourth overall if he hadn't had two mechanical failures at the last four races.

Dovizioso, more circumspect than his younger team-mate, was almost always slower. After a stellar start to the season, which he explained away as a mirage caused by the best Honda and Yamaha riders still getting up to speed, he seemed to go backwards. The GP15 may have ended Ducati's spell as pitlane jokers but there was still plenty of work to do. At first both riders complained of a lack of corner-exit grip, then later on a lack of braking stability. As Dovizioso observed, if you make one area of the bike better, you will make another worse.

Like Iannone, Bradley Smith was another rider transformed. In 2014 the Briton had been the only rider to crash more than the Italian, but Smith went into 2015 with a different mindset. He slowly built up confidence and chipped away at the lap times. As a result he was the best satellite rider of the year and he left team-mate Pol Espargaro for dead. Espargaro – contracted directly to Yamaha, unlike Smith – had a very average second season in the class of kings. It's hard to see the Spaniard taking the next step to the factory team unless he can turn things around as Smith did.

Elder brother Aleix had a better time on the new Suzuki. Great things were not expected of the all-new GSX-RR but the bike surprised everyone. Although the in-line four lacked straight-line speed all year, usually to the tune of 7mph, its easy turning and sweet handling gave adequate compensation at some tracks. Espargaro said the bike's chassis character reminded him of a 250 – that's racing's highest compliment.

Even more impressive on the Suzuki was rookie Maverick

Viñales, who gave the team its best result of the year in Australia, where he finished less than seven seconds behind winner Marquez. Ironically, Phillip Island is MotoGP's fastest track but its fast, flowing layout hides a horsepower deficit better than anywhere.

This was Viñales' third different class in as many years: Moto3 champ in 2013, top Moto2 rookie in 2014 and top MotoGP rookie in 2015. His impressive acclimatisation in the class of kings suggests there's a gang of Moto2 and Moto3 youngsters who will soon be able to run with the best in the premier class.

Johann Zarco dominated Moto2 like no one since Marquez in 2012. The former Red Bull Rookies champ had exactly the right combination to work with Dunlop's very different 2015 front tyre – a Kalex chassis with WP suspension. And he had changed his technique to suit – gone was the hammer-and-tongs style he brought to Moto2 in 2012 and in its place was a much smoother ride that worked perfectly with the Dunlop front.

Even more impressive in Moto2 was newcomer Alex Rins, who took over from Viñales in Sito Pons' team and rode a rookie season that matched his compatriot's 2014 campaign.

Defending champion Tito Rabat struggled until Öhlins worked out how to get the best out of the latest Dunlop front at Aragón. But by then his crown had already gone.

There was burgeoning talent aplenty in Moto3 too. Danny Kent was a new man, dominating the first two-thirds of the season with an uncanny ability to be in the right place at the right time in a class where the podium was usually covered by a few tenths. Such was his speed and race-craft that he had MotoGP teams queuing to take him to MotoGP in 2016, just as HRC had done with Jack Miller. Kent turned down the offers and will return to Moto2 in 2016, this time with the

Kiefer team, who won the 2011 crown with Stefan Bradl.

Significantly, Kent was Britain's first motorcycling Grand Prix world champion since Barry Sheene in 1977. The 22-year-old is also the first British title winner since Dorna commenced its programme of helping non-Latins into MotoGP with Chaz Davies more than a decade ago.

Miguel Oliveira (the first Portuguese rider to win a GP), Enea Bastianini and Niccolò Antonelli were Moto3's other new names who shone brightly. Antonelli is a member of the VR46 Academy for young riders who will carry the torch for Rossi once the sport's greatest-ever exponent retires, a moment that can't be far away now.

ABOVE They got along at the start of the year – Rossi and Lorenzo share a joke

BELOW Lorenzo and Marquez maintained a friendly relationship, fuelling the conspiracy theorists

RIDERS' RIDER
OF THE YEAR 2015

Every rider who rode in more than one MotoGP race votes in our annual poll. This year's result is more different than ever from the official championship table

The rules are simple: list your top six MotoGP riders of the year and don't vote for yourself. The editor then tallies up the votes, scoring six points for a first place down to one point for a sixth.

As usual our unique poll has some fascinating differences from the world championship table, not least in the winner. For only the second time in 12 years (the previous occasion was 2006) the world champion isn't the top man in our poll – Valentino Rossi takes the honours despite not winning the title. Our poll had the two works Yamaha riders a long way clear of the pack, as there were only three riders who

didn't pick one of them as their favourite.

As this is a secret ballot, we cannot tell you who voted for whom, but there are some definite trends that we can report. As in previous years, when a world champion shows signs of fallibility, his vote plummets. It happened to Valentino in the Ducati years, and it happened to Marc Marquez this year. Amazingly, not one of Marc's rivals voted him number one. There was also a marked reluctance among Marc's fellow graduates of Moto2 to put him anywhere near the top.

Interestingly, there doesn't seem to be any correlation between nationality and voting patterns. It's noticeable, however, that Open

2nd JORGE LORENZO

3rd ANDREA IANNONE

4th MARC MARQUEZ

5th DANI PEDROSA

6th BRADLEY SMITH

7th MAVERICK VIÑALES

8th DANILO PETRUCCI

9th NICKY HAYDEN

10th CAL CRUTCHLOW

Class riders do tend to include a significant percentage of their fellows.

Among the riders with statistically significant numbers of votes, the man who comes out notably higher than his championship position is Andrea Iannone, who is third as opposed to fifth. One voter put him as high as second and four had him fourth, but he earned his high placing because all but three riders voted him somewhere in their top six. Surprisingly, his peers put him above both Repsol Honda riders despite both having won races – something Andrea has yet to achieve.

Marquez and Pedrosa are separated by only one point, which is nowhere near reflective of

their 36-point gulf in the championship. The other men highly rated by their rivals are Danilo Petrucci and Maverick Viñales.

There may be some sentiment at work in Nicky Hayden's ninth place. Unusually, the only man in our top ten who is in the same position as in the real table is Bradley Smith.

The vast majority of voters did as asked, although not everyone picked a full six, and some tried to sneak in riders from other classes. The most memorable response came from one of the year's notable under-achievers, who shall remain nameless. When asked for his top six he replied that he didn't want to vote. Actually, he said, 'I don't give a ****.'

2015 TOP TEN

1st	VALENTINO ROSSI	149
2nd	JORGE LORENZO	125
3rd	ANDREA IANNONE	70
4th	MARC MARQUEZ	63
5th	DANI PEDROSA	62
6th	BRADLEY SMITH	33
7th	MAVERICK VIÑALES	28
8th	DANILO PETRUCCI	15
9th	NICKY HAYDEN	9
10th	CAL CRUTCHLOW	8

It's the most extreme test of man and machine. MotoGP is the battleground and Yamaha the victors.
Jorge Lorenzo is champion. Yamaha has the team crown. And the YZR-M1 is the machine. But the real winners are those that ride with Yamaha and have choosen the multi award winning YZF-R1 as their steed. Because the living, breathing heart of the MotoGP inspired YZF-R1 is ready to fuse with yours.

The super lightweight 998cc superbike's 179kg body and 200ps mechanical soul are one with its aluminium Deltbox frame. The YZF-R1's M1 inspired electronic sensors and controls combined with the next generation 6-axis IMU give you total control to let your emotions ride free. The motorcycle is the rider, the rider is the motorcycle. Yamaha R1. We R1

www.yamaha-motor.eu/uk

 RAC YAMALUBE f

TECH REVIEW
NEIL SPALDING

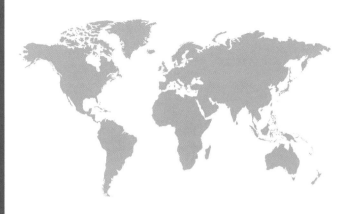

FIVE AGES OF BRIDGESTONE

From nowhere at the turn of the century, Bridgestone fought its way to the very top of motorcycle racing

Bridgestone had kept a low-level presence in racing for years, concentrating mostly on the Japanese championship, but in 2000, with the prospect of MotoGP raising the profile of motorcycle racing, the company decided to develop tyres to allow it to compete in racing's new top class.

TESTING AND RACING

The initial strategy included running a test team at many GP tracks to develop a good base tyre. Then, in 2002, with Erv Kanemoto and Nobuatsu Aoki, Bridgestone went racing, competing for a year with its own Honda NSR500. The first time the tyres went on a four-stroke was in 2003, on a Honda RC211V with Makoto Tamada. Tamada's time on Bridgestones saw a great improvement in their performance, culminating in a couple of wins in 2004. For 2004 Suzuki and Kawasaki decided to move over to Bridgestones, from Michelin and Dunlop respectively. Bridgestone now had three types of tyre for three types of bike. The company was learning fast, but none of its customers could realistically be regarded as championship contenders.

The 2004 season wasn't without its trials. There were a few instances of Bridgestone tyres losing tread at inopportune times: Kenny Roberts' Suzuki had tread delamination issues during pre-season testing in Sepang, Shinya Nakano's Kawasaki had a high-speed blow-out on the main straight at Mugello, and later that same day at Mugello Tamada also had tread delaminate. These incidents were a serious blow to Bridgestone's reputation but the company went back to its design team and started again. The new family of tyres that appeared just a few months later were heavier and stiffer, setting the design trend for Bridgestone for the next decade.

COMPETITION

Bridgestone was now in a classic Catch 22 situation, without
top-level teams and riders who couldn't win consistently – and
unless Bridgestone won consistently no one would take the
risk of running with them. Honda and Yamaha weren't about
to move – the Michelin system worked for them – and no one
in those factories wanted to take the risk of having their main
championship challengers sitting on unproven tyres.

Then along came Ducati. After its first two years of
MotoGP competition, Ducati could be considered a serious
player, and it had also deduced that the Michelins it had been
using were better suited to the Hondas and Yamahas, and
not its own bike. Ducati had also worked out that if Michelin
had a problem then both Honda and Yamaha would be
similarly affected. Ducati's decision to throw in its lot with
Bridgestone meant that it would benefit from tyres designed
and developed specifically for its bike. When Michelin had a
bad day, Ducati would be ready and waiting.

Michelin did have bad days, just as we all have bad
days. The dynamics of tyre competition are quite special,
and make a big difference to the whole motorcycle racing
story. Racing tyres are the ultimate specialisation in racing.
To get the very best from a race tyre, it will be operating on
exactly the surface it was built for, at exactly the right track
surface temperature and under exactly the right loads. Each
manufacturer has its own research into the racing surface of
each track, and ways of predicting how it will change before
the next race.

Given that the weather is beyond anyone's control, that
the track isn't going to change, and that the bike and rider
are only capable of limited changes on the day, the tyre
manufacturer is the one that makes the big difference. For
European races Michelin approached this problem by building

several different specifications, all of which it thought might
be good enough. These tyres were then distributed to
Michelin's contracted riders and their feedback was taken
over the first two days of practice. Michelin then analysed its
engineers' reports and built, on the Saturday evening, tyres
that were a combination of the most successful parts of the
various specifications. These tyres were then transported to
the circuit overnight in a Renault Espace.

There were enough special tyres for the top riders only;
the rest had to make do with the cast-offs from the test tyres
brought for practice. It therefore paid to be among the chosen
ones as far as tyre quality and competitiveness went. Clearly
being based in Europe was a massive advantage to Michelin,
but it was also clear that the company's race strategy and
business model didn't work for races outside Europe.

Ducati saw this business model as an opportunity. It was
on the verge of being really competitive with its 990cc V4,
but as things stood Ducati was on the same tyres as its major
opposition. New to MotoGP, Ducati saw an opportunity to
differentiate itself from its opposition, and knowing that
Michelin would be less competitive away from Europe
was a bonus.

To start the relationship on a strong note, Bridgestone
came up with some superb qualifiers for the tests at the end
of the 2004 season, and Ducati used them during closed-
season testing to set some particularly fast laps. Allowing
those times to be published may well have backfired on both
Ducati and Bridgestone, because it clearly stimulated Michelin
to come up with some new ideas. Although Bridgestone
increased the pace of its development, Michelin completely
dominated MotoGP in 2005 until the Motegi round in
early autumn. There, for the first time, Bridgestone had a
competitive factory bike on its tyres as well as the home

advantage, and away from home Michelin was weak. Ducati won at Motegi and again in the race that followed at Sepang. The gamble had paid off.

With Ducati on board, Bridgestone stopped making tyres for the Hondas. Everything was put into developing a tyre to beat Michelin, and that development came at a cost. Bridgestone had to make its tyres more than a week before each race and its database of circuit surfaces was only a couple of years old. The solution was to test at each circuit in the weeks before each race. Test teams were formed by each of Bridgestone's bike manufacturers and riders were hired, all at immense cost. But when combined with a technical effort to make tyres that would work well over a broad heat range, it started to bear fruit.

In 2006 Bridgestone-equipped Ducatis won four races. The first victory, Loris Capirossi's at Jerez, was a clear warning to Michelin, a Bridgestone win on territory that Michelin could have previously claimed as its own. Later in the year Capirossi also won at Brno and Motegi. Then Troy Bayliss stunned everyone by winning the end-of-season race at Valencia on a one-off ride. Bridgestone was now capable of winning regularly in Michelin's back yard.

DOMINATION

Then came the 800s. The step from 990cc to 800cc engines for 2007 meant that the bikes would work in a very different way. Instead of the flamboyant style of the 990s – big speed, driving deep into a corner, squaring off the corner, blasting out – the 800s encouraged higher speed at the apex of a corner, describing a bigger arc and working the edges of the tyres far harder.

New rules were agreed to reduce costs. Bridgestone's pre-race testing had to cease and Michelin lost the ability to deliver tyres to a circuit after the Thursday before the race. There would also be a cap of 31 tyres per rider per GP. Both the Bridgestone and Michelin riders had to request their choice of tyres on the Thursday afternoon, before a wheel was turned. This meant that Bridgestone's long-term concentration on tyres that could deal with a broad range of temperatures and conditions was starting to pay off. Dunlop was allowed to bypass these restrictions as it hadn't won a race for years, but there was the proviso that Dunlop, too, would have to adhere to the new regulations if it won two races.

Bridgestone's initial '800' tyres were brilliant, especially those developed for the Ducatis. Bridgestone had correctly assessed the likely change in riding style and its tyres were stiffer and more capable of taking the new cornering loads. The Ducati version worked particularly well, allowing Casey Stoner to fire the bike off each corner apex and carry the resulting speed all the way down the following straight. Bridgestone's tyres for Kawasaki and Suzuki, however, weren't quite as effective.

It took Michelin until mid-season to find a tyre specification that could compete, but by then the damage had been done. Valentino Rossi had seen enough of Stoner's ability to fire his bike down the straights to know he needed the same tyres for the following year. He didn't just want Bridgestones, he wanted Ducati-spec Bridgestones – and he got them after extended negotiation between Bridgestone and Yamaha.

During pre-season testing the new tyres worked well on the Yamaha, but it wasn't until the first race of 2008 at Qatar that their true characteristics were revealed. Yamaha and Rossi's crew chief, Jerry Burgess, initially set up their bike as if it was on Michelins and the Bridgestone tyres started to lose rear traction after just six laps. To maintain their grip, the Bridgestone rears needed more load on them than the

TOP Tohru Ubukata was Bridgestone's genius. Working with Ducati, he was responsible for the development of some very special tyres

ABOVE Several different factories used Bridgestones, all specially designed for them, but the Ducati versions were adopted as the control tyres

BOTTOM Once Rossi was using the Bridgestones designed for Ducati, he had to change the weight distribution so that the Yamaha worked like the rear-heavy Ducati

ABOVE With Michelin tyres, it was preferable for a bike to have front/rear weight distribution of 52/48, but the Bridgestones designed for the Ducati needed 48/52. Yamaha's solution was to move the rear axle forwards and also to extend the front

BOTTOM Jorge Lorenzo's style of ultra-smooth, long arcs relies on durable edge grip – Bridgestone has delivered

equivalent Michelins, just as they had on the Ducati for which they were designed.

Over the next four races the weight in Valentino's bike was moved backwards, the rear axle went forward, and the forks were raked out more. After three races a shorter swing arm arrived, and just as an experiment a new chassis that allowed the front wheel to be moved even further forward was tried for one session, but it wasn't needed. The original chassis, with the forks adjusted fully forward and also with additional offset, was just right. At the back, however, the shorter swing arm allowed a further 20mm of adjustment, and that proved invaluable. Rossi could now load up the tyres as if he was riding a Ducati.

Michelin started 2008 well with regular wins from Jorge Lorenzo and Dani Pedrosa as Rossi, Burgess and Yamaha worked out how to get the Bridgestone to give of its best in a Yamaha chassis and Ducati sorted out troublesome new electronics. Once Rossi and Stoner were back up to speed, however, Michelin seemed to drop the ball. By Brno it was going so badly with Michelin that Honda decided to swap Pedrosa to Bridgestone mid-season.

CONTROL

By the end of 2008 it was all over. Dorna felt that it wasn't acceptable to have one tyre manufacturer so dominant that half the teams couldn't get a look in, and therefore decided that for 2009 everyone would run on 'control tyres' from one manufacturer. Although Michelin still wanted to race, the French company didn't approve of the control-tyre concept and declined to put in an offer when the invitation came to submit a bid. Faced with a *fait accompli*, Bridgestone conceded to provide control tyres.

Bridgestone's decision was reached just as the world's stock markets crashed, and it's a pretty safe bet that had everything happened at a different time the deal would have been far harder to put together. Bridgestone decided to keep costs to a minimum and set the range at two types of slick tyre and one or two types of wet tyre. There would be different tyres to suit different circuits, but the basic construction was to be one of the 'Ducati' designs that had proved so successful for both Ducati and Yamaha in 2007 and 2008. The specific build was the thin-carcass, high-temperature version specially developed to deal with the long corners and heat of Catalunya. That decision was to have a major impact on several careers.

The first control-tyre race, the delayed 'Qatar wet race', was won by Stoner on the début of the carbon-chassis Ducati. That in itself was a notable event. Over the races that followed, however, it became obvious that the Ducati had problems – it wasn't heating its tyres sufficiently and crashes became commonplace. Yamaha seemed to understand the needs of the control tyres best, but its people were surprised that so much change was needed.

Bridgestone had made a tyre that was part of the problem, rather than the previous style of having been part of the solution.

The 2009 season was one of frantic activity as riders and factories worked out the differences involved in the control-tyre relationship and then tried to understand what the tyres needed, before having to try to deliver the chassis changes required for the best performance. Everyone was in totally uncharted waters. Until this point, teams had gone racing with their motorcycles and expected their tyre supplier to make tyres that would allow their bikes to work. Now that relationship was completely reversed.

From the perspective of making the introduction of a

control-tyre regime a fair competition, the choice of low heat retention was a very good one. Ducati had tyres that suited the engine layout of its bikes but not their dramatic change of chassis rigidity – that was up to Ducati to work out and resolve. The rest of the teams had tyres for which their bikes could be developed to suit. Given the massive change that control tyres represented, it was well managed. The cost burden, however, had moved, from being shared between the motorcycle manufacturers and tyre companies to being fully carried by the motorcycle manufacturers – and normally that isn't cheap.

As Ducati struggled to get tyre temperatures up, Honda was making new chassis. Two years would pass, however, before Honda was fully competitive again, and it is arguable that Ducati has only started to understand what was required in the more recent past. Stoner certainly could ride the rigid carbon-frame Ducati but he alone seemed to have the reactions to catch the front end as it started to fold.

There was one major issue with the chosen tyre specification – its designed-in tendency to reject heat. This guaranteed not only that everyone had to work on a new chassis set-up but also that the riders had to be very careful to keep the tyres under pressure and therefore hot. If a rider slowed down for just a few corners, most of the grip seemed to evaporate. Crashes on cold tyres became commonplace – and damaging.

FIDDLING AT THE EDGES...

Changing the specifications of a control tyre is fraught with difficulty. It's one thing to change to control tyres in the first place, but quite another to change the design once you have started. In a control-tyre environment the tyres design the bikes, so any change has to be well communicated and must happen during the off-season, as factories and teams have to redevelop their bikes to suit redesigned tyres.

In response to the issues brought by the cold-tyre grip problem, Bridgestone supplied new tyres for 2012. These had softer sidewalls so that the flexing of the tyre carcass generated heat. It was a major change and it didn't get unanimous support. In particular Honda was very upset, and HRC vice-president Shuhei Nakamoto at one point threatened to sue Bridgestone. Honda's worries were real and based on the packaging of its new 1,000cc bike. Typically, however, Yamaha found a quick fix, realising that the new tyres worked well if its bikes were made rather longer than before.

Honda's problem was much more serious. The new 1,000cc rules required that the bore of the new engines had to stay unchanged at 81mm, so any increase in capacity had to come from stroking the engine, and that in turn involved raising the cylinder heads by about 5mm. Honda didn't want to do this because it wanted to keep the height of the bike's centre of gravity exactly where it was. Honda's solution was to widen the vee of its engine, from 75 degrees to 90 degrees. This provided the desired lowering of the cylinder heads but made the engine slightly longer. It was a design that would have definitely worked on the 'old' control Bridgestones, but to be suddenly presented with a new and unknown tyre design just as that new engine was being débuted wasn't what Honda wanted to hear. By mid-season, however, Honda had a new chassis, one that worked better with the new softer-carcass Bridgestones. This episode underlines the mantra that 'the tyre designs the bike', and that includes the layout of the engine.

The next issue was the arrival in 2012 of the era of Claiming Rule Teams (CRT). The CRT bikes, which used less powerful Superbike engines, were a low-cost way of packing out grids. As they didn't stress the Bridgestone tyres sufficiently, CRT bikes always ran on the softest compounds. For 2013 Bridgestone made a special softer compound for these bikes that proved very successful.

For 2014 the CRT class was relaunched as 'Open MotoGP', with engines and bikes from the major manufacturers, and Honda pledged to support the new class by supplying lower-powered versions of its RC213V. At the last minute Yamaha joined in and supplied full-power MotoGP engines and chassis to the class, and that meant Bridgestone had to react again. Having made special softer tyres for the original low-powered CRT bikes, Bridgestone couldn't now allow those tyres to be used on the new 'full-power' Open bikes because they would be under far too much stress.

Bridgestone provided a clear distinction, therefore, between the softest tyre available for the Open Class and the factory category. The problem got worse when Ducati renegotiated its position to get permission to use the softest tyres too. To keep things safe, Bridgestone decided to make all of its tyres harder. The Open 'soft' would therefore be the tyre previously provided for the factory bikes, and so on.

As usual there was a knock-on effect. The new harder tyres for the factory MotoGP group badly affected edge grip and it wasn't until after the Mugello race that a slight revision to the edges of the tyres managed to get that edge grip back. It wasn't applied to all the hard tyres, however, and going into 2015 Bridgestone still used the old construction for several circuits.

Bridgestone's 2015 season was one of record-breaking performance. There were 11 new lap records, 13 new pole-position records, and 12 new race-time records. Bridgestone may have been about to leave, but the company was certainly going to make its successors work hard to go faster.

ABOVE Marc Marquez's style includes extreme lean angles for relatively short periods, but the rest of the time he takes his front tyre to the limit

THE BIKES

YAMAHA
YZR M-1 2015

Yamaha has perfected the step-by-step approach to racing development. Nothing is left untried and most of the time next year's bike is simply last year's made a bit faster. The factory understands slow, patient development. It isn't chasing top speed; it seeks the settings that allow the fastest possible lap times for as long as possible.

This year Yamaha addressed several 'problems' that have affected its bikes in recent years. Last autumn a seamless transmission that allows shifts both up and down the gears was introduced. The addition of seamless down shifts to the bike's repertoire greatly helped its corner entry. The first update was a chassis redesign that allowed both of Yamaha's top riders to have an overall 'feel' that they liked. Lorenzo's long, fast, arc style goes well with a stiff chassis; Rossi has a rather combative riding style and he prefers a more flexible chassis for its more forgiving nature. Yamaha responded by developing a new mainframe and two swing-arm designs: Lorenzo chose the stiffer version, Rossi went for the softer one.

Chassis development didn't stop there. This year's chassis was slightly longer for less load on the front tyre and had a reinforcing crease in the main-beam that improved braking stability without affecting anything else. By mid-season, however, a radical upgrade was introduced that seemingly reduced torsional stiffness (allowing more twisting) around the headstock area by reducing the beam to an I-section, all the while maintaining braking stability. Both works riders adopted the new piece immediately.

Engine performance was exemplary. Yamaha declined to get involved in a horsepower race and instead concentrated on easily usable power, as shown by the fact that Lorenzo was 18th fastest through the speed trap when he won at Mugello. The Yamaha engine simply works well: it's a development of the 990cc unit first seen in 2005, now with a narrower bore, pneumatic valve springs and an ability to finish races on 20 litres of fuel rather than 22.

Tech 3 also ran Yamahas. Pol Espargaro inherited a pair of early 2015 full works chassis and Bradley Smith used late 2014 items. Guy Coulon, Smith's crew chief, performed miracles setting up his bike so that its weight balance was similar to the longer works bikes. He did this by moving Smith's seat position rearwards, with revised foot-peg and handlebar positions.

1 The small lever under the handlebars operates the N-1-2-3-4-5-6 gearbox 'neutral gate'

2 Bradley Smith was moved back on his Tech 3 bike to get the right weight distribution

3 Slash cuts are in: supposedly better for mid-range, definitely better for aerodynamics

4 Jorge Lorenzo used a stiffer swing arm in combination with less stiff axle clamps

HONDA
RC213V 2015

Honda ruled 2014 with a bike that was both powerful and manoeuvrable, a perfect foil for the skills of its lead rider, Mark Marquez. The issue for Honda pre-season was to find a way to deliver more power to see off any attack from Ducati on the straights and to retain the handling that allows Marquez to work his magic. In that, it has to be said that Honda failed.

The Sepang tests saw four different motorcycles lined up for Marquez to test and in addition there were chassis options. Part of the problem was Marquez's ability to ride almost anything improbably fast, rather like his predecessor Casey Stoner. But another part of the problem was Honda's apparent inability to analyse what was required to help Marquez go even faster. Normally a factory would bring one new bike and a good example of the previous year's version; for Honda to have turned up at Sepang with four different bikes merely demonstrated some confusion as to the right design direction.

Both Repsol riders and the two customer teams were provided with machines of similar specification, but the Repsol riders rejected their new 2015 chassis almost immediately. By the time racing started both were on chassis that visually resembled their 2014 bikes, with 2014 fuel tanks and seats retro-fitted. After the first few races Honda provided Cal Crutchlow and Scott Redding with equipment similar to that used by Dani Pedrosa. The major problem once racing started, however, was an engine that was simply too aggressive in its power delivery. This specification was initially chosen as it offered the higher power levels thought to be needed to match the new Ducati on the straights and in the hope that its aggressive traits could be controlled electronically.

Marquez could ride the bike he had chosen, but his performances were more than a little erratic. Once Yamaha had its 2015 specification well sorted, it was obvious that the Honda wasn't right. Marquez lost a lot of points with some impetuous riding in the first few races in Europe, but by Catalunya Honda had accepted that something had to change. MotoGP rules freeze the factory teams' engine designs for the year so the only way out was to change things outside the engine core, and to make the chassis more forgiving. Marquez first got his smaller 2014 exhausts back and probably some changes to the inlets, then he got his old 2014 chassis back and several new, stronger swinging arms also arrived. These mods, along with better electronics introduced before the July cut-off, seemed to give Marquez a bike he could control, but it was clearly still on the edge, as demonstrated by his regular crashes.

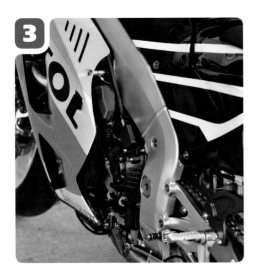

1 The long, large-diameter pipes of 2015 used on Honda's high-horsepower engine

2 The shorter, smaller pipes from 2014 used as part of the 'Marquez engine calm-down package'

3 Marquez was soon back on his 2014 frame…

4 Marquez's initial choice for 2015 – note the bend in the main beam

DUCATI
DESMOSEDICI GP15

After years of under-performing, this year was different. Gigi Dall'Igna had been hired from Aprilia specifically to get Ducati competitive again and Ducati Corse decided to build a completely new motorcycle. Building on the work of previous Ducati Corse chief Bernhard Gobmeier, the new bike was shorter at the front to put more weight on the front tyre. It achieved this with a completely repackaged engine and gearbox unit designed to be both as small as possible and with its various major components put in the optimal positions to get the correct weight distribution. Vitally, the front sprocket was put in the right place to allow the chain to play its important part in extending the suspension as power is applied when exiting corners.

The bike was an immediate success. It now turned in, something that Desmosedecis had always struggled to do. To make sure it did turn in, everything that could affect this area of performance was modified to maximise turn-in potential. Although the engine is a 90-degree V4, which is normally narrow enough not to have a problem with initial rollover into a corner, Ducati decided to reverse-rotate the crankshaft, a practice normally only used for wide in-line four-cylinder engines in order to reduce gyroscopic stability and hasten that roll in. The fairing cowl was redesigned to be as small as possible, with the smallest possible side area, all the better to reduce resistance to that same turn-in. The new chassis had more weight on the front, again to help turn-in.

That same concentration on making the bike turn into corners probably also made it a little unstable under braking, something that troubled Dovizioso especially. A solution came almost fortuitously: a set of small wings designed to improve high-speed stability at circuits like Mugello seemed to calm down the bike, and in all probability they merely mimicked the effect of a more conventional front cowl. As the year went on, Ducati discovered it could maximise off-corner acceleration with ever more wing area, but at the same time the bike seemed to lose its ability to turn in accurately. That same aerodynamic frontal weight bias that prevents wheelies appeared to be overpowering the front tyre going into quick corners. The Ducati is a work in progress, one that hasn't yet delivered on its initial promise.

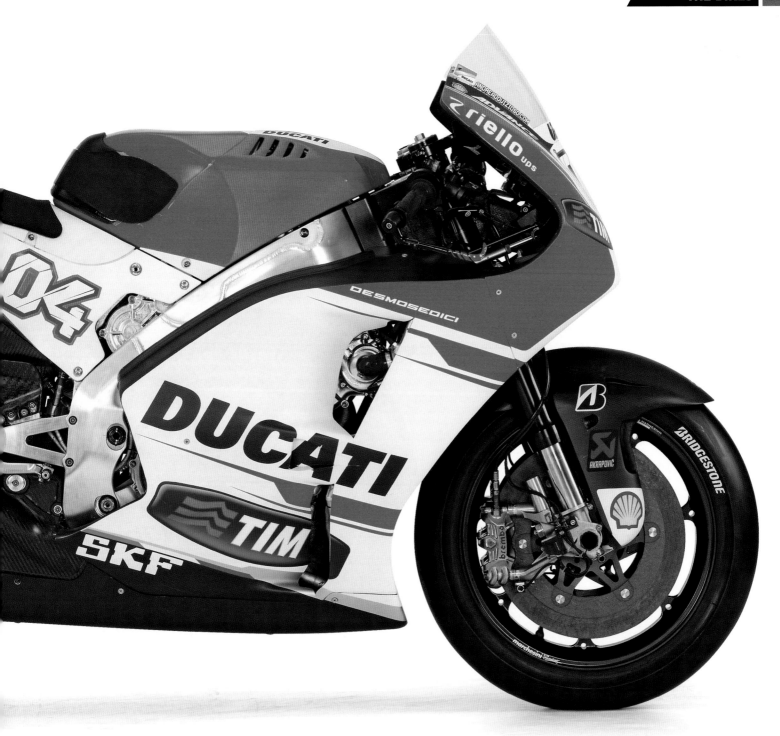

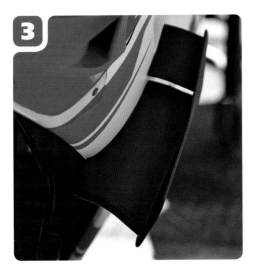

1 The later seat, stronger and with air scoops to keep the pipes cool

2 Shorted pipes led to a little bit of scorched carbonfibre

3 The Mk1 biplane wing; later versions were even bigger

4 Aerodynamic modifications were non-stop all the way through the year

SUZUKI
GSX-RR

Suzuki came back to racing with a new bike, one that had been exhaustively tested on MotoGP circuits for the previous two years. This was a new era for Suzuki: the bike is an in-line four, like the Yamaha, and has a reverse-rotating crossplane crankshaft, also like the Yamaha. The chassis is a very simple-looking twin-beam affair that, if anything, appears a little too spindly.

The bike was deliberately designed to handle well as a first priority, then to be fitted with several different power-up packages through the first year. Once the team's new riders actually got on the bike, it was noticeable just how well it worked in the corners, but they very quickly also highlighted its lack of speed and acceleration. A spectacular pole position at Catalunya greeted the first of the engine upgrades, but it soon became obvious that Suzuki would also need the seamless gearbox that so improved the performance of Honda and Yamaha into and through corners. The Catalunya bikes also benefited from a new, longer swinging arm to keep the bike stable with the additional power.

Suzuki's decision to spend several years away from the sport meant that the company lost some of the impetus in electronic development that regular competition brings, and it's quite possible that the timing of its return was based on the promise of common electronics packages for all by 2016. In addition to being out of competition for several years, Suzuki also had to change from its old (and preferred) Mitsubishi ECU to a Magneti Marelli system. That involved a complete rewrite of the team's MotoGP programming – not a small job for a factory with a tiny racing department.

A further engine upgrade arrived for Aragón, but it didn't get particularly good reviews from the riders. It had been expected that Suzuki would introduce the seamless gearbox at around the same time, but that development was delayed.

1 Suzuki celebrated 30 years of the GSX-R with a fabulous retro paint scheme

2 For the Jerez test Suzuki fitted a torque-monitoring device on Espargaro's bike

3 There was a thinner, more flexible top triple clamp after the initial tests

4 Different pipes came and went; the final versions were from Akrapovic

APRILIA
ART GP15

A prilia decided to develop its new MotoGP bike in public, a brave thing to do, and arrived with slightly modified 65-degree V4 RSV engines in a new chassis. The engines were superbike spec with pneumatic valve springs and beefed-up internals to allow 16,000rpm. Once through testing, the engines proved to be quite reliable, but they're very heavy by MotoGP standards, being based on a street design.

The chassis was based on the ART project bikes. By mid-season they were on their third version with new, much longer front engine mounts. More race-specific, and very adjustable, bodywork also arrived.

The electronics package started off as the works Aprilia superbike set-up, but developed as the year went on. By mid-season a new seamless gearbox was *in situ*, the basic design licensed from British firm Zeroshift, and new dry clutches were also fitted.

Progress was delayed while Marco Melandri went through the nightmare of not finding himself able to trust the tyres. His replacement, Stefan Bradl, was a great improvement, providing good feedback. Together with Alvaro Bautista, Bradl gave the project the direction that's absolutely vital to the development of a new bike.

The bike wasn't particularly powerful, but its main problem was being seriously overweight, by as much as 11kg. The new engine will be a wider vee for a better inlet system, smaller overall, and as much as 8kg lighter. The weight saving alone will make a massive difference.

1 The new Zeroshift seamless gearbox uses a little clutch slip to smooth gear changes, making set-up of the slipper clutch crucial

2 The 2015 Aprilia kept everything central; the ECU went under the fuel tank

3 Longer front engine mounts (compare with the first photo) turned up during the year

HONDA
RC213V-RS

This year's Hondas were a chassis and engine upgrade of last year's steel-valve-spring bikes. The formula was simple: add the power that was missing last year and watch while they go fast. It didn't quite work out, however, as team technicians found Dorna's control software way too complicated and the bike itself proved to be a bit of a handful to ride. Stopping seemed to be a particular problem with several riders complaining that it wasn't possible to set up the throttle system to generate any engine braking, the polar opposite to the works bikes, which seemed to have overly abrupt engine braking. The software for 2016 will hopefully make a big difference.

YAMAHA
M-1

Yamaha's efforts in the Open Class were again down to Forward Racing. The bikes were fast and seemed to be easier to set up than their Honda counterparts. The chassis and swing arms were a bit dated, so there was more weight on the front tyres than with the latest chassis, but they were at least the latest 'web design' with the front engine mount flowing into the main beam. Legal issues affecting the team principal distracted the team badly mid-season, and Stefan Bradl jumped ship to Aprilia. Ex-Kawasaki superbike rider Loris Baz kept going, however, and managed to finish second in the Open Class championship, proving that the Yamaha is easier to ride even if the electronics aren't quite the best.

APRILIA ART
ART GP14

The Aprilia ART didn't really develop that much from the bike used all the way through 2014. The main change was the use of one of the early Aprilia MotoGP chassis after the first few races of the season, with the very unusual 'cutaway beam' chassis (as shown in the photo) finally retired. The replacement looks as though it's virtually the same piece with the section of cutaway chassis welded back in. Engines continued to be the steel-valve-spring versions, guaranteeing maximum revs of around 15,500.

DUCATI
DESMOSEDICI GP14.1

There are a lot of ex-works Ducatis around, testament to the speed of development in Bologna. Avintia had the use of a pair of early 2014 bikes, which had the old 'L' engine held in the chassis as a 'V'. That meant the weight was still biased too far rearwards, even though some 70mm was cut out of the front of the chassis during its development. Ducati, however, had a far better idea of how to set up the Dorna control software than its Open Class opposition, probably because the team's main programs aren't so different.

THE CIRCUIT OF WALES

The Circuit of Wales is a £315m world-class motorsport and destination informed and inspired by nature and regeneration.

A business hub for high-technology excellence in the automotive and technology centres, the Circuit of Wales will provide:

- A state-of-the-art, purpose-built motorcycle Grand Prix circuit and facilities, attracting national and international motorsports

- A centre for low-carbon research and development, providing a base for leading educational institutions

- The home of advance manufacturing, precision engineering and automotive performance companies

- An elite indoor performance academy aimed at developing industry talent

- Leading educational, safety and training automotive infrastructure facilities

- A range of complementary Leisure & Retail offerings in the picturesque Rassau Valley

For further information contact
www.circuitofwales.com

THE RIDERS

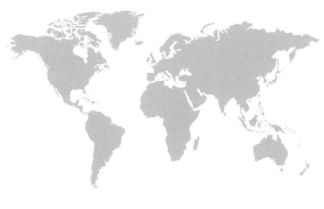

THE SEASON IN FOCUS

From the factory men to the wild cards, every MotoGP rider's season analysed

CHAMPIONSHIP

	Rider	Nation	Team	Points
1	Lorenzo	SPA	Movistar Yamaha MotoGP	330
2	Rossi	ITA	Movistar Yamaha MotoGP	325
3	Marquez	SPA	Repsol Honda Team	242
4	Pedrosa	SPA	Repsol Honda Team	206
5	Iannone	ITA	Ducati Team	188
6	Smith	GBR	Monster Yamaha Tech 3	181
7	Dovizioso	ITA	Ducati Team	162
8	Crutchlow	GBR	LCR Honda	125
9	Espargaro P	SPA	Monster Yamaha Tech 3	114
10	Petrucci	ITA	Octo Pramac Racing	113
11	Espargaro A	SPA	Team Suzuki ECSTAR	105
12	Viñales	SPA	Team Suzuki ECSTAR	97
13	Redding	GBR	EG 0,0 Marc VDS	84
14	Hernandez	COL	Octo Pramac Racing	56
15	Barbera	SPA	Avintia Racing	33
16	Bautista	SPA	Aprilia Racing Team Gresini	31
17	Baz	FRA	Forward Racing	28
18	Bradl	GER	Aprilia Racing Team Gresini	17
	Miller	AUS	LCR Honda	17
20	Hayden	USA	Aspar MotoGP Team	16
21	Pirro	ITA	Ducati Team	12
22	Laverty E	IRL	Aspar MotoGP Team	9
23	Nakasuga	JPN	Yamaha Factory Racing Team	8
	Di Meglio	FRA	Avintia Racing	8
25	Aoyama	JPN	Repsol Honda Team	5
26	Takahashi	JPN	Team HRC with Nissin	4
27	Elias	SPA	Forward Racing	2
	De Angelis	RSM	E-Motion IodaRacing Team	2

> "
> **To feel at one with the road.**
> Colin, 32, Liverpool

> "
> **I love adrenaline and I love to make my family proud.**
> Scott, 22, Gloucestershire

> "
> **To stay focused.**
> Tom, 42, Southampton

That's why I ride.

Why ride with Bennetts?

Recommended by riders[†] • 24 hour claims • Motorcycle insurance specialist
Common modifications covered as standard • Bennetts Exclusives Bonuses*

Get a new quote at **bennetts.co.uk** • 0330 018 5945

#thatswhyiride

Bennetts

1 JORGE LORENZO
MOVISTAR YAMAHA MOTOGP

Seven wins of near perfection made Jorge the most successful rider of the year and paved the way to his third top-class title, making a total of five across all classes.

When Jorge won, the rest had to follow; he was never headed in any of his victories. His wins included four in a row from Jerez to Catalunya that gave him a record total of 108 consecutive laps led, all achieved with total precision.

That precision was best exemplified by his lap for pole position at Valencia, a track at which he had never before set pole in any class. Massive lean angles, amazing corner-entry speeds, and precise, perfect lines allied to a smooth style that doesn't look fast unless you're using a stopwatch – yet Jorge was half a second quicker than

the Hondas on a track that shrinks time gaps. And it was done under extreme pressure.

Jorge started the season slowly. He didn't stand on the rostrum for the first three rounds thanks to a crash helmet malfunction, illness and his tyres, and was always playing catch-up. He did lead the championship briefly, on countback, after Brno, but slipped back at the very next round and came to Valencia seven points behind. Only two men had previously overcome a points deficit at the final round to take a title.

The finale was the best example of how he handled the pressure, for the most part, brilliantly. Yes, he did lose his cool after the Sepang Incident. Yes, he had a moan about tyres at a few races. But for the rest of the year he was simply unflappable.

NATIONALITY Spanish
DATE OF BIRTH 4 May 1987
2015 SEASON 7 wins, 12 rostrums, 5 pole positions, 6 fastest laps
TOTAL POINTS 330

2 VALENTINO ROSSI
MOVISTAR YAMAHA MOTOGP

To come so near a tenth world title and to win five races at the age of 36 against such tough competition was a triumph of motivation and skill.

If Valentino had succeeded, it would have sealed his legacy as the greatest we have ever seen. He has already regained the title once, in 2008 following his sequence of five consecutive wins, and after a two-year gap. Only a few men have regained – as opposed to retained – titles and only Agostini did it with a gap of more than one year. Valentino came close to regaining it after a six-year gap, which would have been a totally unprecedented feat.

As it is, we have to wait and see

again. The man himself says there's no difference between 36 and 37, and after the events of Sepang and the subsequent public wrangling, it's now clear that the rivalries with Lorenzo and Marquez are deeply personal. Valentino's problem is that he's no longer the unbeatable force he was, and Jorge and Marc are not Biaggi and Gibernau.

There were times when Rossi rode as well as he's ever done, and his mastery of tricky tracks and his ability to adapt to circumstances were never better illustrated than at Silverstone. But the stress showed, especially after he couldn't lay a glove on Marquez or Lorenzo at Brno and, crucially, at

NATIONALITY Italian
DATE OF BIRTH 16 February 1979
2015 SEASON 4 wins, 15 rostrums, 1 pole position, 4 fastest laps

3 MARC MARQUEZ
REPSOL HONDA TEAM

NATIONALITY Spanish
DATE OF BIRTH 17 February 1993
2015 SEASON 5 wins, 9 rostrums, 8 pole positions, 7 fastest laps
TOTAL POINTS 242

The reigning champion knew what was going to happen from the very first test of the season. Honda had produced a bike with a 'light-switch' motor. It locked the back wheel when he closed the throttle and spun the rear uncontrollably when he opened it.

Marc won only one race in the first half of the year and that was in Texas, a track where he has never failed. The nadir of his year came with back-to-back crashes at Mugello and Catalunya, the second an almost casual throwaway of his bike on the third lap, ostensibly while trying to pass Lorenzo. Honda responded and, with gritted teeth, gave him back his 2014 chassis, which with a few modifications at least let him ride even if he couldn't replicate the flick-it-in-with-the-back-wheel-in-the-air style of last season.

It wasn't a fix though. Crashes at Silverstone in the wet and then another early one at Aragón wiped out whatever small chance of a championship hat-trick remained. Marc simply couldn't push as he wanted to, especially early in a race.

He did manage to win five races but he also crashed in six, an indication of just how serious his machinery problem was. The last crash was after contact with Rossi in Malaysia, an incident that looks to have soured their relationship for the foreseeable future.

Marc says that he has learned now that sometimes third or fourth places are fine, and it isn't always possible to go for the win or even the rostrum. If he really does think that, then his opposition will be very, very nervous about 2016.

4 DANI PEDROSA
REPSOL HONDA TEAM

NATIONALITY Spanish
DATE OF BIRTH 29 September 1985
2015 SEASON 2 wins, 6 rostrums, 1 pole position
TOTAL POINTS 206

For a man who thought his career could be over after the first race of the year, Dani had a great season. The arm-pump problem that had been afflicting him for over a season returned and he missed three races searching for a cure. As he'd already had two unsuccessful operations, he chose a radical – even speculative – procedure that involved removing the whole muscle sheath as opposed to splitting it to relieve the pressure.

He returned to racing in France, where he crashed but got back on and ran an impressive race pace. Two races later he was back on the rostrum at home in Catalunya.

That looked to be his level, but then in Aragón he engaged Rossi in a ferocious battle for second place and emerged on top. Next time out in

Japan, he won for the first time in over a year and then repeated the medicine in Malaysia, where he set pole and was never headed.

Like his team-mate, Dani also struggled with the Honda in early laps, despite his very different riding style and using a significantly different chassis. However, by the end of the year there was no doubt that the old Pedrosa was back; he was still an Alien.

Dani was also the only one of the top men who emerged from the unsavoury end-of-season events with his dignity intact and his reputation enhanced.

Can Pedrosa finally go through a season uninjured and mount a championship challenge in 2016? Judging by his form in the last five races of this year, why not?

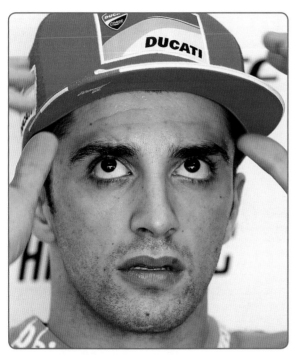

5 ANDREA IANNONE
DUCATI TEAM

NATIONALITY Italian
DATE OF BIRTH 9 August 1989
2015 SEASON 3 rostrums, 1 pole position, 1 fastest lap
TOTAL POINTS 188

The artist formerly known as Crazy Joe reinvented himself as a model professional. In his first season as a factory rider, Iannone got on the rostrum at the very first race and had a lowest dry-weather finish of sixth place.

He made one mistake all season, crashing while pushing to stay with the Hondas at the very last race of the year. His other two non-finishes were due to mechanical problems not of his making, and the reason he lost fourth place overall to the charging Pedrosa at the end of the year. Along the way the leadership of the factory Ducati team moved from Andrea Dovizioso's side of the garage to his.

The highlight of his year was pole and second place (his best result) at home at Mugello, in front of Rossi.

His best race was the Australian GP where he unleashed the top speed of the Desmosedici to fine effect but also made passes at both fast and slow corners, including a very hard pass on Rossi on the last lap.

All this was achieved with a very nasty shoulder injury sustained at a Mugello test. It dislocated again when he was out running and Andrea required surgery immediately after the post-season Valencia test.

If Ducati can adapt its bike to the new control tyres and refine what was a totally new design for this season, and if Andrea can be fully fit for the start of the 2016 season, he seems the most likely man to give Ducati that elusive victory.

The ex-Crazy may even have what it takes to join the Aliens.

6 BRADLEY SMITH
MONSTER YAMAHA TECH 3

Twelve months ago, some considered Bradley Smith lucky to have hung on to his job with Tech 3. This year he repaid the team's faith with a stellar season in which he scored points at every race and always finished within the top ten. He ended the season as top satellite rider by a distance.

His team-mate Pol Espargaro beat him only three times. That matters, as Pol is employed directly by Yamaha and Bradley by the

finish of second place at Misano. He achieved it by staying out on slicks for the whole race while the rest of the field changed bikes twice as the rains came and went. He was stone last at one point, circulating at something like 20 seconds a lap slower than the front-runners on treaded tyres. It was a remarkable feat of bike control, concentration and self-belief. Along with Pol and factory tester Nakasuga, Smith also won the Suzuka Eight Hours for Yamaha.

7 ANDREA DOVIZIOSO
DUCATI TEAM

NATIONALITY Italian
DATE OF BIRTH 23 March 1989
2015 SEASON 5 rostrums, 1 pole position
TOTAL POINTS 162

Dovi started the year as the clear number one rider for the Ducati factory and underlined his status with second places in each of the first three races. Then an electrical glitch at Jerez interrupted his progress before he got back on the rostrum with third place in France.

After that things started to go wrong. In the next four races he suffered two mechanical problems and fell twice. A Dovizioso crash is a very rare thing so these two seemed to indicate serious problems. It must be remembered that the Desmosedici was a new design for the 2015 season that turned a wheel for the first time at the second Sepang test, so the early-season form of Dovi and the new bike was deeply impressive.

So what went wrong? After the summer break, Dovi returned to the rostrum just once, and that was in the wet at Silverstone. More often than not he was fifth or sixth, but not in touch with the front group. The low point was 13th in Australia while his new team-mate Andrea Iannone battled in the lead group. Dovi was back to the old Ducati problem of the bike not turning.

Even his soft-tyre-assisted qualifying went downhill. After pole position at Qatar, he was on the front row three more times, but the last time was at Mugello. After the summer break his best efforts only put him on the second row, and only twice.

One of Ducati's jobs over winter is to restore Andrea's faith in the Desmosedici. After that Dovi's job will be to catch up with his team-mate.

8 CAL CRUTCHLOW
LCR HONDA

NATIONALITY British
DATE OF BIRTH 29 October 1985
2015 SEASON 1 rostrum
TOTAL POINTS 125

No-one riding a Honda had an easy year, and Cal was no exception. He knew from the first test that the bike would be 'difficult'. Three front-end crashes in a row from France to Catalunya give an indication of just how difficult.

The trouble with being on a satellite team is that you're unlikely to get much help through the season. There were also problems with the team's naming sponsor hitting legal problems, so halfway through the year Cal was riding for plain old LCR Honda.

He was, however, responsible for one of the best moments of the year, a beautifully calculated last-corner move on Iannone in Argentina to take third place, Cal's only rostrum of the year. He looked set for at least third at Silverstone too, a track that's never

been kind to Cal, only to be skittled by his team-mate. Valencia was the other race where Cal's practice and qualifying promised at least fourth place, but his number-one bike developed a fault on the grid and he started the race from the back on his second machine.

He didn't have any front-row starts but there were eight second-row qualifications. Not a lot of luck went his way this season.

The good news is that for the first time in three years Cal is going to stay with the same team for another season. He has a very experienced race engineer in Christophe Bourguignon and Lucio Cecchinello runs a model satellite team. That consistency can do no harm, and provided Honda does its bit Cal should have a better time in 2016.

9 POL ESPARGARO
MONSTER YAMAHA TECH 3

NATIONALITY
Spanish

DATE OF BIRTH
10 June 1991

TOTAL POINTS
114

Pol's second year in MotoGP didn't deliver as expected. He didn't once start on the front row or finish on the rostrum, and he was comfortably out-performed by his team-mate Bradley Smith. As Pol is contracted directly to Yamaha he received some machinery updates, whereas Smith is a team employee and didn't – so this makes next year crucial for Pol. Will he do as Smith did in his third year in the class and deliver? Pol certainly believes the change to Michelins will aid his cause. All the top riders' contracts are up for renewal at the end of the 2016 season and Pol must perform if he's to become a factory rider.

10 DANILO PETRUCCI
OCTO PRAMAC RACING

NATIONALITY
Italian

DATE OF BIRTH
24 October 1990

2015 SEASON
1 rostrum

TOTAL POINTS
113

One of the surprises of the year. Having slimmed down for his first year on a satellite team bike, Danilo delivered in spectacular fashion. The highlight was his second place in the wet at Silverstone where he harassed Rossi for the lead, but he was top Ducati rider again at San Marino and Malaysia as well as a permanent threat to the established order in qualifying, where he used the soft tyre to good effect. Fifth at Indianapolis was his best grid position. And it was all done with great good humour and a permanent smile. Watch him next year.

11 ALEIX ESPARGARO
TEAM SUZUKI ECSTAR

NATIONALITY
Spanish

DATE OF BIRTH
30 July 1989

2015 SEASON
1 pole position

TOTAL POINTS
105

Ostensibly the lead rider in Suzuki's return, Aleix never gave less than 100 per cent and was rewarded with pole position at home in Barcelona as well as two other front-row starts. His best finish was sixth place. The second half of his season was more difficult as the Suzuki's lack of a seamless gearbox and some top-end horsepower was shown up more and more. However, both rider and bike performed in excess of most people's expectations and Aleix was always combative. The only thing he has to worry about is his team-mate, who was delivering results on a par with Aleix's by season's end.

12 MAVERICK VIÑALES
TEAM SUZUKI ECSTAR

NATIONALITY
Spanish

DATE OF BIRTH
12 January 1995

TOTAL POINTS
97

We knew he was good, but not that good. The Rookie of the Year moved up to MotoGP after just one season in Moto2 to join Suzuki's return to racing. Frankly, not many people thought it was a good career move, but they were all wrong. By Catalunya Maverick was on the front row, finishing sixth. By Brno he was racing with the satellite Yamahas. By the end of the season he was looking like the faster man in the Suzuki garage. There haven't been many better rookie seasons, and by the end of next year he will be at the top of the factory teams' shopping lists.

13 SCOTT REDDING
EG 0,0 MARC VDS

NATIONALITY
British

DATE OF BIRTH
4 January 1993

2015 SEASON
1 rostrum

TOTAL POINTS
84

It's difficult to put a gloss on what was a disappointing season that saw Scott's target of top-ten finishes achieved only five times. The highlight for him was third place in mixed conditions at Misano, while his next best result was sixth in the wet at Silverstone. In the dry, however, he never found confidence or feeling with the bike. Part of the problem may have been down to both team and rider never having previously run a factory bike, and there was a rookie crew chief. In 2016 Scott will ride for Pramac Ducati on a bike that will fit him better and suit his style.

14 YONNY HERNANDEZ
OCTO PRAMAC RACING

NATIONALITY
Colombian

DATE OF BIRTH
25 July 1988

TOTAL POINTS
56

Rode the 2014 Ducati but didn't really improve on his impressive first year with the Pramac team. Yonny's career-best finish of seventh came in 2014, while his best in 2015 was eighth. He twice qualified fifth thanks to bravery on the soft tyre, but only managed a top-ten finish five times (a slight improvement on 2014), four of those before the summer break. Scott Redding will take his ride in 2016, but Yonny has another year left on his factory Ducati contract and has been placed in Aspar's team, which will be moving back to Ducati. Another rider for whom next season will be crucial.

15 HECTOR BARBERA
AVINTIA RACING

NATIONALITY
Spanish

DATE OF BIRTH
2 November 1986

TOTAL POINTS
33

This was the last year of the race-within-a-race that started with CRT and is now thankfully extinct. The Open Class bikes used Dorna's unified software, with Avintia Ducatis and Forward Yamahas leading the way ahead of customer Hondas. Hector fought off a challenge from Loris Baz and won the class eight times. His season was a model of consistency, something that wouldn't have seemed very likely for him a couple of years ago. He failed to finish only once and was outside the points just five times in a field containing 17 factory-option bikes – so some weekends it wasn't easy to score a point.

16 ALVARO BAUTISTA
APRILIA RACING TEAM GRESINI

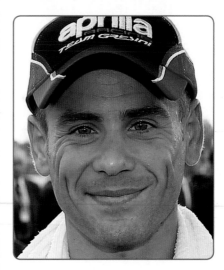

NATIONALITY
Spanish

DATE OF BIRTH
21 November 1984

TOTAL POINTS
31

Led the Aprilia factory's comeback, a year earlier than originally planned and with a bike that was more superbike than MotoGP machine. It didn't get a dry clutch until after the summer break, although a seamless gearbox arrived impressively early. Despite the bike being seriously overweight and lacking power, Alvaro scored points an impressive 13 times and only failed to finish once. Those who thought he'd fade away after his years on top machinery were very wrong. The highlights were two tenth places in very different races: first at a scorching Catalunya (where he stayed upright in a crash fest) and then at a soaking Silverstone (where his experience told).

17 LORIS BAZ
FORWARD RACING

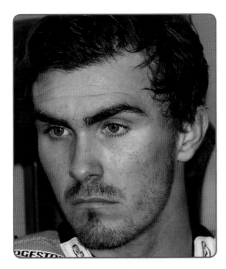

NATIONALITY
French

DATE OF BIRTH
1 February 1993

TOTAL POINTS
28

The tall Frenchman had an impressive rookie year. In the Open Class Loris was the only man to give Hector Barbera a hard time and he even led that championship after San Marino, where he rode brilliantly to fourth place, only a few seconds off the rostrum. There were also six other points-scoring rides. All this has to be seen against the background of turmoil within his team, Forward Racing, which meant that he missed the Indianapolis GP. The team won't be back in MotoGP next season but Loris will be, on a Pramac Ducati alongside Scott Redding. It'll fit him a bit better than the Yamaha.

18 STEFAN BRADL
APRILIA RACING TEAM GRESINI

NATIONALITY
German

DATE OF BIRTH
29 November 1989

TOTAL POINTS
17

Stefan started the year with Forward Racing on a Yamaha M-1 but jumped ship when the team's legal troubles started. After breaking his wrist at Assen, he missed his home race, then reappeared at Indianapolis as an Aprilia rider, replacing Marco Melandri. Stefan promptly out-qualified his new team-mate, Alvaro Bautista, and kept doing so, although the Spaniard outraced him everywhere except Malaysia. Aprilia was delighted with its surprise signing and his excellent technical feedback. The factory promptly retained him for 2016, when he and Alvaro will have a proper GP bike, not the modified superbike of this year.

19 JACK MILLER
LCR HONDA

NATIONALITY
Australian

DATE OF BIRTH
18 January 1995

TOTAL POINTS
17

Jack stepped up from Moto3 to MotoGP without bothering with Moto2. Was it a good idea? Well, he finished above all other riders on customer Hondas, scoring points in six races and winning the Open Class at home in Australia. Would it have been reasonable to expect anything more? Probably not. The loss of the LCR team's main sponsor didn't help, and in 2016 the team will only run one bike – for Cal Crutchlow. As Jack is contracted directly by Honda, he has been placed for next season with the Marc VDS team, alongside rookie Tito Rabat. So far he has done very little wrong.

20 NICKY HAYDEN
ASPAR MOTOGP TEAM

NATIONALITY
American

DATE OF BIRTH
30 July 1981

TOTAL POINTS
16

The 2006 world champion bowed out of MotoGP with a year on Aspar's customer Honda. There were still doubts about his wrist, but Nicky twice finished top of the Open Class, at Le Mans and Silverstone. He now moves on to the World Superbike Championship with Honda, with an eye on the target of becoming the first man to win world titles in both series. It's a measure of the regard in which Hayden is held that he was inaugurated as a MotoGP legend at the final GP of the year. MotoGP's loss is very much World Superbike's gain – and there won't be an American rider in the paddock next year.

21 MICHELE PIRRO
DUCATI TEAM

NATIONALITY Italian
DATE OF BIRTH 5 July 1986
TOTAL POINTS 12

Ducati's test rider had his three scheduled wild-card appearances at the two Italian rounds and Valencia. He scored points twice with an impressive eighth at Mugello his best finish.

22 EUGENE LAVERTY
ASPAR MOTOGP TEAM

NATIONALITY Irish
DATE OF BIRTH 3 June 1986
TOTAL POINTS 9

His rookie year in MotoGP, and on a difficult bike. Eugene's best finish was 12th at Catalunya but his best ride was 14th at Aragón, where he was top Open Class finisher.

23 K. NAKASUGA
YAMAHA FACTORY RACING TEAM

NATIONALITY Japanese
DATE OF BIRTH 9 August 1981
TOTAL POINTS 8

By far the most impressive wild card, Yamaha's factory tester finished eighth at home in Japan on what looked like a 2016 model M-1. Won the Suzuka Eight Hours with Pol Espargaro and Bradley Smith.

24 MIKE DI MEGLIO
AVINTIA RACING

NATIONALITY French
DATE OF BIRTH 17 January 1988
TOTAL POINTS 8

His second season with Avintia wasn't much easier than the first, and he scored one point less than in 2014. The 125cc world champion of 2008 moves on to be an Aprilia test rider.

25 HIROSHI AOYAMA
AB MOTORACING

NATIONALITY Japanese
DATE OF BIRTH 25 October 1981
TOTAL POINTS 5

Now HRC's test rider, Hiro acted as a replacement rider twice; first for Dani Pedrosa in the factory team and then on Karel Abraham's customer bike, scoring points once in four rides.

26 T. TAKAHASHI
TEAM HRC WITH NISSIN

NATIONALITY Japanese
DATE OF BIRTH 26 November 1989
TOTAL POINTS 4

Honda's young gun, twice a winner of the Suzuka Eight Hours, made his MotoGP début as a wild card at Motegi and finished 12th on an RCV with Nissin brakes and Showa suspension. Impressive.

27 TONI ELÍAS
FORWARD RACING

NATIONALITY Spanish
DATE OF BIRTH 26 March 1983
TOTAL POINTS 2

Replaced Abraham at Indianapolis and reappeared as a Forward Racing rider for the last five races of the year. The ex-Moto2 world champion had one points-scoring ride in Malaysia.

28 ALEX DE ANGELIS
E-MOTION IODARACING TEAM

NATIONALITY Sammarinese
DATE OF BIRTH 26 February 1984
TOTAL POINTS 2

Managed the small miracle of two points-scoring rides on Ioda Racing's old ART before having a horrible accident in Japan. Despite multiple fractures, he was back in the paddock in Valencia.

KAREL ABRAHAM
AB MOTORACING

NATIONALITY Czech
DATE OF BIRTH 2 January 1990

Started the year on a customer Honda with Nissin brakes and Showa suspension. Had nearly got it sorted when a crash at Catalunya broke his foot badly and ended his season.

KOUSUKE AKIYOSHI
AB MOTORACING

NATIONALITY Japanese
DATE OF BIRTH 12 January 1975

Honda's veteran superbike star replaced the injured Karel Abraham at Motegi and finished 19th – pretty impressive at 40 years of age. More than likely his last GP appearance.

CLAUDIO CORTI
ATHINA FORWARD RACING

NATIONALITY Italian
DATE OF BIRTH 25 June 1987

Claudio was an injury replacement in the Forward team for Bradl at the Sachsenring and was then given the ride after the German moved to Aprilia. After three races, 'Shorts' was then himself replaced by Elias.

DAMIAN CUDLIN
E-MOTION IODARACING TEAM

NATIONALITY Australian
DATE OF BIRTH 19 October 1982

Damian rode the Ioda ART in Japan and Malaysia as replacement for de Angelis after the San Marino rider was hurt in Japan. Got the go-ahead only after it was clear that de Angelis was recovering well.

MICHAEL LAVERTY
APRILIA RACING TEAM GRESINI

NATIONALITY British
DATE OF BIRTH 7 June 1981

Aprilia's test rider stood in at short notice at the German Grand Prix after Marco Melandri left the team – the MotoGP race didn't coincide with Michael's British Superbike Championship duties.

MARCO MELANDRI
APRILIA RACING TEAM GRESINI

NATIONALITY Italian
DATE OF BIRTH 7 August 1982

Seconded from Aprilia's World Superbike Championship team against his will. Predictably suffered horribly, never qualifying with more than two bikes behind him nor getting remotely near a point.

BROC PARKES
E-MOTION IODARACING TEAM

NATIONALITY Australian
DATE OF BIRTH 24 December 1981

Broc was the second of the veteran Aussie guns for hire to get a ride on Ioda's ART. He deputised for the convalescing Alex de Angelis at the final race of the year at Valencia.

ANTHONY WEST
AB MOTORACING

NATIONALITY Australian
DATE OF BIRTH 17 July 1981

After being sacked by his Moto2 team following Misano, Ant rode Karel Abraham's AB Cardion customer Honda at the last three races of the year but wasn't able to score any points.

AUTODROMO INTERNAZIONALE DEL
MUGELLO

Gran Premio d'Italia TIM
22 Maggio
2016

Tickets: www.ticketone.it

Info: www.mugellocircuit.it Mugello Circuit MugelloCircuit

THE RACES

COMMERCIAL BANK GRAND PRIX OF QATAR
LOSAIL INTERNATIONAL CIRCUIT

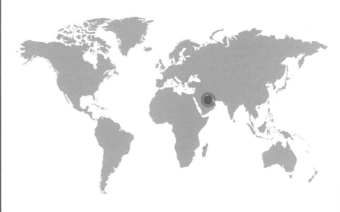

TALES OF THE UNEXPECTED

Valentino Rossi won the season opener, followed by two Ducatis as Honda hit problems

It would be wrong to call Valentino Rossi's victory unexpected. After all, he has three victories in Qatar on his CV plus second places for the past two years. Last season he was beaten by Marc Marquez by just over a quarter of a second, having started from tenth on the grid. Although Qatar can be an unreliable form guide, Rossi hadn't been off the podium since Japan 2014 and to see him win a close fight after starting eighth definitely wasn't a quirk. It was exhilarating and it was fantastic to watch, but it wasn't surprising – unlike just about everything else that happened.

For starters, Rossi was chased over the line by Andrea Dovizioso, who set his personal best lap of the race on the final lap on Ducati's new Desmosedici. It was a measure of just how improved the Ducati was that Dovi, rather than being ecstatic with a result he couldn't have dreamed of over the previous two seasons, was mildly disappointed that he didn't win. The new Ducati, it's worth remembering, was first seen in public at the second Sepang pre-season test and was effectively a complete redesign of the 2014 model. Gigi Dall'Igna, who was installed as general manager of Ducati Corse the previous season, looked on calmly as Andrea Iannone made it a near-perfect début with his first podium in MotoGP. This wasn't just a result of Dall'Igna's undoubted engineering prowess, but also reflected his skills as a manager of the talent he found when he joined the Bologna factory.

The other brand-new bike, the Suzuki GSX-RR, also surprised everyone. Following some embarrassing blow-ups in testing, it was glacier-slow in a straight line but Aleix Espargaro and Maverick Viñales both scored points. There was talk of a faulty batch of components

ABOVE Suzuki's new GSV-RR surprised everyone and both riders scored points – this is Aleix Espargaro in typical pose

RIGHT Marco Melandri returned to MotoGP with Aprilia but it wasn't a happy reunion

OPPOSITE Marc Marquez runs wide at the very first corner of the year – and the pattern for Honda's problems is set

causing those testing failures, but it was blindingly obvious that Suzuki was being very cautious with its power settings. Riders of other marques reported that there was nothing wrong with any other aspect of the Suzuki's performance; it handled and clearly had good side grip and traction, but could certainly cope with a bit more horsepower.

The form of the factory Hondas was also a surprise, but not a positive one. Marquez didn't get pole, but this was thought to be due to Dovizioso's use of the softer tyre allowed by the rule concessions. With three Ducatis on the first two rows of the grid, it was assumed that Marquez would have something in hand for race day – but he didn't. At the first corner he got pushed out and ended up at the back of the field. It looked like a rider error, and Marc admitted as much, although later in the season Honda management muttered about a bike problem, presumably with the clutch. Marquez then cut through the field in typically brutal fashion – Bautista was one unhappy victim – but lapped at around the same pace as Lorenzo, suggesting that he couldn't have overhauled the leaders anyway.

Another change evident at Qatar was that the Open Class bikes didn't look like makeweights. The Hondas, now with pneumatic valves, were much quicker; Forward again had last year's Yamahas; and Avintia ran two 14.1-spec Ducatis, one of which Hector Barbera used to be best in the Open Class in both qualifying and the race, but he had to fight right to the final corner.

The second riders of the Yamaha and Honda factory teams both faded in the closing stages, but for very dissimilar reasons. Lorenzo looked like he could go with

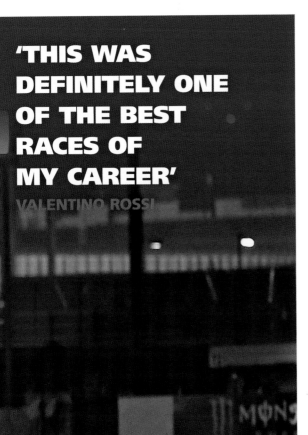

'THIS WAS DEFINITELY ONE OF THE BEST RACES OF MY CAREER'

VALENTINO ROSSI

ABOVE Marquez charged back through the field to fifth place; here he closes on Yonny Hernandez on the Pramac Ducati

BELOW Hector Barbera won the Open Class on a Ducati 14.1

the Ducatis and even chase his team-mate and challenge for the win, but his vision was partially obscured when the lining of his crash helmet moved. Yamaha management were, to put it mildly, unamused. What happened to Pedrosa? Team manager Livio Suppo came clean after the race: it was the return of arm pump and, crucially, in the twice-operated-on right arm. It had been afflicting Dani for nearly a year and he now said he couldn't go on racing like this. He had spent winter

looking for advice and every doctor he'd consulted told him it was highly inadvisable to operate for a third time.

Several questions immediately came to mind. First, did this mean the end of Dani's career? And secondly, what would it mean for Honda's team and the constructors' championship? The name of Casey Stoner was mentioned as a potential stand-in; and as the Aussie had announced his participation in the Suzuka 8 Hours just before the paddock assembled in Qatar, the suggestion wasn't greeted with the ridicule it once would have attracted.

The travails of Pedrosa, Lorenzo and Marquez ensured that there were no Spaniards on the podium, a fact that may not have been much remarked upon had a Spaniard finished in the top three in Moto2 or Moto3 – but that didn't happen either. All of a sudden French, British and German racers looked like they could be contenders not just for the occasional race win, but for titles. It was nearly ten years since a Spaniard failed to stand on a podium over a Grand Prix weekend (China 2005), and nearly as long since the MotoGP podium was populated entirely by Italians (Japan 2006).

'It was a long, long time ago this happened,' said a triumphant Rossi. 'I know, because I was there also.' And that seemingly glib comment hides one of the great truths about Valentino's record – his longevity at the top level. This is a hallmark of a true great and Rossi, now 36, is way over the age at which other multiple champions have retired – yet his motivation remains undimmed. His delight at winning the first race of the season was as intense as it ever has been. Again, this isn't a surprise – but no less astonishing.

A LEVEL PLAYING FIELD

By achieving a double rostrum, added to the one Dovizioso scored in Texas in 2014, Ducati lost the first of the concessions allowed to factories that have not won a dry race for two seasons. At the start of the year, Ducati – like Suzuki and Aprilia – entered as a Factory Option team and was thus able to use its own engine software. Unlike Honda and Yamaha, Ducati also had 24 litres of petrol, a softer tyre allocation, unlimited testing, 12 engines for the season (as opposed to five) and no freeze on development. All of those benefits are designed to allow factories new to MotoGP to get up to speed.

Ducati's three dry rostrum finishes (Crutchlow's at Aragón and Dovi's at Assen were achieved in the mixed conditions of flag-to-flag races) triggered the loss of the first concession. From Texas onwards, the works and Pramac bikes would lose two litres of fuel. As the Avintia team's bikes are entered in the Open class, they use the 'spec' software and were therefore unaffected. The next trigger point is three dry-weather wins, which would see the soft-tyre concession removed.

Ducati was unperturbed by the loss of the two litres, although when the red bikes blasted past the Yamaha on the front straight it did look as if they had dusted off their old sector-fuelling software and taken advantage of the favourable fuel allowance.

The concessions system will go on into the 2016 season with a few tweaks. Factories will score three concession points for a win, two for a second place and one for a third place. Racking up six points will immediately lose the right to unlimited testing and all other concessions the following year. Any factory not scoring a rostrum during the season will get the full set of concessions the following year.

At the same time, the GP Commission decided that for 2016 all bikes not operating under concessions will have 22 litres of fuel per race, seven engines for the season, and a lower minimum weight of 157kg (reduced by 1kg).

BELOW The new Ducati was a revelation. Andrea Dovizioso started from pole position and then raced at the front with the Yamahas

COMMERCIAL BANK GRAND PRIX OF QATAR
LOSAIL INTERNATIONAL CIRCUIT
ROUND 1
MARCH 29

OFFICIAL TIMEKEEPER

RACE RESULTS

CIRCUIT LENGTH 3.343 miles

NO. OF LAPS 22

RACE DISTANCE 73.546 miles

WEATHER Dry, 22°C

TRACK TEMPERATURE 28°C

WINNER Valentino Rossi

FASTEST LAP 1m 55.267s, 104.390mph, Valentino Rossi

LAP RECORD 1m 55.135s, 104.452mph, Casey Stoner (2008)

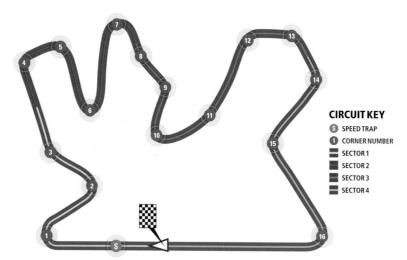

CIRCUIT KEY
- Ⓢ SPEED TRAP
- ① CORNER NUMBER
- ▬ SECTOR 1
- ▬ SECTOR 2
- ▬ SECTOR 3
- ▬ SECTOR 4

TYRE OPTIONS

FRONT

FRONT COMPOUNDS
SOFT (**S**), MEDIUM (**M**), HARD (**H**)

REAR

REAR COMPOUNDS
SOFT (**S**), MEDIUM (**M**), HARD (**H**)

SEVERITY RATING

<MILD   SEVERE>

BRIDGESTONE

QUALIFYING

	Rider	Nation	Motorcycle	Team	Time	Pole +
1	Dovizioso	ITA	Ducati	Ducati Team	1m 54.113s	
2	Pedrosa	SPA	Honda	Repsol Honda Team	1m 54.330s	0.217s
3	Marquez	SPA	Honda	Repsol Honda Team	1m 54.437s	0.324s
4	Iannone	ITA	Ducati	Ducati Team	1m 54.521s	0.408s
5	Hernandez	COL	Ducati	Pramac Racing	1m 54.675s	0.562s
6	Lorenzo	SPA	Yamaha	Movistar Yamaha MotoGP	1m 54.711s	0.598s
7	Smith	GBR	Yamaha	Monster Yamaha Tech 3	1m 54.732s	0.619s
8	Rossi	ITA	Yamaha	Movistar Yamaha MotoGP	1m 54.851s	0.738s
9	Petrucci	ITA	Ducati	Pramac Racing	1m 54.876s	0.763s
10	Espargaro P	SPA	Yamaha	Monster Yamaha Tech 3	1m 55.004s	0.891s
11	Espargaro A	SPA	Suzuki	Team Suzuki ECSTAR	1m 55.035s	0.922s
12	Crutchlow	GBR	Honda	CWM LCR Honda	1m 55.123s	1.010s
13	Viñales	SPA	Suzuki	Team Suzuki ECSTAR	1m 55.246s	Q1
14	Redding	GBR	Honda	EG 0,0 Marc VDS	1m 55.428s	Q1
15	Barbera	SPA	Ducati	Avintia Racing	1m 55.604s	Q1
16	Di Meglio	FRA	Ducati	Avintia Racing	1m 55.729s	Q1
17	Hayden	USA	Honda	Aspar MotoGP Team	1m 55.756s	Q1
18	Bradl	GER	Yamaha	Athinà Forward Racing	1m 55.791s	Q1
19	Laverty E	IRL	Honda	Aspar MotoGP Team	1m 55.848s	Q1
20	Abraham	CZE	Honda	AB Motoracing	1m 55.892s	Q1
21	Bautista	SPA	Aprilia	Aprilia Racing Team Gresini	1m 56.187s	Q1
22	Miller	AUS	Honda	CWM LCR Honda	1m 56.287s	Q1
23	Baz	FRA	Yamaha	Athinà Forward Racing	1m 56.454s	Q1
24	De Angelis	RSM	ART	Octo IodaRacing Team	1m 56.793s	Q1
25	Melandri	ITA	Aprilia	Aprilia Racing Team Gresini	1m 57.934s	Q1

1 VALENTINO ROSSI
Rolled back the years with a win from the third row of the grid. As in previous years at Qatar, Vale was able to cut through the pack but this time he didn't just get on the rostrum, he won under immense pressure from Dovizioso's Ducati.

2 ANDREA DOVIZIOSO
An amazing début for the GP15 Desmosedici. Dovi set pole and ran at the front for the entire race. He lost out in the final duel with Rossi despite setting his personal best lap on the final lap. There was just a tinge of disappointment at not taking the win, but Dovi did manage a smile.

3 ANDREA IANNONE
His maiden podium in MotoGP on his first race as a factory rider, making it a double podium for the GP15 Desmosedici on début. Further proof of Andrea's maturing skiulls.

4 JORGE LORENZO
In a rostrum position and feeling like he could go for the win when, four laps from the flag, a problem with his helmet partially obscured his vision and forced him to slow.

5 MARC MARQUEZ
Ran wide at the first corner and rejoined in last place. Marc got through the Open

Class and the satellite bikes but was running much the same lap times as the leaders and couldn't get to the front group.

6 DANI PEDROSA
Lost ground late on in the race thanks to the return of arm pump, for which he was operated on less than 12 months previously. There would be serious consequences.

7 CAL CRUTCHLOW
Top satellite bike and the finishing position could have been even better but for a crash in qualifying. Looked at home on the Honda. Still a promising first ride on the Honda.

8 BRADLEY SMITH
Not sure whether to be happy about finishing for the first time at Losail or to be miffed about just missing out on being top satellite bike – but pleased to beat his team-mate.

9 POL ESPARGARO
Struggled throughout the weekend with electronics settings, particularly traction control, with compromised acceleration and a knock-on effect on anti-wheelie.

10 YONNY HERNANDEZ
His best weekend in MotoGP. Used the softer tyre superbly in qualifying then

ran with the leading group for the first five laps. Thankfully untroubled by his pre-season shoulder injury.

11 ALEIX ESPARGARO
Scored points on Suzuki's return to MotoGP but unimpressed with finishing outside the top ten and only too well aware that the bike lacks power. Everyone else was seriously impressed.

12 DANILO PETRUCCI
Made it a great weekend for the Pramac team. Lost pace dramatically in the middle of the race before recovering strongly.

LAP CHART

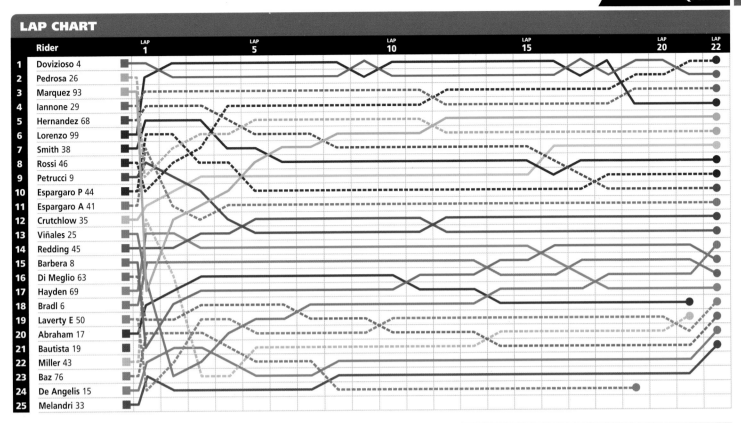

	Rider						
1	Dovizioso 4						
2	Pedrosa 26						
3	Marquez 93						
4	Iannone 29						
5	Hernandez 68						
6	Lorenzo 99						
7	Smith 38						
8	Rossi 46						
9	Petrucci 9						
10	Espargaro P 44						
11	Espargaro A 41						
12	Crutchlow 35						
13	Viñales 25						
14	Redding 45						
15	Barbera 8						
16	Di Meglio 63						
17	Hayden 69						
18	Bradl 6						
19	Laverty E 50						
20	Abraham 17						
21	Bautista 19						
22	Miller 43						
23	Baz 76						
24	De Angelis 15						
25	Melandri 33						

(LAP 1, LAP 5, LAP 10, LAP 15, LAP 20, LAP 22)

RACE

	Rider	Motorcycle	Race time	Time +	Fastest lap	Avg. speed	B
1	Rossi	Yamaha	42m 35.717s		1m 55.267s	103.6mph	H/M
2	Dovizioso	Ducati	42m 35.891s	0.174s	1m 55.495s	103.6mph	M/M
3	Iannone	Ducati	42m 37.967s	2.250s	1m 55.514s	103.5mph	M/M
4	Lorenzo	Yamaha	42m 38.424s	2.707s	1m 55.428s	103.5mph	M/M
5	Marquez	Honda	42m 42.753s	7.036s	1m 55.661s	103.3mph	M/M
6	Pedrosa	Honda	42m 46.472s	10.755s	1m 55.798s	103.1mph	M/M
7	Crutchlow	Honda	42m 48.101s	12.384s	1m 55.926s	103.1mph	H/M
8	Smith	Yamaha	42m 48.631s	12.914s	1m 56.091s	103.0mph	H/M
9	Espargaro P	Yamaha	42m 48.748s	13.031s	1m 56.067s	103.0mph	H/M
10	Hernandez	Ducati	42m 53.152s	17.435s	1m 56.037s	102.8mph	H/M
11	Espargaro A	Suzuki	42m 55.618s	19.901s	1m 56.375s	102.8mph	H/M
12	Petrucci	Ducati	43m 00.149s	24.432s	1m 56.493s	102.6mph	H/M
13	Redding	Honda	43m 07.749s	32.032s	1m 55.855s	102.3mph	H/M
14	Viñales	Suzuki	43m 09.180s	33.463s	1m 56.616s	102.2mph	M/M
15	Barbera	Ducati	43m 09.342s	33.625s	1m 56.738s	102.2mph	H/M
16	Bradl	Yamaha	43m 09.661s	33.944s	1m 57.127s	102.2mph	H/M
17	Hayden	Honda	43m 14.687s	38.970s	1m 56.778s	102.0mph	H/S
18	Laverty E	Honda	43m 22.287s	46.570s	1m 57.442s	101.7mph	H/M
19	Di Meglio	Ducati	43m 34.928s	59.211s	1m 57.237s	101.2mph	H/S
20	De Angelis	ART	43m 50.698s	1m 14.981s	1m 59.323s	99.4mph	M/S
21	Melandri	Aprilia	44m 23.860s	1m 48.143s	1m 57.509s	87.8mph	H/M
22	Baz	Yamaha	43m 25.153s	3 laps	1m 57.509s	87.8mph	H/M
NF	Abraham	Honda	41m 22.439s	1 lap	1m 56.891s	101.8mph	H/S
NF	Miller	Honda	41m 23.031s	1 lap	1m 57.175s	101.8mph	H/M
NF	Bautista	Aprilia	–	–	–	–	M/S

CHAMPIONSHIP

	Rider	Nation	Team	Points
1	Rossi	ITA	Movistar Yamaha MotoGP	25
2	Dovizioso	ITA	Ducati Team	20
3	Iannone	ITA	Ducati Team	16
4	Lorenzo	SPA	Movistar Yamaha MotoGP	13
5	Marquez	SPA	Repsol Honda Team	11
6	Pedrosa	SPA	Repsol Honda Team	10
7	Crutchlow	GBR	CWM LCR Honda	9
8	Smith	GBR	Monster Yamaha Tech 3	8
9	Espargaro P	SPA	Monster Yamaha Tech 3	7
10	Hernandez	COL	Pramac Racing	6
11	Espargaro A	SPA	Team Suzuki ECSTAR	5
12	Petrucci	ITA	Pramac Racing	4
13	Redding	GBR	EG 0,0 Marc VDS	3
14	Viñales	SPA	Team Suzuki ECSTAR	2
15	Barbera	SPA	Avintia Racing	1

13 SCOTT REDDING
A difficult début on the satellite Honda. Scott targeted a top-ten finish but fell short, with turning being his main problem.

14 MAVERICK VIÑALES
Not surprisingly, the rookie was more excited than his team-mate about finishing outside the top ten. He lost traction control early on but decided to continue.

15 HECTOR BARBERA
Used a setting they only tried in warm-up and suffered at the start with a lack of rear grip. Rode around the problems and came out on top of a last-lap battle with both Bradl and Viñales.

16 STEFAN BRADL
Spent most of the race fighting with Barbera but lost the lead of the Open Class when he outbraked himself at the last corner and lost two places.

17 NICKY HAYDEN
Went with the soft tyre and was able to chase down Redding, but when the tyre wore the traction control cut in far too often.

18 EUGENE LAVERTY
Excellent progress in practice ruined by electronics problems in the race. The bike didn't know where it was on track.

19 MIKE DI MEGLIO
Confused by the bike not behaving the same way on race day as it did in qualifying. Also suffered severe vibrations plus the old Ducati problem of the bike not wanting to turn.

20 ALEX DE ANGELIS
Treated the weekend as a test session. The race was the longest distance Alex had ever done on the bike. Pleased to finish and gain data but not happy that he was unable to fight with the group in front.

21 MARCO MELANDRI
Ruefully remarked that it wasn't the fastest race of his life but grateful for the data from his first truly long run on the new Aprilia.

22 LORIS BAZ
Despite having a mangled little finger from a practice crash, he started well but had to pit to change his front tyre. A fraught MotoGP début.

ALVARO BAUTISTA
Had his brake lines severed by Marquez as he came past after his bad start. Distinctly unimpressed.

KAREL ABRAHAM
Scooped up by Miller on the last lap, a fitting end to a lacklustre weekend.

JACK MILLER
Obviously still coming to terms with the bike in practice and qualifying. Crashed in the race trying a highly optimistic last-lap manoeuvre.

RED BULL GRAND PRIX OF THE AMERICAS
CIRCUIT OF THE AMERICAS

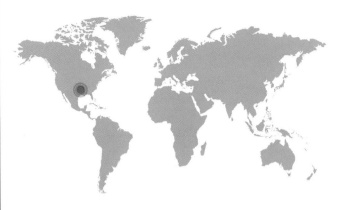

NEW WORLD DOMINATION

Marc Marquez won again in the USA but not by the expected margin, with Ducati and Dovi second

The only predictable thing about the Grand Prix of the Americas was the winner. Marc Marquez duly continued his winning run in the USA – six races, six victories – but only after the most remarkable pole-position lap anyone could remember as well as a serious challenge from both Yamaha and Ducati.

Given the nature of the Austin circuit and the way Hondas have dominated in the past, another runaway win wouldn't have been surprising. Marc's margin of victory, however, was under two and a half seconds from second-placed Andrea Dovizioso and just over three seconds from third-placed Valentino Rossi – all of which compares interestingly with 2014 when Marquez was 21 seconds ahead of the next non-Honda (third-placed Dovi). In 2013 Marquez took his maiden MotoGP win here, again in front of his team-mate and over three seconds ahead of an on-form Jorge Lorenzo.

There were other strange aspects to the Grand Prix of the Americas that gave it a slightly bizarre feeling that was a little at odds with the usual air of efficiency. First there was the absence of, or faulty distribution of, medics that delayed Friday practice. Then came a stray dog that was nearly collected by Maverick Viñales during MotoGP practice, causing another delay; a local rescue charity christened the hound Moto and found it a home. Then there was another hold-up thanks to fog, and bad weather in the form of heavy rain continued to disrupt practice and also affected race day. There was a setback before the MotoGP race when a pedestrian bridge decided to dump the rainwater that had accumulated on its roof onto the track beneath. Thankfully, the promised race-day storms failed to materialise, and all three classes produced fine racing.

ABOVE The first corner was interesting: Bradley Smith and Valentino Rossi made daring moves around the outside

RIGHT Qatar hadn't been a fluke for Ducati: Dovizioso led the early laps then fought with Rossi after Marquez went past

OPPOSITE Alex de Angelis celebrated starting his 250th GP; his first race was Imola 1999 in the 125cc class

While it should be noted that front-tyre wear was a major issue last year, and this year some riders again suffered serious wear on the right side of their front tyres, anything other than a Marquez win was almost unthinkable. Not that all was rosy in the Honda camp. The shock announcement from Dani Pedrosa after the Qatar race that he was suffering from arm pump and was off to seek a cure meant factory tester Hiro Aoyama took over the second Repsol machine. Pedrosa, having said that all doctors he consulted had advised against further surgery, managed to find a surgeon willing to undertake a radical and invasive procedure. The prognosis was uncertain and he certainly wouldn't be back quickly.

There was much debate over whether Casey Stoner would be called back into action. The man himself said publicly that he was willing to race in Texas and Argentina to help out his friend Pedrosa, but HRC gritted their teeth and turned down the offer on the grounds that there wasn't enough time to test. As the engineer he would have worked with was a rookie, 'at least one test' would have been necessary to give him a bike with which he could fight for the rostrum. Anything less than that, said HRC's Shuhei Nakamoto, would have been unthinkable.

Aoyama was nowhere near competitive, leading many to wonder if the team and constructors' championship titles were already impossible for Honda to retain. At least Marquez rode a smart race, taking the lead off Dovizioso on lap five and maintaining a small gap once he was sure of the track conditions, which were much altered by overnight rain. The only

'I'M REALLY HAPPY FOR THIS VICTORY AFTER WHERE I FINISHED IN QATAR'

MARC MARQUEZ

ABOVE Hayden was first customer Honda rider, but not the Open Class winner

OPPOSITE Rossi and Marquez share a joke

BELOW Hiro Aoyama, the Honda test rider, replaced Dani Pedrosa

fight was for second place: Rossi got past Dovi but hit this track's old problem of front-tyre abrasion and had to concede the place again five laps from the flag. Thanks to Ducati having scored three dry-weather rostrums inside a year, its factory bikes – Pramac's as well as those of the works – were racing with two litres less fuel; Gigi Dall'Igna insisted that this wasn't a problem and everyone believed him.

Then both Dovi and Andrea Iannone ran out of fuel on the slow-down lap (going up the hill to the first corner) and we weren't so sure. Ducati Corse at first conceded that its bikes had run out of fuel but soon changed its mind, citing another 'tank-related issue'. It turned out that the small but significant amount of fuel left in the tank after the flag had become vaporised when the riders slowed because cooling airflow, always critical on the Desmosedici, was no longer up to the job. That rear cylinder head makes a very effective hotplate.

Lorenzo was again strangely anonymous, coming through to fourth place past a feisty Andrea Iannone and Bradley Smith, who benefited from a particularly brave run round the outside at the first corner. The Englishman hung on to be top satellite bike, ahead of Cal Crutchlow, who won that particular fight at Qatar; you had the impression that this one would run and run. Hector Barbera again made good use of his 2014-model Ducati to win the Open Class decisively.

Marquez's victory may have seemed like a return to the status quo, but it didn't feel like that in the paddock post-race. The Ducatis' form in the first race of the year obviously wasn't a fluke and neither was that of Rossi. Whatever the new Desmosedici was capable of producing, Dovizioso looked capable of using 100 per cent of it, while Rossi, the nine-times champion, was rolling back the years after a period of reinvention, not least of his riding style.

Valentino's Qatar form clearly wasn't a blip: he was again in command at Yamaha and ruling the media with all his old flair and gusto. Could he really put together a genuine championship challenge? No one was inclined to bet against him.

LAP OF THE GODS

Marc Marquez was just starting the first flying lap of his second qualifying run when a warning lamp illuminated on his dash – a lamp that said 'Stop. Now.' Marc did as he was told and rolled to a halt, propping the bike against the pit wall. When he left the pits he'd been on pole; he was now seventh and less than four minutes of the session remained.

Marc vaulted the wall – no mean feat as it's as high as he is tall – and ran 100 metres up pitlane in full kit. His other bike was ready and he exited pitlane with just 2 minutes 20 seconds available to do his out lap if he were to get another chance at pole; a decent race lap is around 2 minutes 20 seconds. He made it with three seconds to spare with Andrea Dovizioso on his tail. Dovi was fastest man and must have thought he had his second pole of the year. He wanted to follow Marc 'to look at the line, to see some secrets'.

Andrea then had the best seat in the house to observe the most astonishing lap MotoGP has seen. You didn't need to be that close to see the massive mistake at Turn 10 followed by an out-of-control moment braking for Turn 11. Everywhere

else Marquez just looked like he was going to crash. At the line he was quickest by over a third of a second; the next third of a second covered six riders. How do you do that after your concentration has been vaporised and then running a decent 100 metres in leathers? An air of disbelief settled

over the Circuit of the Americas.

Dovi was not immune: 'So many mistakes…' he reported, speaking even more quietly than usual and shaking his head slowly. 'But so fast…'

Later, Marquez calmly announced that the bike was set up all wrong and was using the wrong front tyre.

RED BULL GRAND PRIX OF THE AMERICAS
CIRCUIT OF THE AMERICAS
ROUND **2**
APRIL 12

OFFICIAL TIMEKEEPER

RACE RESULTS

CIRCUIT LENGTH 3.427 miles

NO. OF LAPS 21

RACE DISTANCE 71.967 miles

WEATHER Dry, 27°C

TRACK TEMPERATURE 36°C

WINNER Marc Marquez

FASTEST LAP 2m 04.251s, 99.233mph, Andrea Iannone

LAP RECORD 2m 03.575s, 99.792mph, Marc Marquez (2014)

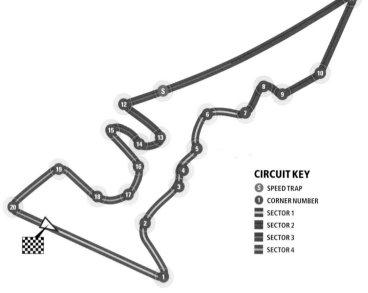

CIRCUIT KEY

- **S** SPEED TRAP
- **1** CORNER NUMBER
- SECTOR 1
- SECTOR 2
- SECTOR 3
- SECTOR 4

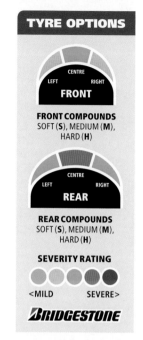

TYRE OPTIONS

FRONT

FRONT COMPOUNDS
SOFT (**S**), MEDIUM (**M**), HARD (**H**)

REAR

REAR COMPOUNDS
SOFT (**S**), MEDIUM (**M**), HARD (**H**)

SEVERITY RATING

<MILD   SEVERE>

BRIDGESTONE

QUALIFYING

	Rider	Nation	Motorcycle	Team	Time	Pole +
1	Marquez	SPA	Honda	Repsol Honda Team	2m 02.135s	
2	Dovizioso	ITA	Ducati	Ducati Team	2m 02.474s	0.339s
3	Lorenzo	SPA	Yamaha	Movistar Yamaha MotoGP	2m 02.540s	0.405s
4	Rossi	ITA	Yamaha	Movistar Yamaha MotoGP	2m 02.573s	0.438s
5	Crutchlow	GBR	Honda	CWM LCR Honda	2m 02.613s	0.478s
6	Redding	GBR	Honda	EG 0,0 Marc VDS	2m 02.674s	0.539s
7	Iannone	ITA	Ducati	Ducati Team	2m 02.792s	0.657s
8	Espargaro A	SPA	Suzuki	Team Suzuki ECSTAR	2m 02.869s	0.734s
9	Espargaro P	SPA	Yamaha	Monster Yamaha Tech 3	2m 03.161s	1.026s
10	Smith	GBR	Yamaha	Monster Yamaha Tech 3	2m 03.440s	1.305s
11	Petrucci	ITA	Ducati	Pramac Racing	2m 03.741s	1.606s
12	Viñales	SPA	Suzuki	Team Suzuki ECSTAR	2m 03.754s	1.619s
13	Barbera	SPA	Ducati	Avintia Racing	2m 03.926s	Q1
14	Bradl	GER	Yamaha	Athinà Forward Racing	2m 04.275s	Q1
15	Hernandez	COL	Ducati	Pramac Racing	2m 04.313s	Q1
16	Di Meglio	FRA	Ducati	Avintia Racing	2m 04.392s	Q1
17	Laverty E	IRL	Honda	Aspar MotoGP Team	2m 04.875s	Q1
18	Aoyama	JPN	Honda	Repsol Honda Team	2m 05.086s	Q1
19	Miller	AUS	Honda	CWM LCR Honda	2m 05.156s	Q1
20	Baz	FRA	Yamaha	Athinà Forward Racing	2m 05.214s	Q1
21	Abraham	CZE	Honda	AB Motoracing	2m 05.261s	Q1
22	Hayden	USA	Honda	Aspar MotoGP Team	2m 05.569s	Q1
23	Bautista	SPA	Aprilia	Aprilia Racing Team Gresini	2m 05.595s	Q1
24	De Angelis	RSM	ART	Octo IodaRacing Team	2m 06.145s	Q1
25	Melandri	ITA	Aprilia	Aprilia Racing Team Gresini	2m 07.267s	Q1

1 MARC MARQUEZ
Six races in the USA, six wins. But it wasn't as simple as that; first, there was the most amazing pole lap ever; then in the race he didn't lead every lap. It took Marc a while to understand the track conditions, changed by overnight rain, then to deal with Dovizioso.

2 ANDREA DOVIZIOSO
Led the race for the first four laps until he was passed by Marquez. Then involved in a race-long fight with Rossi, settled by Dovi's pass five laps from the flag. Second in the points table. Not bad for a brand new motorcycle.

3 VALENTINO ROSSI
Had to manage the front tyre, which wasn't in a good state at the end of the race, and so couldn't fend off Dovizioso after a race-long dice with the Ducati man. Nevertheless, retained his championship lead.

4 JORGE LORENZO
Taking antibiotics for bronchitis and, not surprisingly, not feeling race-fit. However, he got a good start only to get tangled in the first-corner fracas. After that he followed Iannone up to and past Smith before taking fourth three laps from the flag.

5 ANDREA IANNONE
Held up by the Redding/Espargaro incident on lap one, losing four seconds. Fought back well but worked his front tyre hard and had no defence against Lorenzo.

6 BRADLEY SMITH
Top satellite rider from tenth on the grid largely thanks to a brave round-the-outside move at Turn 1 that put him fourth. Forgot to alter the traction-control map thus overheating his tyre and losing pace.

7 CAL CRUTCHLOW
Didn't take full advantage of his second-row start. Tangled in the first-lap crash but

had made unspecified mistakes in set-up and definitely wasn't happy.

8 ALEIX ESPARGARO
Unhappy with his finishing position but definitely content to close the gap to the winner to under 20 seconds. As in Qatar, suffered badly from rear-wheel chatter.

9 MAVERICK VIÑALES
Not surprisingly, the mixed conditions made set-up difficult for the rookie. Pleased that he improved on his Qatar position but thought he made the wrong tyre choice.

10 DANILO PETRUCCI
Diced with Viñales for much of the race, losing out to the Spaniard two laps from home.

11 HIROSHI AOYAMA
Replaced Pedrosa on the factory Honda, and rode it in completely dry conditions for the first time in the race.

12 HECTOR BARBERA
Top Open Class bike in qualifying and the race. Not happy in the mixed conditions. Spent the race dicing with Aoyama's factory Honda and finished nine seconds ahead of the next Open bike.

LAP CHART

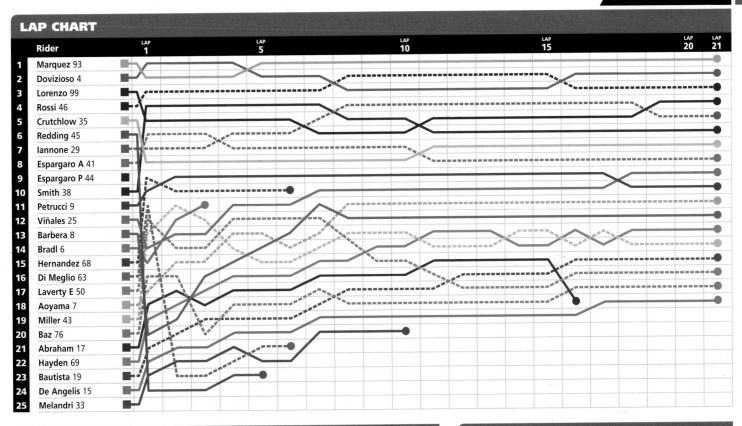

	Rider	LAP 1	LAP 5	LAP 10	LAP 15	LAP 20	LAP 21
1	Marquez 93						
2	Dovizioso 4						
3	Lorenzo 99						
4	Rossi 46						
5	Crutchlow 35						
6	Redding 45						
7	Iannone 29						
8	Espargaro A 41						
9	Espargaro P 44						
10	Smith 38						
11	Petrucci 9						
12	Viñales 25						
13	Barbera 8						
14	Bradl 6						
15	Hernandez 68						
16	Di Meglio 63						
17	Laverty E 50						
18	Aoyama 7						
19	Miller 43						
20	Baz 76						
21	Abraham 17						
22	Hayden 69						
23	Bautista 19						
24	De Angelis 15						
25	Melandri 33						

RACE

	Rider	Motorcycle	Race time	Time +	Fastest lap	Avg. speed	฿
1	Marquez	Honda	43m 47.150s		2m 04.563s	98.6mph	H/M
2	Dovizioso	Ducati	43m 49.504s	2.354s	2m 04.323s	98.5mph	M/M
3	Rossi	Yamaha	43m 50.270s	3.120s	2m 04.543s	98.4mph	H/M
4	Lorenzo	Yamaha	43m 53.832s	6.682s	2m 04.753s	98.3mph	M/M
5	Iannone	Ducati	43m 54.734s	7.584s	2m 04.251s	98.2mph	M/M
6	Smith	Yamaha	43m 57.707s	10.557s	2m 04.583s	98.2mph	M/M
7	Crutchlow	Honda	44m 04.117s	16.976s	2m 05.133s	98.0mph	H/M
8	Espargaro A	Suzuki	44m 06.175s	19.025s	2m 04.535s	97.9mph	M/M
9	Viñales	Suzuki	44m 25.720s	38.570s	2m 06.146s	97.1mph	H/M
10	Petrucci	Ducati	44m 28.946s	41.796s	2m 05.512s	97.0mph	M/M
11	Aoyama	Honda	44m 34.349s	47.199s	2m 06.753s	96.8mph	M/M
12	Barbera	Ducati	44m 34.489s	47.339s	2m 06.633s	96.8mph	M/M
13	Hayden	Honda	44m 43.634s	56.484s	2m 06.791s	96.5mph	M/M
14	Miller	Honda	44m 43.881s	56.731s	2m 06.076s	96.5mph	M/M
15	Bautista	Aprilia	44m 44.522s	57.372s	2m 06.618s	96.4mph	M/S
16	Laverty E	Honda	44m 46.048s	58.898s	2m 07.000s	96.4mph	M/M
17	Baz	Yamaha	44m 55.937s	1m 08.787s	2m 07.352s	96.0mph	M/M
18	De Angelis	ART	45m 09.386s	1m 22.236s	2m 07.316s	95.6mph	M/M
NF	Abraham	Honda	34m 12.000s	5 laps	2m 06.903s	96.1mph	M/M
NF	Melandri	Aprilia	22m 02.076s	11 laps	2m 09.256s	93.3mph	M/M
NF	Hernandez	Ducati	12m 41.408s	15 laps	2m 06.076s	97.1mph	H/M
NF	Di Meglio	Ducati	13m 03.065s	15 laps	2m 06.786s	94.4mph	H/M
NF	Redding	Honda	11m 09.010s	16 laps	2m 06.855s	92.1mph	H/M
NF	Bradl	Yamaha	6m 23.675s	18 laps	2m 06.070s	96.4mph	M/M
NF	Espargaro P	Yamaha	–	–	–	–	M/M

CHAMPIONSHIP

	Rider	Nation	Team	Points
1	Rossi	ITA	Movistar Yamaha MotoGP	41
2	Dovizioso	ITA	Ducati Team	40
3	Marquez	SPA	Repsol Honda Team	36
4	Iannone	ITA	Ducati Team	27
5	Lorenzo	SPA	Movistar Yamaha MotoGP	26
6	Smith	GBR	Monster Yamaha Tech 3	18
	Crutchlow	GBR	CWM LCR Honda	18
8	Espargaro A	SPA	Team Suzuki ECSTAR	13
9	Pedrosa	SPA	Repsol Honda Team	10
	Petrucci	ITA	Pramac Racing	10
11	Viñales	SPA	Team Suzuki ECSTAR	9
12	Espargaro P	SPA	Monster Yamaha Tech 3	7
13	Hernandez	COL	Pramac Racing	6
14	Aoyama	JPN	Repsol Honda Team	5
	Barbera	SPA	Avintia Racing	5
16	Hayden	USA	Aspar MotoGP Team	3
	Redding	GBR	EG 0,0 Marc VDS	3
18	Miller	AUS	CWM LCR Honda	2
19	Bautista	SPA	Aprilia Racing Team Gresini	1

13 NICKY HAYDEN
Made up places after a bad start and won a group dice. Nicky described it as 'a small victory' in his 200th GP.

14 JACK MILLER
Points in his second MotoGP race and got as high as 11th at one point. He was too hard on his tyres to have the ability to fight in the closing stages.

15 ALVARO BAUTISTA
Delighted to score the team's first point of the year. Managed his soft tyre cleverly to ensure he had pace in the second half of the race.

16 EUGENE LAVERTY
Again suffered when the tyres dropped off in the second half of the race but had a good fight with Miller for a while.

17 LORIS BAZ
Stayed with the group for the first half of the race but suffered from front-tyre wear and dropped away.

18 ALEX DE ANGELIS
The changing conditions didn't help the team get a good set-up. Alex had serious problems with the tyres from the early laps. Brought the bike home in the hope the data gathered would be of use.

DID NOT FINISH

SCOTT REDDING
Qualified on the second row but fell at Turn 11 after making contact with Lorenzo and took out Pol Espargaro. Restarted but lost his left footrest.

POL ESPARGARO
Taken out on the first lap when Redding crashed and the Honda scooped him up.

YONNY HERNANDEZ
Started well but didn't have race pace with the hard tyre. Crashed at the final corner of lap eight when he lost the rear.

KAREL ABRAHAM
Retired when his gear lever broke six laps from the flag.

MARCO MELANDRI
Gearbox problems forced him to retire after 11 laps.

MIKE DI MEGLIO
Lost the front and crashed twice.

STEFAN BRADL
Fell after he was touched by Miller who was attempting a repass.

DID NOT RACE

DANI PEDROSA
Announced after Qatar that he was suffering from arm pump and 'couldn't race like this'. Replaced by Aoyama while he sought a cure.

ARGENTINA
ROUND 3

G.P. RED BULL DE LA REPÚBLICA ARGENTINA
TERMAS DE RÍO HONDO

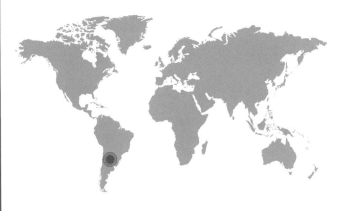

OLD DOG, OLD TRICKS

Valentino Rossi handed out a hard lesson to Marc Marquez, while Ducati and Suzuki impressed again

Age and experience, goes the saying, always trump youth and enthusiasm. It certainly applied to the closing laps of the Argentine GP as Valentino Rossi, using Bridgestone's new, ultra-hard rear tyre, closed down Marc Marquez, who'd gone with the softer option. Having been eighth on the first lap, The Doctor took second place behind runaway leader Marquez just before half distance and then set about closing a gap of more than four seconds. He started by snipping away the odd tenth of a second but by lap 20 of the 25 he was taking three-quarters of a second a lap. One can only imagine what Marquez was thinking as he checked his pitboard every lap.

Rossi caught the Spaniard two laps from home and next time round made his move. The Honda twitched on the brakes at the end of the straight and went wide; Rossi went through cleanly. The following corner, Turn 6, is a big, wide-open, left-handed sweeper where Marquez, exiting the tight right, tried to squeeze up the inside only to have the door firmly shut. There was definitely contact. Then as both men accelerated across the track, aiming for the distant apex, Rossi's back wheel and Marquez's rear wheel came together with the inevitable result. Marquez slid a good way up the track, eventually got to his feet and sprinted – genuinely sprinted – to his bike. There was a small tantrum when he realised his race was over.

To his credit, Marc said all the right things afterwards, although clearly he was far from happy. The phrase 'Valentino has always been my reference, I always learn things from him' was certainly open to more than one interpretation. Most agreed it was a racing incident, with many similarities to the Zarco/

'I THINK HE [MARQUEZ] MADE A MISTAKE AND HE CRASHED'
VALENTINO ROSSI

Simeon coming-together in the Moto2 race in Texas – and that's exactly how Race Direction saw it. Some people were suspicious of Rossi's glance over his right shoulder just before the incident, but it's doubtful that he could see Marquez at that moment and his action looked like a response to Marc's barge on the exit of the right-hander.

All of which tended to obscure what a clever race Valentino rode. He knew from the first day that he would be racing on the ultra-hard tyre and again he seemed to sacrifice qualifying in order to fully understand how the tyre would behave. The answer was that it would be difficult at the start but its longevity would be vital. Marquez and his crew were less sure and changed to the hard tyre on the grid. After Marquez crashed, TV pictures showed that his rear tyre was starting to break up – more evidence of how well Rossi and his team were working and how calm Valentino had been in executing his plan.

Honda's honour was upheld by Cal Crutchlow, who snatched third place from an equally impressive Andrea Iannone with a beautifully executed last-corner pass. Cal came from way back to power up the inside of the penultimate right-hander and had enough pace to hold on round the outside of the final left. A rostrum on his third ride on the Honda from fourth on the grid was impressive enough, but factor in that he had missed the Argentinian round in 2014 through injury and it looks even better.

Andrea Dovizoso's third second place in three races, plus Iannone's result, showed just how far Ducati had progressed since the previous season. Any suspicions

LEFT & INSET Fire down below! Hernandez's Ducati engine burns, the suspension linkage melts and Yonny finds himself sitting on the rear tyre

ABOVE Danilo Petrucci leads Stefan Bradl and Maverick Viñales in a midfield dice

qualifying. Yes, Suzuki had access to a softer tyre than the other Japanese factory bikes but Aleix's team was brave enough to copy Marquez's two-stop strategy and use three tyres. Encouragingly, Maverick Viñales also went straight to the final qualifying session. Other riders confirmed that the Suzuki handled superbly, with great edge grip, and could certainly deal with the extra power it needed, but the bike's immediate problem was severe chatter when the rear tyre started to wear, but only in right-handers.

At least Aleix got the holeshot and led round to the straight, where, of course, he was blown away by Marquez. Jorge Lorenzo also got past on the opening lap, but that was as good as it got for him. Crutchlow got him next time round and Jorge began a slow slide back. Seventh was Suzuki's best finish so far, but team and rider were mildly disappointed.

If Marquez had any malevolent thought, he kept it to himself. But the question now was how he would cope with discovering that Valentino wasn't his best friend after all. Of course, a lad as intelligent as Marc had worked that out already, although he still tends to defer to the nine-times champ in public, as in the press conference after this race. However, most if not all of what he said – especially to the Spanish media – is very much open to interpretation. Mutterings from inside the Honda tent certainly implied that the Marquez camp was far from happy.

Valentino was ecstatic. He went to the rostrum wearing an Argentine national football shirt bearing the number ten of Diego Maradonna, a hero in Italy as well as at home. It probably wasn't a coincidence that Valentino was shooting for his tenth world title.

ABOVE & BELOW
Cal Crutchlow (below) was third and Jack Miller was top finisher in the Open Class – hence the joy in *parc fermé* for the LCR team

about the fuelling problems in Texas were laid to rest, helped, no doubt, by Gigi Dall'Igna returning home between races and arriving at Buenos Aires airport with large boxes containing new tanks. This time the Ducatis made it all the way round the slow-down lap.

The other achievement that might have gone under the radar was Aleix Espargaro's second place in

CASEY AND HONDA

As both Repsol Hondas failed to make it to the flag, it's a fair bet that HRC wished that it could have taken up Casey Stoner's offer to ride in the GPs of the Americas and Argentina. The reasons for HRC's refusal are interesting and worth exploring in some detail.

They came to light after Casey used Twitter to express his disappointment that he wouldn't be racing: 'Sorry to everyone but I am not racing next weekend, it would have been an honour to ride for Honda.' He followed up on that one by saying he wasn't planning on winning, just helping out his friend Dani Pedrosa. Despite having spent a year begging Casey to come back, HRC's Shuhei Nakamoto confirmed that he had had no option but to refuse the offer.

The main reason was that Honda couldn't countenance putting Casey in a race unless he had a set-up capable of getting him on the rostrum. Anything less wasn't acceptable. That would mean, said Nakamoto-san, 'at least one test'. The situation was compounded by the fact that Casey's old race engineer, Cristian Gabbarini, was now with Jack Miller, and Pedrosa's race engineer, Ramon Aurin, was a rookie. 'A very good engineer,' said Nakamoto, 'but a rookie.'

After the news broke that Pedrosa wouldn't be back for Jerez, Nakamoto-san enlarged on his comments about the amount of testing needed, emphasising the 'at least' in 'at least one test'. And that, he said, couldn't be fitted into the 2015 schedule. So no Casey this season.

Not that anyone was ever saying that Stoner would come back to racing full-time. He could justify helping out his friend but had no interest in a full-time return, as he made clear himself when he attended the Catalan race later in the season. However, with both of its factory riders having problems, Honda already looked to be in serious trouble in the Teams' and Constructors' Championships, both of which are of great importance in Japan. How strange that the one company that could have had a Plan B for this sort of circumstance declined to find a way to do so.

RIGHT Marc Marquez contemplates that coming-together; he was far from convinced that it was just a racing incident

G.P. RED BULL DE LA REPÚBLICA ARGENTINA
TERMAS DE RÍO HONDO
ROUND 3
APRIL 19

RACE RESULTS

CIRCUIT LENGTH 2.986 miles

NO. OF LAPS 25

RACE DISTANCE 74.650 miles

WEATHER Dry, 29°C

TRACK TEMPERATURE 36°C

WINNER Valentino Rossi

FASTEST LAP 1m 39.019s, 108.553mph, Valentino Rossi (record)

PREVIOUS LAP RECORD 1m 39.233s, 108.305mph, Dani Pedrosa (2014)

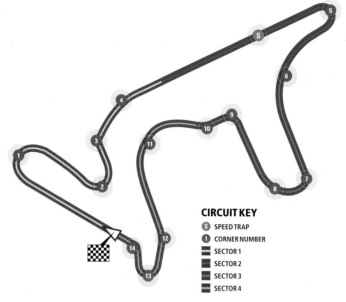

CIRCUIT KEY

S SPEED TRAP
1 CORNER NUMBER
■ SECTOR 1
■ SECTOR 2
■ SECTOR 3
■ SECTOR 4

QUALIFYING

	Rider	Nation	Motorcycle	Team	Time	Pole +
1	Marquez	SPA	Honda	Repsol Honda Team	1m 37.802s	
2	Espargaro A	SPA	Suzuki	Team Suzuki ECSTAR	1m 38.316s	0.514s
3	Iannone	ITA	Ducati	Ducati Team	1m 38.467s	0.665s
4	Crutchlow	GBR	Honda	CWM LCR Honda	1m 38.485s	0.683s
5	Lorenzo	SPA	Yamaha	Movistar Yamaha MotoGP	1m 38.485s	0.683s
6	Dovizioso	ITA	Ducati	Ducati Team	1m 38.520s	0.718s
7	Petrucci	ITA	Ducati	Pramac Racing	1m 38.786s	0.984s
8	Rossi	ITA	Yamaha	Movistar Yamaha MotoGP	1m 38.890s	1.088s
9	Viñales	SPA	Suzuki	Team Suzuki ECSTAR	1m 39.187s	1.385s
10	Smith	GBR	Yamaha	Monster Yamaha Tech 3	1m 39.197s	1.395s
11	Redding	GBR	Honda	EG 0,0 Marc VDS	1m 39.380s	1.578s
12	Barbera	SPA	Ducati	Avintia Racing	1m 40.526s	2.724s
13	Hernandez	COL	Ducati	Pramac Racing	1m 39.405s	Q1
14	Laverty E	IRL	Honda	Aspar MotoGP Team	1m 39.434s	Q1
15	Aoyama	JPN	Honda	Repsol Honda Team	1m 39.715s	Q1
16	Bradl	GER	Yamaha	Athinà Forward Racing	1m 39.734s	Q1
17	Abraham	CZE	Honda	AB Motoracing	1m 39.758s	Q1
18	Espargaro P	SPA	Yamaha	Monster Yamaha Tech 3	1m 39.808s	Q1
19	Bautista	SPA	Aprilia	Aprilia Racing Team Gresini	1m 39.828s	Q1
20	Hayden	USA	Honda	Aspar MotoGP Team	1m 39.876s	Q1
21	Miller	AUS	Honda	CWM LCR Honda	1m 39.888s	Q1
22	Baz	FRA	Yamaha	Athinà Forward Racing	1m 39.972s	Q1
23	Di Meglio	FRA	Ducati	Avintia Racing	1m 40.133s	Q1
24	Melandri	ITA	Aprilia	Aprilia Racing Team Gresini	1m 40.403s	Q1
25	De Angelis	RSM	ART	Octo IodaRacing Team	1m 40.485s	Q1

1 VALENTINO ROSSI
This race was yet another contender for his best ever. Knew he would be using the extra-hard tyre right from the first session. Seemed unconcerned about qualifying and executed his plan perfectly on race day, crossing a big gap when the tyre came in and provoking an error from Marquez.

2 ANDREA DOVIZIOSO
His third second place in three races, maintaining Andrea's position in the championship table. Rated it his best race so far as the track is difficult for Ducati and tyre drop-off severe.

3 CAL CRUTCHLOW
Rode a really clever race to conserve some grip for the final stages which he then used to put a great pass on Iannone in the final corner for his first rostrum on the Honda.

4 ANDREA IANNONE
Showed a little inexperience by changing the engine map too late to deal with mid-race problems.

5 JORGE LORENZO
Started well and was up to third. However, Jorge, unlike his team-mate, couldn't use the extra-hard rear tyre and dropped back to extend his run of non-podium finishes.

6 BRADLEY SMITH
His second successive sixth place followed another disappointing qualifying and a clever race, despite his attempt to go round the outside at Turn 1 not working this time.

7 ALEIX ESPARGARO
Disappointed with his finishing position after qualifying second. Hampered by the lack of top speed and by rear-wheel chatter.

8 POL ESPARGARO
Not a bad recovery from 18th on the grid! Sprayed with oil when Hernandez's bike blew, causing Pol to lose touch with his brother and his team-mate.

9 SCOTT REDDING
Better than Qatar; worse than Texas. Using the extra-hard rear tyre may have been a mistake, but he was able to fight off Viñales on last lap.

10 MAVERICK VIÑALES
Went straight to the second qualifying session for the first time, but, like his team-mate, had hoped for a better result. Maverick's feeling for the bike got better as the race went on and his lap times at the end were seriously impressive.

11 DANILO PETRUCCI
Suffered with a full tank and tyre wear but was fast at the end – although his last-corner pass on Aoyama cost him a penalty point.

12 JACK MILLER
Top Open bike thanks to a last-corner pass on Barbera. Had to do a lot of passing from his grid position, 21st, and destroyed his tyre, but not bad for his third MotoGP race.

13 HECTOR BARBERA
Qualified as top Open bike and fought with Miller for the race 'win' for the second half of the race. Hector lost out on the final lap after several passes and repasses.

LAP CHART

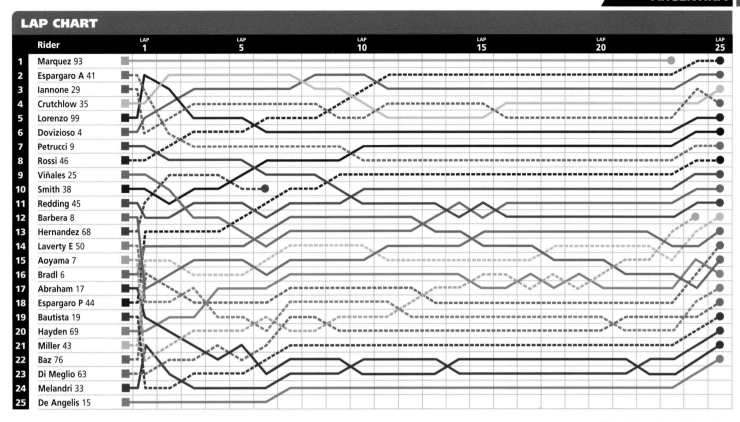

	Rider	LAP 1	LAP 5	LAP 10	LAP 15	LAP 20	LAP 25
1	Marquez 93						
2	Espargaro A 41						
3	Iannone 29						
4	Crutchlow 35						
5	Lorenzo 99						
6	Dovizioso 4						
7	Petrucci 9						
8	Rossi 46						
9	Viñales 25						
10	Smith 38						
11	Redding 45						
12	Barbera 8						
13	Hernandez 68						
14	Laverty E 50						
15	Aoyama 7						
16	Bradl 6						
17	Abraham 17						
18	Espargaro P 44						
19	Bautista 19						
20	Hayden 69						
21	Miller 43						
22	Baz 76						
23	Di Meglio 63						
24	Melandri 33						
25	De Angelis 15						

RACE

	Rider	Motorcycle	Race time	Time +	Fastest lap	Avg. speed	🅱
1	Rossi	Yamaha	41m 35.644s		1m 39.019s	107.7mph	H/XH
2	Dovizioso	Ducati	41m 41.329s	5.685s	1m 39.495s	107.4mph	H/H
3	Crutchlow	Honda	41m 43.942s	8.298s	1m 39.474s	107.3mph	H/H
4	Iannone	Ducati	41m 43.996s	8.352s	1m 39.507s	107.3mph	M/XH
5	Lorenzo	Yamaha	41m 45.836s	10.192s	1m 39.595s	107.2mph	H/H
6	Smith	Yamaha	41m 55.520s	19.876s	1m 40.058s	106.8mph	H/XH
7	Espargaro A	Suzuki	41m 59.977s	24.333s	1m 40.261s	106.6mph	M/H
8	Espargaro P	Yamaha	42m 03.314s	27.670s	1m 40.287s	106.5mph	H/XH
9	Redding	Honda	42m 10.041s	34.397s	1m 40.524s	106.2mph	M/XH
10	Viñales	Suzuki	42m 10.452s	34.808s	1m 40.432s	106.2mph	M/H
11	Petrucci	Ducati	42m 15.850s	40.206s	1m 40.566s	105.9mph	H/H
12	Miller	Honda	42m 18.298s	42.654s	1m 40.854s	105.9mph	H/H
13	Barbera	Ducati	42m 18.373s	42.729s	1m 40.567s	105.9mph	M/H
14	Baz	Yamaha	42m 18.497s	42.853s	1m 40.927s	105.8mph	H/H
15	Bradl	Yamaha	42m 18.681s	43.037s	1m 40.593s	105.8mph	H/H
16	Hayden	Honda	42m 18.896s	43.252s	1m 40.921s	105.8mph	H/H
17	Laverty E	Honda	42m 19.044s	43.400s	1m 40.900s	105.8mph	H/H
18	Di Meglio	Ducati	42m 19.452s	43.808s	1m 40.865s	105.8mph	M/H
19	Bautista	Aprilia	42m 20.522s	44.878s	1m 41.067s	105.8mph	M/H
20	Melandri	Aprilia	42m 31.880s	56.236s	1m 41.471s	105.3mph	M/H
21	Abraham	Honda	42m 39.015s	1m 03.371s	1m 41.507s	105.0mph	H/H
22	De Angelis	ART	42m 44.088s	1m 04.444s	1m 41.613s	104.8mph	M/H
NC	Aoyama	Honda	40m 34.659s	1 lap	1m 40.500s	105.9mph	M/H
NC	Marquez	Honda	38m 15.720s	2 laps	1m 39.071s	107.7mph	H/H
NC	Hernandez	Ducati	10m 08.383s	19 laps	1m 40.395s	106.0mph	H/H

CHAMPIONSHIP

	Rider	Nation	Team	Points
1	Rossi	ITA	Movistar Yamaha MotoGP	66
2	Dovizioso	ITA	Ducati Team	60
3	Iannone	ITA	Ducati Team	40
4	Lorenzo	SPA	Movistar Yamaha MotoGP	37
5	Marquez	SPA	Repsol Honda Team	36
6	Crutchlow	GBR	CWM LCR Honda	34
7	Smith	GBR	Monster Yamaha Tech 3	28
8	Espargaro A	SPA	Team Suzuki ECSTAR	22
9	Espargaro P	SPA	Monster Yamaha Tech 3	15
10	Viñales	SPA	Team Suzuki ECSTAR	15
11	Petrucci	ITA	Pramac Racing	15
12	Pedrosa	SPA	Repsol Honda Team	10
	Redding	GBR	EG 0,0 Marc VDS	10
14	Barbera	SPA	Avintia Racing	8
15	Hernandez	COL	Pramac Racing	6
	Miller	AUS	CWM LCR Honda	6
17	Aoyama	JPN	Repsol Honda Team	5
18	Hayden	USA	Aspar MotoGP Team	3
19	Baz	FRA	Athinà Forward Racing	2
20	Bradl	GER	Athinà Forward Racing	1
	Bautista	SPA	Aprilia Racing Team Gresini	1

14 LORIS BAZ
His first points in MotoGP. Struggled with a full tank but his feeling improved and Loris ran good, consistent lap times.

15 STEFAN BRADL
Problems with the electronics and tyres after ten laps meant he went from contending for the Open victory to struggling with no feel in the final laps.

16 NICKY HAYDEN
Battled back from a bad start and difficulties with the full tank to be in contention for top Open bike only to go wide on the brakes at the final corner.

17 EUGENE LAVERTY
The race didn't live up to Eugene's impressive qualifying performance. Loss of feel and grip from the rear tyre was the main problem as the suspension didn't perform as it had in practice.

18 MIKE DI MEGLIO
Better in the race than qualifying. Raced with the big Open group but lost out in the final laps after contact with Laverty.

19 ALVARO BAUTISTA
Too cautious in the first part of the race to be within range of a point at the finish despite having conserved his tyre well.

20 MARCO MELANDRI
Like his team-mate, careful at the start of the race so unable to score points. Same problems as before but closer to the winner than in the first two races.

21 KAREL ABRAHAM
Another non-score, again thanks to technical problems that appeared for the first time immediately after the start. Acceleration out of corners suffered most.

22 ALEX DE ANGELIS
It all went downhill after good practice. Lack of grip meant he qualified last and he ran off-track on the first lap of the race.

DID NOT FINISH

HIROSHI AOYAMA
Was 11th when clipped by Petrucci on the last lap.

MARC MARQUEZ
Opened up a big lead only to be closed down by Rossi. Tried to bite back when the Yamaha came past but tagged Rossi's back wheel and fell.

YONNY HERNANDEZ
Looking good until oil leaking onto the exhaust caused a fire, which caused the rear suspension to collapse.

DID NOT RACE

DANI PEDROSA
Recovering from the operation he had to cure arm pump. Replaced for the second race by Aoyama.

GRAN PREMIO bwin
DE ESPAÑA
CIRCUITO DE JEREZ

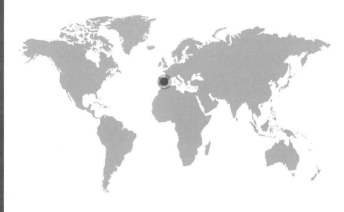

LORENZO'S LAND

Jorge Lorenzo added another dimension to an already enthralling season with a dominating win

It's great to have Jorge back. It's even better to have his ego back. If you've watched him over the years you'll know that, like all top sportsmen, he's at his best when he's feeling confident. That's a statement of the obvious, but the point is that most sports folk hide their true feelings quite effectively. Not Jorge.

Afflicted by problems with his crash helmet, bronchitis and tyres over the first three races, he arrived at Jerez following the longest rostrum-free run of his MotoGP career apart from the crash-prone streak of his rookie year. Jerez is the track where he'd previously had four poles and two victories – now make that five and three. He led every lap. He broke his own lap record by over three-quarters of a second. He lowered the race record by 20 seconds. And he established himself as a championship contender again. His gap to Rossi at the top was now 20 points – no longer a scary number.

There was never any doubt because there couldn't be. For Jorge to fail here would have been unthinkable, so he didn't think it. At the pre-event press conference his opening remark was 'I am in perfect condition, so no excuses.' Once he'd dominated qualifying with the first ever lap of Jerez below 1:38.0, nearly 0.4 second quicker than anyone else, he knew 'everything is possible'.

'I rode many impressive lap times in my career, but this one is very special. A 1:37.9 with these temperatures is very impressive and I am very satisfied,' he said at the front-row press conference. His concluding remark was a belter, delivered straight-faced with no hint of irony: 'I can do great things.' Nobody laughed.

And so he went out on race day and indeed did great things, adding a new dimension to an already fascinating season. Welcome back to Lorenzo's Land.

'WE HAVE RECOVERED
THE FEELING AND THE
ABILITY TO GO FAST'

JORGE LORENZO

Jorge's whole weekend was copybook perfect. Start from pole, get the holeshot, break the lap record on the first flying lap, and circulate with metronomic regularity. Ignoring the first and last laps, he opened with two laps in the 1:38 bracket, then 16 in the 1:39s and eight in the 1:40s. The slowest lap, his penultimate at 1:40.214, was 1.479 seconds slower than his new lap record of 1:38.735. Even his final lap would have been counted if Jorge hadn't taken time to wave to fans on the hillsides around the Nieto and Peluqui corners.

Jorge's team-mate, championship leader Valentino Rossi, qualified in the middle of the second row but lost time early on fighting with Pol Espargaro – which is exactly why Jorge's qualifying prowess is important. Lorenzo did have one piece of luck, however, in that Marc Marquez wasn't quite race-fit. The little finger on his left hand had been broken in a dirt-tracking accident, when he'd had a small crash and a friend ran over his hand. That happened at about 2pm on the Saturday between the Argentinian and Spanish GPs, and he was in theatre by around 5pm to have the break pinned. Not unnaturally, he started the weekend steadily, going from three-quarters of a second off the pace in FP1 to an eighth of a second by the end of Friday. By Saturday, Marc was looking as competitive as ever, even if he didn't put in any long runs. He even had a crash at Turn One in qualifying, sliding off with the injured hand held well out of harm's way. All that did was make him abandon the three-run strategy he pioneered at Jerez the previous year. However, Rossi, Lorenzo, Crutchlow and Aleix Espargaro all used it, with varying degrees of success.

In the race, Marc latched onto the rear of Lorenzo's Yamaha and hung on for longer than anyone expected.

ABOVE Although he started on the front row, Andrea Iannone had the engine's rain map selected and dropped to last before fighting back to sixth

OPPOSITE Scott Redding continued to find the factory Honda a tricky proposition but scored points for the third time in four races

LEFT Lorenzo started from pole, led every lap, and set the fastest lap of the race

ABOVE Jack Miller leads Andrea Dovizioso, who ran wide early in the race and had to recover through the field to ninth

BELOW Pol Espargaro had his best race of the season so far with a solid fifth place on his Tech 3 Yamaha

OPPOSITE Jorge Lorenzo got to stand on the podium for the first time this season following two fourths and a fifth place

That's how it looked, anyway. In fact Marc knew after five laps that although his finger wasn't a problem, he was over-compensating for the injury with his right arm. In fact he had to worry about Valentino Rossi, who closed to under a second with six laps to go. 'I thought it was going to be Argentina all over again,' said Marc, but this time Valentino couldn't close him down.

Rossi didn't know whether to be happy that he'd extended his championship lead or worry about how long it took him to find a set-up. It was like the old days, with changes being tested in Sunday morning warm-up. The set-up was good, but you got the impression that it wasn't good enough for Valentino as he looked to defend his points lead. One interesting point was that race day was much hotter than the rest of the weekend, something that in the past has worked for the Hondas and against the Yamahas, with their reliance on edge grip – this is especially true of Lorenzo. If Jorge had any problems, no-one could see them. Cal Crutchlow's fourth place also looked good, but surely would have been a rostrum if he'd qualified decently. In the Open Class, Hector Barbera reasserted his authority after Jack Miller's interruption in Argentina.

When the race was over, one journalist asked Jorge Lorenzo how it felt to be back. That got a quizzical stare and a measured response: 'I haven't been away.' Which, strictly speaking, was true. Two fourths and one fifth place in the first three races of the year hardly represent a meltdown, but Jorge's gaps to the leaders in those races were significant. Yes, there may have been extenuating circumstances, but it was nearly as bad a start to the year as 12 months previously. And now, with one victory, he was suddenly a contender again.

GEOFF DUKE, 1923–2015

Motorcycle racing lost its first modern champion with the death of Geoff Duke just before the weekend of the Spanish GP. His record of wins and six world titles – two on 350cc Nortons, one on the 500cc Manx Norton and three in a row on Gilera's 500cc fours – is impressive enough, but doesn't do full justice to his achievements.

As a rider he was smooth and precise as well as tough – the Italians called him 'The Iron Duke'. He introduced a new level of professionalism, typified by his pioneering of one-piece leathers, and worked with Rex McCandless to develop the first modern motorcycle chassis, the Norton Featherbed.

As the only man to win the top title on a British single-cylinder bike, he worked with legendary team manager Joe Craig and ex-pat Polish engineer Leo Kuzmicki to extend the competition life of the Manx Norton. Then he controversially defected to Italy, where he persuaded the Gilera factory to adopt the same design principles.

With Gilera he became the first man to win three 500cc titles

in a row, from 1953 to 1955 (the photo above shows him in '55). He was also the first rider to win two titles in a season (350cc and 500cc in 1951 for Norton) and the first to win the 500cc title on two different makes of motorcycle. He was awarded the OBE in 1953.

Duke started with Norton's trials team before taking to tarmac in 1948 in the Junior Clubmans TT. He won the Senior Manx GP the following year and

the Senior TT in 1950 – his first Grand Prix win. He also raced sports cars with some success and ran his own team, Scuderia Duke, after retiring from competition.

Away from the track, he retired to the Isle of Man where he was involved in several successful business ventures, including the first roll-on/roll-off ferry to serve the island and the pioneering company Duke Video.

GRAN PREMIO bwin DE ESPAÑA
CIRCUITO DE JEREZ
ROUND 4
MAY 3

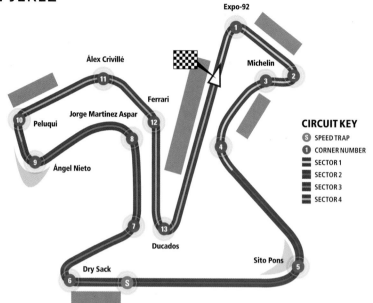

CIRCUIT KEY
- **S** SPEED TRAP
- **1** CORNER NUMBER
- SECTOR 1
- SECTOR 2
- SECTOR 3
- SECTOR 4

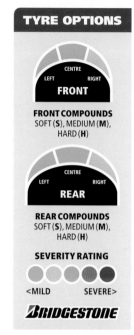

TYRE OPTIONS

FRONT

FRONT COMPOUNDS
SOFT (**S**), MEDIUM (**M**),
HARD (**H**)

REAR

REAR COMPOUNDS
SOFT (**S**), MEDIUM (**M**),
HARD (**H**)

SEVERITY RATING

<MILD   SEVERE>

BRIDGESTONE

RACE RESULTS

CIRCUIT LENGTH 2.748 miles

NO. OF LAPS 27

RACE DISTANCE 74.205 miles

WEATHER Dry, 26°C

TRACK TEMPERATURE 30°C

WINNER Jorge Lorenzo

FASTEST LAP 1m 38.735s,
100.165mph, Jorge Lorenzo (record)

PREVIOUS LAP RECORD 1m 39.565s,
99.357mph, Jorge Lorenzo (2013)

QUALIFYING

	Rider	Nation	Motorcycle	Team	Time	Pole +
1	Lorenzo	SPA	Yamaha	Movistar Yamaha MotoGP	1m 37.910s	
2	Marquez	SPA	Honda	Repsol Honda Team	1m 38.300s	0.390s
3	Iannone	ITA	Ducati	Ducati Team	1m 38.468s	0.558s
4	Espargaro P	SPA	Yamaha	Monster Yamaha Tech 3	1m 38.539s	0.629s
5	Rossi	ITA	Yamaha	Movistar Yamaha MotoGP	1m 38.632s	0.722s
6	Espargaro A	SPA	Suzuki	Team Suzuki ECSTAR	1m 38.638s	0.728s
7	Crutchlow	GBR	Honda	CWM LCR Honda	1m 38.714s	0.804s
8	Dovizioso	ITA	Ducati	Ducati Team	1m 38.823s	0.913s
9	Hernandez	COL	Ducati	Pramac Racing	1m 39.464s	1.554s
10	Smith	GBR	Yamaha	Monster Yamaha Tech 3	1m 39.491s	1.581s
11	Petrucci	ITA	Ducati	Pramac Racing	1m 39.789s	1.879s
12	Redding	GBR	Honda	EG 0,0 Marc VDS	1m 39.825s	1.915s
13	Barbera	SPA	Ducati	Avintia Racing	1m 39.569s	Q1
14	Viñales	SPA	Suzuki	Team Suzuki ECSTAR	1m 39.603s	Q1
15	Bautista	SPA	Aprilia	Aprilia Racing Team Gresini	1m 39.612s	Q1
16	Aoyama	JPN	Honda	Repsol Honda Team	1m 39.866s	Q1
17	Laverty E	IRL	Honda	Aspar MotoGP Team	1m 39.974s	Q1
18	Hayden	USA	Honda	Aspar MotoGP Team	1m 40.025s	Q1
19	Bradl	GER	Yamaha	Athinà Forward Racing	1m 40.166s	Q1
20	Abraham	CZE	Honda	AB Motoracing	1m 40.177s	Q1
21	Baz	FRA	Yamaha	Athinà Forward Racing	1m 40.280s	Q1
22	Miller	AUS	Honda	CWM LCR Honda	1m 40.365s	Q1
23	Di Meglio	FRA	Ducati	Avintia Racing	1m 40.817s	Q1
24	De Angelis	RSM	ART	Octo IodaRacing Team	1m 41.108s	Q1
25	Melandri	ITA	Aprilia	Aprilia Racing Team Gresini	1m 41.273s	Q1

1 JORGE LORENZO
An exhibition of near-perfection from the first free-practice session to the last lap of the race. Jorge and Yamaha agreed to take up the option for another year together in 2016 and he responded with a touch of his old genius.

2 MARC MARQUEZ
Managed the broken little finger on his left hand brilliantly to take a few points back from Rossi. Naturally, he overworked his right arm and when he had to rest it Rossi closed in, but Marc was able to prevent what he thought was going to be a repeat of Argentina.

3 VALENTINO ROSSI
Not happy despite taking his 200th podium finish in Grand Prix racing. Didn't get set-up perfect, thought he might catch Marquez but had a couple of warnings from the tyres and had to settle for third.

4 CAL CRUTCHLOW
Happy to be top satellite bike again. Knew he couldn't catch Rossi so managed the gap to Pol Espargaro.

5 POL ESPARGARO
His best result of the season so far. Qualified well, started brilliantly, and fought first with Rossi and then with

Crutchlow. May have tried too hard while third but despite arm pump was able to manage the gap to Iannone.

6 ANDREA IANNONE
Switched to the 'rain map' rather than launch control at the start, so had to do the whole race with it as changing is complicated. Managed a great ride under the circumstances.

7 ALEIX ESPARGARO
Suzuki brought some upgrades and made progress with their chatter. Lack of power is no longer a problem, according to Aleix, it's managing the power they've got.

8 BRADLEY SMITH
After three crashes, eighth place at a track he doesn't enjoy was a relief. Closed down on Aleix Espargaro – hard tyre versus soft tyre – late in the race.

9 ANDREA DOVIZIOSO
Ran off-track at the final corner of the second lap and rejoined in last place.

10 YONNY HERNANDEZ
His second top-ten finish of the year came as a relief after two disappointing races. Preserved his tyres well, battled entertainingly with his team-mate in the second half of the race.

11 MAVERICK VIÑALES
His race was compromised by a crash in qualifying but it was another impressive weekend for the rookie, despite a bad start from 14th on the grid.

12 DANILO PETRUCCI
He was the leading Ducati in the early laps but couldn't stay with Iannone when he came past. Diced with his team-mate but was caught by Viñales on the last lap.

13 SCOTT REDDING
Happier with the front but still missing out badly on corner exit. Relying on the Monday test for a cure.

LAP CHART

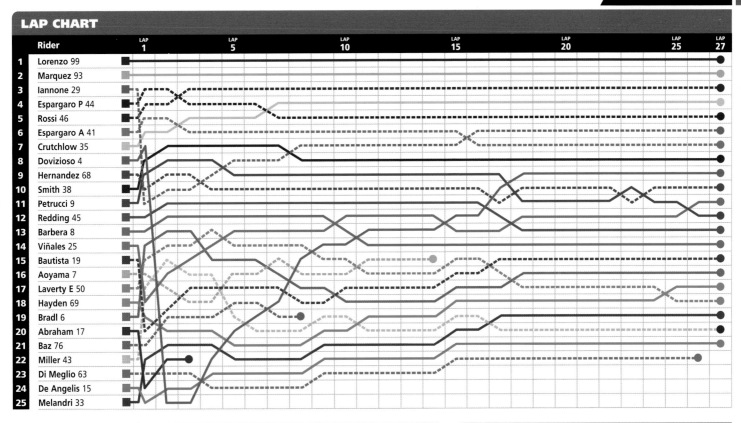

	Rider						
1	Lorenzo 99						
2	Marquez 93						
3	Iannone 29						
4	Espargaro P 44						
5	Rossi 46						
6	Espargaro A 41						
7	Crutchlow 35						
8	Dovizioso 4						
9	Hernandez 68						
10	Smith 38						
11	Petrucci 9						
12	Redding 45						
13	Barbera 8						
14	Viñales 25						
15	Bautista 19						
16	Aoyama 7						
17	Laverty E 50						
18	Hayden 69						
19	Bradl 6						
20	Abraham 17						
21	Baz 76						
22	Miller 43						
23	Di Meglio 63						
24	De Angelis 15						
25	Melandri 33						

RACE

	Rider	Motorcycle	Race time	Time +	Fastest lap	Avg. speed	B
1	Lorenzo	Yamaha	44m 57.246s		1m 38.735s	99.0mph	H/M
2	Marquez	Honda	45m 02.822s	5.576s	1m 38.823s	98.8mph	H/M
3	Rossi	Yamaha	45m 08.832s	11.586s	1m 39.186s	98.6mph	H/M
4	Crutchlow	Honda	45m 19.973s	22.727s	1m 39.444s	98.2mph	H/M
5	Espargaro P	Yamaha	45m 23.866s	26.620s	1m 39.169s	98.1mph	H/M
6	Iannone	Ducati	45m 24.267s	27.021s	1m 39.829s	98.1mph	H/M
7	Espargaro A	Suzuki	45m 32.691s	35.445s	1m 39.444s	97.7mph	M/S
8	Smith	Yamaha	45m 33.542s	36.296s	1m 40.139s	97.7mph	H/M
9	Dovizioso	Ducati	45m 39.179s	41.933s	1m 40.000s	97.5mph	H/M
10	Hernandez	Ducati	45m 48.318s	51.072s	1m 39.882s	97.2mph	H/M
11	Viñales	Suzuki	45m 48.920s	51.674s	1m 40.638s	97.1mph	M/S
12	Petrucci	Ducati	45m 49.667s	52.421s	1m 40.199s	97.1mph	H/M
13	Redding	Honda	45m 50.298s	53.052s	1m 40.317s	97.1mph	H/M
14	Barbera	Ducati	45m 50.446s	53.200s	1m 40.722s	97.1mph	H/S
15	Bautista	Aprilia	45m 54.590s	57.344s	1m 40.548s	96.9mph	H/S
16	Bradl	Yamaha	45m 56.264s	59.018s	1m 40.714s	96.9mph	H/M
17	Hayden	Honda	45m 58.752s	1m 01.506s	1m 41.292s	96.8mph	H/S
18	Laverty E	Honda	46m 00.409s	1m 03.163s	1m 40.766s	96.7mph	H/S
19	Melandri	Aprilia	46m 04.141s	1m 06.895s	1m 41.321s	96.6mph	H/S
20	Miller	Honda	46m 11.428s	1m 14.182s	1m 40.715s	96.4mph	H/S
21	De Angelis	ART	46m 24.078s	1m 26.832s	1m 41.755s	95.9mph	H/S
22	Di Meglio	Ducati	45m 28.537s	1 lap	1m 41.576s	94.3mph	H/S
NC	Aoyama	Honda	23m 47.434s	13 laps	1m 40.949s	97.0mph	H/H
NC	Baz	Yamaha	13m 40.421s	19 laps	1m 40.887s	96.4mph	H/M
NC	Abraham	Honda	5m 14.679s	24 laps	1m 41.562s	94.3mph	H/S

CHAMPIONSHIP

	Rider	Nation	Team	Points
1	Rossi	ITA	Movistar Yamaha MotoGP	82
2	Dovizioso	ITA	Ducati Team	67
3	Lorenzo	SPA	Movistar Yamaha MotoGP	62
4	Marquez	SPA	Repsol Honda Team	56
5	Iannone	ITA	Ducati Team	50
6	Crutchlow	GBR	CWM LCR Honda	47
7	Smith	GBR	Monster Yamaha Tech 3	36
8	Espargaro A	SPA	Team Suzuki ECSTAR	31
9	Espargaro P	SPA	Monster Yamaha Tech 3	26
10	Viñales	SPA	Team Suzuki ECSTAR	20
11	Petrucci	ITA	Pramac Racing	19
12	Redding	GBR	EG 0,0 Marc VDS	13
13	Hernandez	COL	Pramac Racing	12
14	Pedrosa	SPA	Repsol Honda Team	10
15	Barbera	SPA	Avintia Racing	10
16	Miller	AUS	CWM LCR Honda	6
17	Aoyama	JPN	Repsol Honda Team	5
18	Hayden	USA	Aspar MotoGP Team	3
19	Baz	FRA	Athinà Forward Racing	2
20	Bautista	SPA	Aprilia Racing Team Gresini	2
21	Bradl	GER	Athinà Forward Racing	1

14 HECTOR BARBERA
A perfect weekend. Top Open Class finisher in among factory bikes and well clear of the second Open man.

15 ALVARO BAUTISTA
The Aprilia team's first point of the year was reward for a much-improved weekend in practice, qualifying and the race. It might have been better but for a coming-together with Barbera on the first lap.

16 STEFAN BRADL
Handicapped both by a touch of flu and using the harder tyre. Nevertheless, second Open bike home.

17 NICKY HAYDEN
Couldn't run the pace he expected in the first half of the race. Was more consistent in the second part and made up a couple of places.

18 EUGENE LAVERTY
His set-up had a lot of weight on the rear to cure traction problems, but that meant he was fighting the front all race. That led to arm pump early on, and it got worse.

19 MARCO MELANDRI
Like his team-mate, Marco had a much-improved weekend. Handicapped by bad qualifying and getting stuck behind Miller.

20 JACK MILLER
Another Honda rider who had problems with grip. Ran wide mid-race and lost touch with the group. Tried to get back but realised he would crash, so brought the bike home.

21 ALEX DE ANGELIS
Never found a set-up to cope with the lack of grip, then lost touch with the field when he avoided the crashing di Meglio.

22 MIKE DI MEGLIO
Crashed when he lost the front at Turn 1. Got back on but took a long time to regain his confidence.

DID NOT FINISH

HIROSHI AOYAMA
The only rider to chose the harder rear tyre. Maintained it was the correct decision but made a mistake and crashed at mid-distance.

LORIS BAZ
Crashed at the final corner just before half distance while pushing to stay with Laverty and Bradl.

KAREL ABRAHAM
Still no points. Getting desperate after another crash.

DID NOT RACE

DANI PEDROSA
Still recovering from his arm-pump operation. Replaced by Aoyama for the third time.

FRANCE
ROUND 5

MONSTER ENERGY GRAND PRIX DE FRANCE
LE MANS

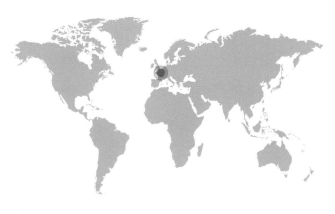

MASTER BLASTER

Jorge Lorenzo won again as it became clear that Honda, and Marc Marquez in particular, had serious problems

It's taken for granted nowadays that we don't really understand how a season is unfolding until we get back to Europe and the tracks the teams know so well. So at Le Mans it was no surprise that Jorge Lorenzo reprised his Jerez win, and again wasn't headed in the race. The surprise, or rather shock, was what happened to reigning champion Marc Marquez, the man who won at Le Mans 12 months previously and sat on pole position this time.

Despite that pole position, Marquez's Honda never looked settled. It was making shapes as usual, but not the shapes you expect. It looked twitchier, nervous. There was none of the standard – for Marc – corner-entry style where the rear wheel waves from side to side as he pitches the thing in before it has time to settle, yet still finds the apex. When he can do that, you see smooth, controlled movements – impossible for other riders, granted, but still smooth. At Le Mans, however, if he got his bike out of shape going into a corner, it suddenly and viciously snapped back into line, usually resulting in Marc running on. None of this was enough to stop him finding a stunning lap for pole position, just three-quarters of a second faster than anything he'd managed before, but the problems were back on the first lap of the race.

Marquez was punted wide by Andrea Iannone on the run through Turn 1 and then tried a highly optimistic lunge up the inside at the left-handed entry to the Dunlop chicane. Often as not, this is the sort of manoeuvre that Marc gets away with, but not this time; he let both factory Ducatis through to chase after hole-shot man Jorge Lorenzo. Usually this wouldn't have been a problem as Marc would have hunted them down before half-distance. This time, though, both Valentino Rossi and Bradley Smith came past him in the next four laps as Marc

'WITH NOBODY IN FRONT I CAN BRAKE PERFECTLY'

JORGE LORENZO

lapped over a second slower than the leaders. He did get faster, but only fast enough to fight for fourth with Iannone and Smith, some 20 seconds behind Lorenzo.

The man who did challenge the leader was Rossi, who made another stunning charge from the third row of the grid thanks mainly to a set-up fix thrown in for warm-up – just like the old days with Jerry Burgess. Valentino closed on his team-mate but never got much nearer than two seconds as Lorenzo controlled the gap from half-distance. Behind the Yamahas, Andrea Dovizioso rode to another rostrum finish, his fourth in five races.

The other Andrea was lucky to start the race, and not many thought he would figure. Iannone had two big crashes during testing at Mugello on the Monday before this GP and suffered a dislocated shoulder. Amazingly, he found the strength to indulge in a ferocious battle with Marquez, with Smith involved too. It was as graphic an illustration of Marquez's woes as you could imagine; every pass was met with an instant repass, the double champion unable to dispense with the injured Italian in his first year as a works rider. There was also the biggest moment you can imagine on the brakes when Marc got up to them for the first time. His bike twitched instantly and madly going into the Chemin aux Boeufs chicane. Somehow he saved it but had to make up ground again.

And it wasn't just Marc's bike. The other Hondas were having serious trouble too. Dani Pedrosa, back from his arm-pump problems, crashed on the second lap but got going again, and both satellite bikes crashed on the run down the hill to Chapelle, echoing Marquez's complaints about the front end. It must be said that Crutchlow put up his hand and admitted a mistake, but it was very clear

OPPOSITE Dani Pedrosa returned from his arm problems, fell, got back on and lapped at a good pace to finish the race

ABOVE Bradley Smith takes in some last-minute tips

LEFT Andrea Dovizioso leads briefly off the start on his way to third place and a fourth rostrum finish in five races

ABOVE Valentino Rossi chases, but for the second race running Jorge Lorenzo led every lap

BELOW Nicky Hayden flashes a smile after finishing on top of the Open Class

OPPOSITE Marquez's bike problems put him in a highly entertaining fight with Andrea Iannone

that the 2015 version of the RCV was, as Cal said at the first test, 'not an easy bike to ride'.

Interestingly, Pedrosa had a very similar view after his eventful afternoon. The media wanted to talk to him about his arm; he wanted to talk about the bike. No, he didn't know why he'd crashed. Yes, the arm held up well, as demonstrated by the fact that his lap times didn't drop off. Yes, he was very pleased. The bike? He spoke of problems with stability going into corners and traction coming out. He went into some detail and emphasised that work needed to be done if Honda hoped to catch the Ducatis, let alone the Yamahas. Dovizioso provided corroborating evidence when he offered the opinion in the winners' press conference that Marquez's talent had been masking the Honda's failings.

The numbers backed him up. Marquez's race time was very close to his winning time of the previous season. However, Lorenzo's winning time was nearly 20 seconds quicker than his 2014 time, while Dovi's race time was nearly 30 seconds better than his previous year's time! The implications were clear. Yamaha had made subtle but significant improvements over winter. Ducati's new bike, still only five races old, was a massive improvement over its predecessor. Honda had stood still – at best.

HRC boss Shuhei Nakamoto bravely stated that the motor wasn't to blame. In light of his riders' comments, not many people believed him. However, with the technical regulations mandating a freeze on engine development for the season, he had little option but to brazen it out. The question now was this: what could Honda do with electronics to try to ameliorate what seemed to be a fundamental problem with the design of its engine.

WHAT'S WRONG WITH IT?

Honda's problems at Le Mans didn't appear from nowhere. Marc Marquez and the factory knew from the Valencia test that the new motor was too aggressive into and out of corners. Things weren't so bad at the Sepang tests, and perhaps because of the nature of the big, wide-open track and tropical weather conditions, it seemed as if the problems had been sorted out.

The first race of the year, however, left Marc in no doubt that he had a problem. As the Texan and Argentinian races involved much tyre conservation, the problems were again disguised and the rest of the world could be forgiven for overlooking them. At Le Mans, though, the low-grip track, a big temperature change and short gearing conspired to make the RCV a nightmare. Even more confusingly, the rise in track temperature on race day didn't benefit Honda as might usually be expected.

Clearly, Marquez could still pull out a blindingly fast lap when it was needed, but what he couldn't do was string 20 of them together.

He described the corner-entry problem as 'locking up' – in other words

when he shuts the throttle and goes down the gearbox the rear wheel can't keep up. Going out of corners, the rear spins up too easily. Both symptoms could be simplistically explained by a low-inertia crankshaft, which stops spinning instantly when the throttle is

closed, but in reality the cause is likely to be a combination of design factors.

As MotoGP regulations specify that engine design is frozen for the season, it was fair to surmise that Honda had a problem that was going to be difficult to solve.

MONSTER ENERGY GRAND PRIX DE FRANCE
LE MANS
ROUND 5
MAY 17

RACE RESULTS

CIRCUIT LENGTH 2.597 miles

NO. OF LAPS 28

RACE DISTANCE 72.812 miles

WEATHER Dry, 18°C

TRACK TEMPERATURE 32°C

WINNER Jorge Lorenzo

FASTEST LAP 1m 32.879s, 100.786mph, Valentino Rossi (record)

PREVIOUS LAP RECORD 1m 33.548s, 100.041mph, Marc Marquez (2014)

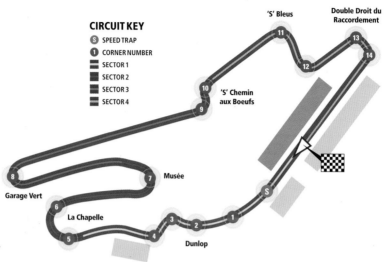

CIRCUIT KEY
- S SPEED TRAP
- 1 CORNER NUMBER
- SECTOR 1
- SECTOR 2
- SECTOR 3
- SECTOR 4

QUALIFYING

	Rider	Nation	Motorcycle	Team	Time	Pole +
1	Marquez	SPA	Honda	Repsol Honda Team	1m 32.246s	
2	Dovizioso	ITA	Ducati	Ducati Team	1m 32.749s	0.503s
3	Lorenzo	SPA	Yamaha	Movistar Yamaha MotoGP	1m 32.846s	0.600s
4	Crutchlow	GBR	Honda	CWM LCR Honda	1m 32.897s	0.651s
5	Iannone	ITA	Ducati	Ducati Team	1m 33.001s	0.755s
6	Smith	GBR	Yamaha	Monster Yamaha Tech 3	1m 33.299s	1m 053s
7	Rossi	ITA	Yamaha	Movistar Yamaha MotoGP	1m 33.352s	1m 106s
8	Pedrosa	SPA	Honda	Repsol Honda Team	1m 33.419s	1m 173s
9	Petrucci	ITA	Ducati	Pramac Racing	1m 33.556s	1m 310s
10	Espargaro A	SPA	Suzuki	Team Suzuki ECSTAR	1m 33.665s	1m 419s
11	Hernandez	COL	Ducati	Pramac Racing	1m 33.714s	1m 468s
12	Espargaro P	SPA	Yamaha	Monster Yamaha Tech 3	1m 33.724s	1m 478s
13	Viñales	SPA	Suzuki	Team Suzuki ECSTAR	1m 34.245s	Q1
14	Hayden	USA	Honda	Aspar MotoGP Team	1m 34.267s	Q1
15	Redding	GBR	Honda	EG 0,0 Marc VDS	1m 34.551s	Q1
16	Bradl	GER	Yamaha	Athinà Forward Racing	1m 34.575s	Q1
17	Di Meglio	FRA	Ducati	Avintia Racing	1m 34.833s	Q1
18	Miller	AUS	Honda	CWM LCR Honda	1m 34.858s	Q1
19	Barbera	SPA	Ducati	Avintia Racing	1m 34.870s	Q1
20	Abraham	CZE	Honda	AB Motoracing	1m 34.940s	Q1
21	Laverty E	IRL	Honda	Aspar MotoGP Team	1m 34.947s	Q1
22	Baz	FRA	Yamaha	Athinà Forward Racing	1m 35.456s	Q1
23	Bautista	SPA	Aprilia	Aprilia Racing Team Gresini	1m 35.458s	Q1
24	De Angelis	RSM	ART	Octo IodaRacing Team	1m 35.680s	Q1
25	Melandri	ITA	Aprilia	Aprilia Racing Team Gresini	1m 37.522s	Q1

1 JORGE LORENZO
Two wins in a row after missing out on the podium put Jorge right back in the mix. This win was just as impressive as Jerez: he took the lead at the second corner and pulled out half a second in the first lap, after which he didn't lap outside the 1:33 bracket until the last lap.

2 VALENTINO ROSSI
Completed a perfect day for Yamaha but Valentino's inability to get up to Jorge despite setting the fastest lap showed that his problem with qualifying remains. Vale credited a big change on Sunday morning for his ability to be competitive.

3 ANDREA DOVIZIOSO
Got the holeshot but was immediately passed by Lorenzo. Held off Rossi until mid-distance but a distinct drop in rear grip prevented a counter attack. Another rostrum, but slightly disappointed.

4 MARC MARQUEZ
Never looked comfortable all weekend despite qualifying on pole. There was a massive improvement in warm-up, but the warmer track didn't deliver for Honda; instead it produced front-end grip problems. Had a massive moment on the first lap and another while dicing with Iannone and Smith.

5 ANDREA IANNONE
Rode despite dislocating his left shoulder in testing the previous week. He was fine for ten laps but then had to compensate with his right arm. Nevertheless, he had an entertaining dice with Marquez and Smith.

6 BRADLEY SMITH
Much-improved qualifying gave him the chance to race for fourth place. Diced with Marquez and Iannone but was pushed out by Marquez's final lunge at Dunlop chicane.

7 POL ESPARGARO
A great race after looking lost in practice and qualifying. Quickly settled in seventh

and had a lonely race managing the gap to Hernandez. Suffered arm pump and had an operation the following week.

8 YONNY HERNANDEZ
Went straight to the second qualifying session and ran in the top ten all race without any problems.

9 MAVERICK VIÑALES
Had to be content with ninth after a very promising Sunday morning warm-up suggested he could take advantage of the warmer conditions. However, Maverick gave away several positions at the second corner and spent the race fighting back.

10 DANILO PETRUCCI
Still having difficulty with the bike on a full tank at the start of the race. Then a worn rear tyre meant he couldn't fight off Viñales at the close.

11 NICKY HAYDEN
Topped the Open Class for the first time this season. Electronics problems caused problems for the last ten laps.

12 LORIS BAZ
Delighted to be second Open bike at his first home Grand Prix. Raced with a special livery and found he could lap consistently faster than in practice.

LAP CHART

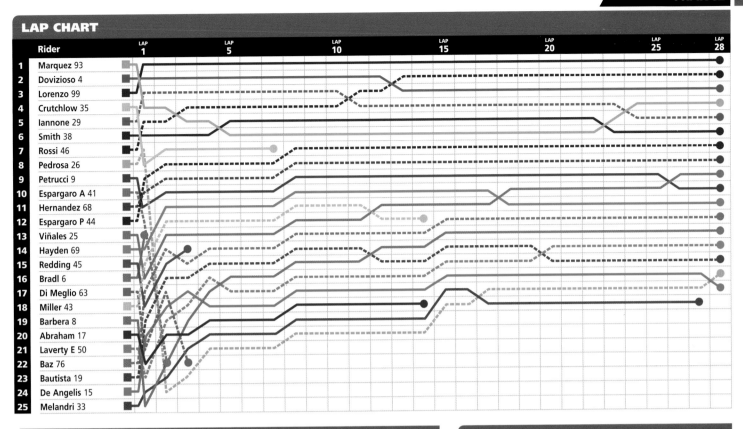

	Rider	LAP 1	LAP 5	LAP 10	LAP 15	LAP 20	LAP 25	LAP 28
1	Marquez 93							
2	Dovizioso 4							
3	Lorenzo 99							
4	Crutchlow 35							
5	Iannone 29							
6	Smith 38							
7	Rossi 46							
8	Pedrosa 26							
9	Petrucci 9							
10	Espargaro A 41							
11	Hernandez 68							
12	Espargaro P 44							
13	Viñales 25							
14	Hayden 69							
15	Redding 45							
16	Bradl 6							
17	Di Meglio 63							
18	Miller 43							
19	Barbera 8							
20	Abraham 17							
21	Laverty E 50							
22	Baz 76							
23	Bautista 19							
24	De Angelis 15							
25	Melandri 33							

RACE

	Rider	Motorcycle	Race time	Time +	Fastest lap	Avg. speed	
1	Lorenzo	Yamaha	43m 44.143s		1m 33.004s	99.9mph	S/S
2	Rossi	Yamaha	43m 47.963s	3.820s	1m 32.879s	99.7mph	S/S
3	Dovizioso	Ducati	43m 56.523s	12.380s	1m 33.039s	99.4mph	S/S
4	Marquez	Honda	44m 04.033s	19.890s	1m 33.310s	99.1mph	S/S
5	Iannone	Ducati	44m 04.380s	20.237s	1m 33.035s	99.1mph	S/S
6	Smith	Yamaha	44m 05.288s	21.145s	1m 33.559s	99.0mph	S/S
7	Espargaro P	Yamaha	44m 19.636s	35.493s	1m 33.940s	98.5mph	S/S
8	Hernandez	Ducati	44m 23.744s	39.601s	1m 34.427s	98.4mph	S/S
9	Viñales	Suzuki	44m 25.714s	41.571s	1m 34.477s	98.3mph	S/S
10	Petrucci	Ducati	44m 26.932s	42.789s	1m 34.495s	98.2mph	S/S
11	Hayden	Honda	44m 37.779s	53.636s	1m 34.418s	97.9mph	S/XS
12	Baz	Yamaha	44m 44.760s	1m 00.617s	1m 34.936s	97.6mph	S/XS
13	Barbera	Ducati	44m 48.415s	1m 04.272s	1m 34.768s	97.5mph	S/S
14	Laverty E	Honda	44m 49.402s	1m 05.259s	1m 35.219s	97.4mph	S/XS
15	Bautista	Aprilia	44m 49.658s	1m 05.515s	1m 34.863s	97.4mph	S/XS
16	Pedrosa	Honda	45m 05.050s	1m 20.907s	1m 34.083s	96.9mph	S/S
17	De Angelis	ART	45m 05.806s	1m 21.663s	1m 35.595s	96.9mph	S/XS
18	Melandri	Aprilia	44m 22.904s	1 lap	1m 36.986s	94.9mph	S/XS
NC	Miller	Honda	22m 19.390s	14 laps	1m 34.503s	97.8mph	S/XS
NC	Abraham	Honda	22m 44.150s	14 laps	1m 35.756s	96.1mph	S/S
NC	Crutchlow	Honda	11m 05.352s	21 laps	1m 33.585s	98.5mph	S/S
NC	Redding	Honda	4m 53.755s	25 laps	1m 34.226s	95.6mph	S/S
NC	Di Meglio	Ducati	5m 24.444s	25 laps	1m 35.876s	86.6mph	S/S
NC	Espargaro A	Suzuki	3m 24.384s	26 laps	–	91.6mph	S/S
NC	Bradl	Yamaha	1m 43.349s	27 laps	–	90.5mph	S/S

CHAMPIONSHIP

	Rider	Nation	Team	Points
1	Rossi	ITA	Movistar Yamaha MotoGP	102
2	Lorenzo	SPA	Movistar Yamaha MotoGP	87
3	Dovizioso	ITA	Ducati Team	83
4	Marquez	SPA	Repsol Honda Team	69
5	Iannone	ITA	Ducati Team	61
6	Crutchlow	GBR	CWM LCR Honda	47
7	Smith	GBR	Monster Yamaha Tech 3	46
8	Espargaro P	SPA	Monster Yamaha Tech 3	35
9	Espargaro A	SPA	Team Suzuki ECSTAR	31
10	Viñales	SPA	Team Suzuki ECSTAR	27
11	Petrucci	ITA	Pramac Racing	25
12	Hernandez	COL	Pramac Racing	20
13	Redding	GBR	EG 0,0 Marc VDS	13
14	Barbera	SPA	Avintia Racing	13
15	Pedrosa	SPA	Repsol Honda Team	10
16	Hayden	USA	Aspar MotoGP Team	8
17	Baz	FRA	Athinà Forward Racing	6
18	Miller	AUS	CWM LCR Honda	6
19	Aoyama	JPN	Repsol Honda Team	5
20	Bautista	SPA	Aprilia Racing Team Gresini	3
21	Laverty E	IRL	Aspar MotoGP Team	2
22	Bradl	GER	Athinà Forward Racing	1

13 HECTOR BARBERA
Just grateful to get away with a few points from a weekend where the team used an aggressive map and a new chassis.

14 EUGENE LAVERTY
His first points in MotoGP. Despite two practice crashes he got a good set-up (very different from previous races) then fought back from running on at the second corner.

15 ALVARO BAUTISTA
Another point. Good on new tyres and at the end of the race, but the bike was unstable in the middle of the race.

16 DANI PEDROSA
The comeback from his arm operation. Crashed on lap two but remounted to lap at impressive pace for the entire race.

17 ALEX DE ANGELIS
Happy to have split the factory Aprilias but lost touch with the group containing Barbera when di Meglio crashed in front of him. Continued to lap at the same pace as the group, so it could have been considerably better.

18 MARCO MELANDRI
Never happy, and in the race hampered by gearbox problems.

DID NOT FINISH

JACK MILLER
After a good start he dealt well with the universal Honda problem of lack of front grip. Tried to stay with Viñales when the Suzuki came past but crashed at Dunlop on lap 15.

CAL CRUTCHLOW
Crashed at Turn 6 but blamed it on his own mistake rather than the lack of front grip. His foot slipped off the rear brake and he grabbed too much front brake.

KAREL ABRAHAM
Stopped yet again by a mechanical problem. Pulled in on the 14th lap.

SCOTT REDDING
Another Honda rider who lost the front end, this time going down the hill towards Chapelle.

MIKE DI MEGLIO
Lost a lot of time when he came together with Viñales on the first lap, then crashed at Chemin aux Boeufs on the second lap.

ALEIX ESPARGARO
Stopped by a clutch problem before his hand injury – from a massive Saturday crash – made itself felt. He was operated on the following week.

STEFAN BRADL
Started well but was the first victim of Turn 6 when he lost the front on the second lap.

GRAN PREMIO D'ITALIA TIM
AUTODROMO DEL MUGELLO

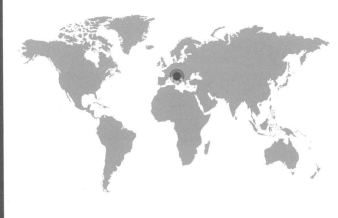

COMEBACK COMPLETED

They came to worship Valentino Rossi, but had to make do with booing Jorge Lorenzo's third win in a row

Mugello always looks stunning but this year it looked even more beautiful than usual. Maybe it was the Italian expectation in the run-up to the event: Valentino Rossi leading the championship, Ducati competitive. Surely victory was possible for Valentino, who hadn't won at Mugello since his legendary seven-in-a-row run came to an end in 2008? Surely Ducati was finally in with a chance of winning after so far putting at least one bike on every 2015 rostrum except Jerez. An Italian winning the Italian GP on an Italian bike? That hadn't been done since 1974, when Gianfranco Bonera won at Imola on an MV Agusta. Before the event Ducati even paraded its bikes in Siena's medieval centre in the Piazza del Campo, the site of the Palio horse race, and it's difficult to imagine a more Italian coming-together of traditions.

Unfortunately for the romantics, one other record had been overlooked – Jorge Lorenzo's three Mugello wins in a row 2011–13.

Nevertheless, things started well for Ducati. To no-one's surprise, Andrea Dovizioso was fastest on Friday and then dropped a hint about special qualifying motors. As Ducati races with concessions, among which are 12 motors for the season and no development freeze, this may not have been an idle threat. And indeed the factory bikes did take new motors on Saturday morning and the regular riders both got on the front row with the bonus of factory tester Michele Pirro, racing as a wild card, getting sixth position. It was Andrea Iannone who was fastest, thus becoming the first Italian on an Italian bike to be on pole for an Italian GP since Giacomo Agostini and MV Agusta in 1972. If it were possible, Iannone was in even more pain than he

ABOVE Iannone took his first MotoGP pole and scored a career-best finish

OPPOSITE Rossi and Dovizioso sweep past their fans on the packed banks

BELOW Pirro, the factory test rider, made it three works Ducatis on the grid

was two weeks previously in Le Mans. Since then he'd been diagnosed with a cracked humerus, and needed help to take off his crash helmet, one with a special design. His race prospects didn't look good. As for Ducati's rocket motors, Iannone got pole by following Lorenzo, and Pirro followed Dovi for his sixth position.

Rossi again only managed to qualify on the third row and was now publicly acknowledging that he had to improve this area of his performance and do it quickly in order to stay in front of Lorenzo in the championship, or indeed the race. No-one felt shocked

any longer by Valentino's grid slot; frankly, a front-row start had become a surprise. What was unprecedented was Marc Marquez's 13th place. Not only did he fail to make it through directly to Q2 (see page 89), but he then managed not to finish first or second in Q1! Jorge Lorenzo voiced everyone's thoughts best: 'The first corner here is always...' – a very long pause for thought – 'quite complicated.'

Jorge was right. As expected, Marquez flew up the inside and gained seven places by the time he came out of the first corner. Yonny Hernandez attempted to track him but simply couldn't hold the line and went wide, miraculously not taking anyone with him. The big loser was Rossi, who not only failed to make up ground but actually lost places. Bravest was that other perennial poor qualifier, Bradley Smith, who went round the outside to set up an excellent race.

The biggest controversy of the race happened at the start – right at the start. It appeared to most spectators and TV viewers that Andrea Iannone jumped the start from pole position, so a ride-through penalty was surely going to come his way. Then Karel Abraham was called in for the same offence. As Race Direction announces penalties in grid order, Iannone was evidently in the clear. HRC sent some senior management for a none-too-gentle word with Race Director Mike Webb. It turned out that Iannone was very, very lucky. Mugello's red lights above the start line use old-fashioned bulbs, not LEDs, so the glow lingers longer. Forensic analysis of the pictures showed that the Italian hadn't gone before Webb turned the lights off – by the tiniest of margins. Webb's office

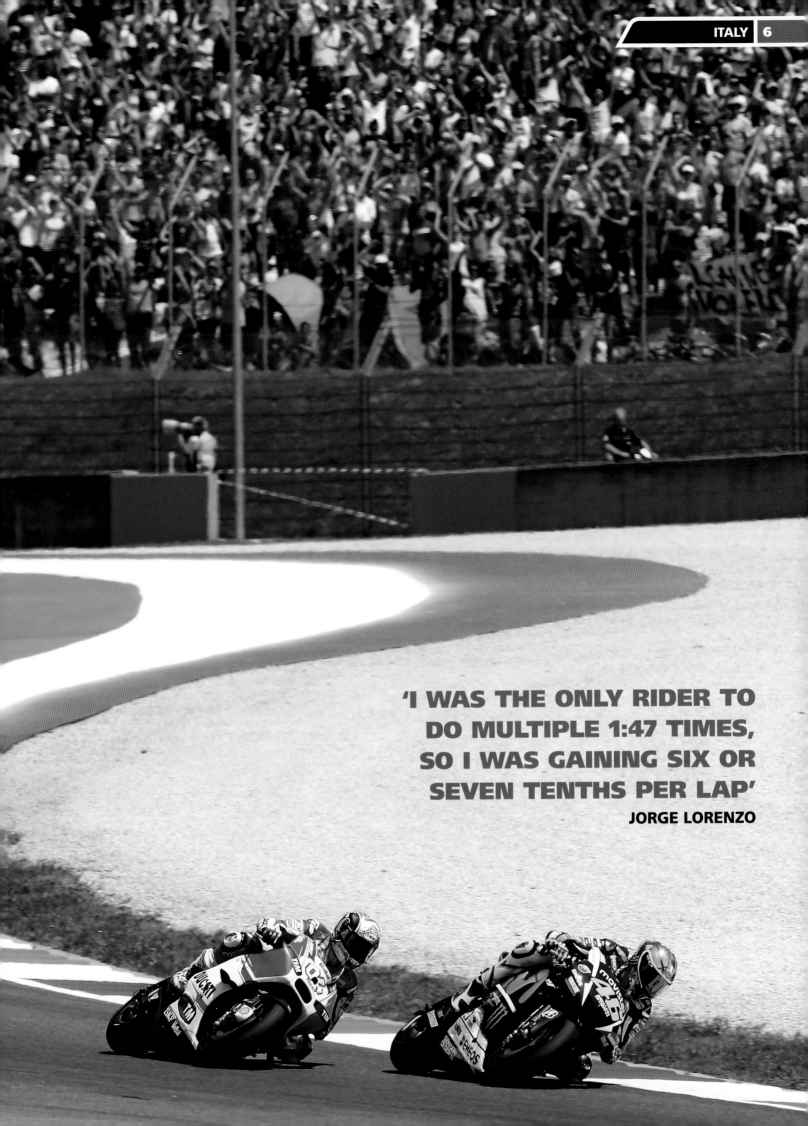

'I WAS THE ONLY RIDER TO
DO MULTIPLE 1:47 TIMES,
SO I WAS GAINING SIX OR
SEVEN TENTHS PER LAP'

JORGE LORENZO

door allegedly suffered as the deputation departed.

Over 90,000 fans, the overwhelming majority wearing yellow, then suffered as the inevitable happened. Lorenzo put in another of those millimetre-perfect performances to lead every lap. Marquez got up to second on the third lap but Lorenzo rode away from him at half a second a lap and, to make it worse, Marc then came under attack from the factory Ducatis. First Dovi went past, but as he started to fade due to vibration, which would put him out, Iannone took over second place. Marquez managed to stay with Iannone, but with increasing difficulty. The inevitable happened at Turn 1 on the 17th lap.

In his post-mortem, Marc noted that he didn't have the same problems on corner exit as at Le Mans, probably because of the nature of the course. But braking into corners was definitely still an issue. He was, he said, getting 'no support from the rear' and therefore having to load the front more and more. For the opening laps, when there was a bit of grip at the back, he could ride at the leaders' pace, but once grip dropped off he started over-working the front. He visibly struggled to get the thing turned at the end of the main straight a few times before it finally slid away from him.

Miraculously, Iannone didn't fade and his second place was a career-best finish in MotoGP. Rossi was again quick at the end of the race but too far back to threaten his team-mate. The locals roundly booed Jorge on the rostrum, an experience he appeared to relish.

ABOVE Loris Baz's 12th place was good enough to top the Open Class

BELOW Eugene Laverty and Alvaro Bautista both made it into the points

OPPOSITE Two Italians on the rostrum; the one in red was the faster

WHY DID MARQUEZ QUALIFY 13TH?

Qualifying is so important in today's MotoGP because gaps between riders are routinely measured in thousandths of a second. So how come Marc Marquez and his team managed to mess up so spectacularly?

The real mistake, says Marc, came in FP3 when the team didn't use a new tyre. Vital work on the electronics to try to improve performance on used tyres distracted them and they missed the cut by nine-thousandths of a second thanks to Maverick Viñales. So far, mildly embarrassing. The job now was to finish in the top two of Q1 and go forward to Q2 to shoot for pole. A minor crash in FP4 didn't help, and neither did the tyre allocation. The intention was to use only one in Q1, thus saving two for Q2.

For unknown reasons, Marc suffered massive wheelspin in the first qualifying session and was second behind the gutsy Aleix Espargaro as it came to an end. The plan appeared to be working; Marc looked safe and was sitting in his pit as the chequered flag came out. Then Yonny Hernandez, using the soft tyre, caught the slipstream of

Loris Baz as he came out of the final corner. Yonny couldn't have timed it better, and suddenly he was top of the session by more than a tenth of a second, thus pushing Marquez back to

third and consigning him to 13th place on the grid.

Unfortunately for Marc, the TV cameras were on him. Not surprisingly, he wasn't happy – and showed it.

GRAN PREMIO D'ITALIA TIM
AUTODROMO DEL MUGELLO
ROUND 6
MAY 31

OFFICIAL TIMEKEEPER

RACE RESULTS

CIRCUIT LENGTH 3.259 miles
NO. OF LAPS 23
RACE DISTANCE 74.959 miles
WEATHER Dry, 25°C
TRACK TEMPERATURE 48°C
WINNER Jorge Lorenzo
FASTEST LAP 1m 47.654s, 108.926mph, Marc Marquez
LAP RECORD 1m 47.639s, 108.989mph, Marc Marquez (2013)

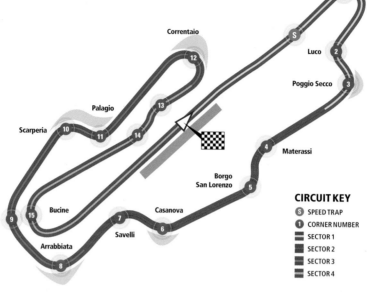

CIRCUIT KEY
- **S** SPEED TRAP
- **1** CORNER NUMBER
- SECTOR 1
- SECTOR 2
- SECTOR 3
- SECTOR 4

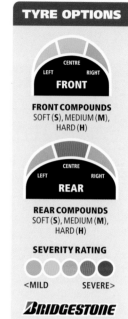

TYRE OPTIONS

FRONT
LEFT | CENTRE | RIGHT

FRONT COMPOUNDS
SOFT (**S**), MEDIUM (**M**), HARD (**H**)

REAR
LEFT | CENTRE | RIGHT

REAR COMPOUNDS
SOFT (**S**), MEDIUM (**M**), HARD (**H**)

SEVERITY RATING
<MILD   SEVERE>

BRIDGESTONE

QUALIFYING

	Rider	Nation	Motorcycle	Team	Time	Pole +
1	Iannone	ITA	Ducati	Ducati Team	1m 46.489s	
2	Lorenzo	SPA	Yamaha	Movistar Yamaha MotoGP	1m 46.584s	0.095s
3	Dovizioso	ITA	Ducati	Ducati Team	1m 46.610s	0.121s
4	Crutchlow	GBR	Honda	CWM LCR Honda	1m 46.657s	0.168s
5	Espargaro A	SPA	Suzuki	Team Suzuki ECSTAR	1m 46.854s	0.365s
6	Pirro	ITA	Ducati	Ducati Team	1m 46.870s	0.381s
7	Pedrosa	SPA	Honda	Repsol Honda Team	1m 46.875s	0.386s
8	Rossi	ITA	Yamaha	Movistar Yamaha MotoGP	1m 46.923s	0.434s
9	Viñales	SPA	Suzuki	Team Suzuki ECSTAR	1m 46.934s	0.445s
10	Espargaro P	SPA	Yamaha	Monster Yamaha Tech 3	1m 47.050s	0.561s
11	Smith	GBR	Yamaha	Monster Yamaha Tech 3	1m 47.090s	0.601s
12	Hernandez	COL	Ducati	Octo Pramac Racing	1m 47.423s	0.934s
13	Marquez	SPA	Honda	Repsol Honda Team	1m 47.240s	Q1
14	Petrucci	ITA	Ducati	Octo Pramac Racing	1m 47.497s	Q1
15	Barbera	SPA	Ducati	Avintia Racing	1m 47.978s	Q1
16	Bradl	GER	Yamaha	Athinà Forward Racing	1m 48.047s	Q1
17	Redding	GBR	Honda	EG 0,0 Marc VDS	1m 48.120s	Q1
18	Baz	FRA	Yamaha	Athinà Forward Racing	1m 48.133s	Q1
19	Hayden	USA	Honda	Aspar MotoGP Team	1m 48.298s	Q1
20	Abraham	CZE	Honda	AB Motoracing	1m 48.366s	Q1
21	Bautista	SPA	Aprilia	Aprilia Racing Team Gresini	1m 48.477s	Q1
22	Di Meglio	FRA	Ducati	Avintia Racing	1m 48.503s	Q1
23	Miller	AUS	Honda	CWM LCR Honda	1m 48.572s	Q1
24	Laverty E	IRL	Honda	Aspar MotoGP Team	1m 48.638s	Q1
25	De Angelis	RSM	ART	E-Motion IodaRacing Team	1m 49.198s	Q1
26	Melandri	ITA	Aprilia	Aprilia Racing Team Gresini	1m 51.391s	Q1

1 JORGE LORENZO
Perfection once more. Qualified only behind the Ducati and led every lap. Booed on the podium but gave every sign of enjoying it. Moved to within six points of his team-mate at the top of the points table.

2 ANDREA IANNONE
His best MotoGP result, and from pole position despite the painful shoulder from his testing crash three weeks earlier. That made itself felt later in the race when Andrea was fending off Rossi.

3 VALENTINO ROSSI
Delighted the home fans with a rostrum finish but again couldn't get on the first two rows of the grid, consigning himself to a battle through the field.

4 DANI PEDROSA
Much more like his old self. Impressive consistency of lap time and a good recovery from an average start. Held third place after his team-mate's crash until Rossi went past.

5 BRADLEY SMITH
Reverted to his old bad-qualifying habits but made up seven places on the first lap.

The race result accurately reflected Brad's form through the weekend.

6 POL ESPARGARO
Received a factory chassis but was still recovering from arm-pump surgery after the previous race. Not happy to finish behind his team-mate but admitted it was probably the best result possible.

7 MAVERICK VIÑALES
Went directly into Q2 and very happy with his best result of the year, which he attributed to a breakthrough in set-up. A little more power would have made him even happier.

8 MICHELE PIRRO
Ducati's test rider entered as a wild card for his first race on the GP15. Qualified sixth to help put Marquez out of Q2 and was the only factory rider to use the soft rear tyre in the race. Achieved his objective of finishing less than 30 seconds behind the winner.

9 DANILO PETRUCCI
Two falls on Saturday made it a difficult day for Danilo, who also struggled with the heat. Happier in the closing laps, and would have been very glad of his ninth place if he'd been offered it before the race!

10 YONNY HERNANDEZ
Suffered with chatter in the early laps but recovered to lap with his team-mate and give the newly christened Octo Pramac team a double top-ten finish.

11 SCOTT REDDING
A difficult weekend that didn't end as well as it started. Team and rider are starting to feel the pressure of expectation.

12 LORIS BAZ
Won the Open Class for the first time. Fought with Redding for over half the race but had to deal with tyre drop-off in the last ten laps. Impressive.

LAP CHART

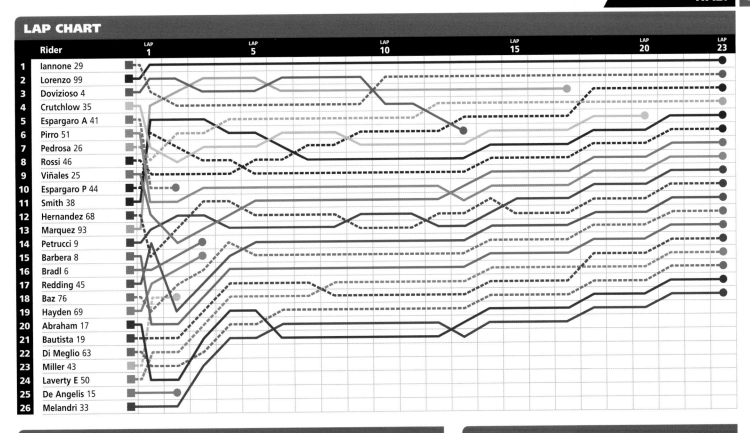

	Rider	LAP 1	LAP 5	LAP 10	LAP 15	LAP 20	LAP 23
1	Iannone 29						
2	Lorenzo 99						
3	Dovizioso 4						
4	Crutchlow 35						
5	Espargaro A 41						
6	Pirro 51						
7	Pedrosa 26						
8	Rossi 46						
9	Viñales 25						
10	Espargaro P 44						
11	Smith 38						
12	Hernandez 68						
13	Marquez 93						
14	Petrucci 9						
15	Barbera 8						
16	Bradl 6						
17	Redding 45						
18	Baz 76						
19	Hayden 69						
20	Abraham 17						
21	Bautista 19						
22	Di Meglio 63						
23	Miller 43						
24	Laverty E 50						
25	De Angelis 15						
26	Melandri 33						

RACE

	Rider	Motorcycle	Race time	Time +	Fastest lap	Avg. speed	B
1	Lorenzo	Yamaha	41m 39.173s		1m 47.700s	107.9mph	M/M
2	Iannone	Ducati	41m 44.736s	5.563s	1m 47.837s	107.7mph	M/M
3	Rossi	Yamaha	41m 45.834s	6.661s	1m 48.173s	107.7mph	M/M
4	Pedrosa	Honda	41m 49.151s	9.978s	1m 48.043s	107.5mph	M/M
5	Smith	Yamaha	41m 54.457s	15.284s	1m 48.415s	107.3mph	H/M
6	Espargaro P	Yamaha	41m 54.838s	15.665s	1m 48.698s	107.2mph	M/M
7	Viñales	Suzuki	42m 02.978s	23.805s	1m 48.774s	106.9mph	M/M
8	Pirro	Ducati	42m 08.325s	29.152s	1m 49.005s	106.7mph	M/S
9	Petrucci	Ducati	42m 11.181s	32.008s	1m 49.007s	106.6mph	M/M
10	Hernandez	Ducati	42m 13.744s	34.571s	1m 49.256s	106.5mph	H/M
11	Redding	Honda	42m 17.726s	38.553s	1m 49.217s	106.3mph	M/M
12	Baz	Yamaha	42m 21.331s	42.158s	1m 49.569s	106.1mph	M/S
13	Barbera	Ducati	42m 23.974s	44.801s	1m 49.662s	106.1mph	M/S
14	Bautista	Aprilia	42m 29.608s	50.435s	1m 49.868s	105.8mph	M/S
15	Laverty E	Honda	42m 32.233s	53.060s	1m 50.053s	105.7mph	M/S
16	Di Meglio	Ducati	42m 54.438s	1m 15.265s	1m 50.525s	104.8mph	M/S
17	Abraham	Honda	42m 54.554s	1m 15.381s	1m 49.602s	104.8mph	M/S
18	Melandri	Aprilia	43m 21.013s	1m 41.840s	1m 52.063s	103.7mph	M/S
NC	Crutchlow	Honda	36m 25.980s	3 laps	1m 48.620s	107.3mph	H/M
NC	Marquez	Honda	30m 54.340s	6 laps	1m 47.654s	107.6mph	H/M
NC	Dovizioso	Ducati	23m 40.721s	10 laps	1m 47.905s	107.3mph	M/M
NC	Bradl	Yamaha	5m 36.736s	20 laps	1m 49.379s	104.5mph	M/S
NC	Hayden	Honda	5m 36.942s	20 laps	1m 49.117s	104.4mph	M/S
NC	Espargaro A	Suzuki	3m 45.870s	21 laps	1m 49.330s	103.8mph	M/M
NC	Miller	Honda	3m 48.048s	21 laps	1m 49.839s	102.8mph	M/S
NC	De Angelis	ART	3m 52.933s	21 laps	1m 52.469s	100.7mph	M/S

CHAMPIONSHIP

	Rider	Nation	Team	Points
1	Rossi	ITA	Movistar Yamaha MotoGP	118
2	Lorenzo	SPA	Movistar Yamaha MotoGP	112
3	Dovizioso	ITA	Ducati Team	83
4	Iannone	ITA	Ducati Team	81
5	Marquez	SPA	Repsol Honda Team	69
6	Smith	GBR	Monster Yamaha Tech 3	57
7	Crutchlow	GBR	CWM LCR Honda	47
8	Espargaro P	SPA	Monster Yamaha Tech 3	45
9	Viñales	SPA	Team Suzuki ECSTAR	36
10	Petrucci	ITA	Octo Pramac Racing	32
11	Espargaro A	SPA	Team Suzuki ECSTAR	31
12	Hernandez	COL	Octo Pramac Racing	26
13	Pedrosa	SPA	Repsol Honda Team	23
14	Redding	GBR	EG 0,0 Marc VDS	18
15	Barbera	SPA	Avintia Racing	16
16	Baz	FRA	Athinà Forward Racing	10
17	Pirro	ITA	Ducati Team	8
	Hayden	USA	Aspar MotoGP Team	8
19	Miller	AUS	CWM LCR Honda	6
20	Aoyama	JPN	Repsol Honda Team	5
	Bautista	SPA	Aprilia Racing Team Gresini	5
22	Laverty E	IRL	Aspar MotoGP Team	3
23	Bradl	GER	Athinà Forward Racing	1

13 HECTOR BARBERA
Not happy on a circuit he loves. Two massive moments in the early laps, so after seeing the Bradl/Hayden crash he concentrated on bringing his bike home.

14 ALVARO BAUTISTA
Best result of the season so far, with the help of a seamless gearbox for the first time.

15 EUGENE LAVERTY
As at Le Mans, he had trouble with the bike but just as in France he scored points. Loss of feel from the front in the final third of the race was the problem.

16 MIKE DI MEGLIO
Found some feel from the front for the first time, but just missed out on his first point.

17 KAREL ABRAHAM
The bad news was a jump-start penalty. The good news was that the team finally looked to have found a cure for its problem with an overheating rear shock.

18 MARCO MELANDRI
The best that can be said is that both of the team's bikes got through the weekend with no technical problems, despite many new parts.

DID NOT FINISH

CAL CRUTCHLOW
The weekend looked promising until Sunday, when he had two big crashes, the first in warm-up and the second in the race, three laps from the flag – Cal was left with a dislocated ankle.

MARC MARQUEZ
Another fraught weekend characterised by Marc overriding a bike that didn't want to turn, resulting in the front tyre giving up in the race. Unbelievably, he didn't even make the second qualifying session.

ANDREA DOVIZIOSO
Forced to retire when his rear sprocket started to break up. Maybe a legacy of the embarrassing crash in warm-up?

STEFAN BRADL
Crashed on lap three when he made contact with Hayden after the Yamaha's rear stepped out.

NICKY HAYDEN
Looking good and confident in his set-up for the conditions, but was collected by Bradl when the German had a moment.

ALEIX ESPARGARO
Taken out by Petrucci at the first corner of lap three. Fortunately, there was no further damage to his injured thumb.

JACK MILLER
Lost the front at the final corner, the culmination of a series of front-end moments that started on the second lap.

ALEX DE ANGELIS
Changed to the softer tyre but found he had massive chatter, which was so bad that he pulled in at the end of the first lap.

GP MONSTER ENERGY DE CATALUNYA
CIRCUIT DE CATALUNYA

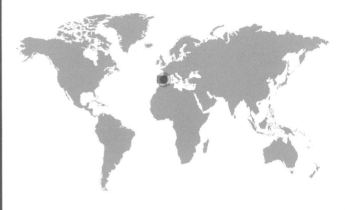

TURNING POINT

Jorge Lorenzo won again and reduced Rossi's lead to just one point – so why was Valentino so happy?

It looked like business as usual – or business as usual since MotoGP returned to Europe. Yamaha dominated, Honda said goodbye to its championship chances, the early promise of both Ducati and Suzuki was forgotten, and Jorge Lorenzo led every lap. There were, however, some interesting developments, not least in the power struggle between Yamaha's factory teams.

What we didn't expect was for Suzuki to be so competitive and for the evolution motor the team brought to Catalunya to propel Aleix Espargaro to pole position and his rookie team-mate Maverick Viñales to second place. The last time that happened was Jerez in 1993 thanks to Kevin Schwantz and Alex Barros. The last time there was a Suzuki on pole was Assen in 2007, Chris Vermeulen the rider.

Who'd have thought it? We've become a little too used to Suzuki, the smallest and most conservative of the Japanese big four, going off half-cocked. Both factory and team made all the right noises about coming back to win but, frankly, we were prepared to be underwhelmed. Reality turned out to be better than anyone's expectation. Aleix and Maverick had looked to be taking a big gamble in choosing to go to the new team rather than, say, Tech 3 or Marc VDS. Catalunya was the seventh race of the year and already their decision looked a lot more clever than anyone expected.

Did we now have a blue rocketship to contend with? Well, no. Suzuki did bring an evolution motor to Barcelona and while the bikes were still notably slower than the other factory entries, the gap was a major improvement on the start of the year, now down to between 5.5mph (race) and 7.7mph (FP3). The riders also reported the power characteristics to be significantly

ABOVE Jorge Lorenzo congratulates Aleix Espargaro on Suzuki's first pole position since Assen 2007

OPPOSITE Marc Marquez wore a Gaudi-inspired helmet design but didn't stay upright long enough for many people to appreciate it

RIGHT It is 450 metres from the start line to the first corner and already the Suzukis have been swallowed up by the pack

improved – a clever trick – but it still wasn't enough to save them from more embarrassment when the red lights went out. The distance from the front row of the Catalunya grid to the first corner is 450 metres, more than enough for the Suzukis to be swamped despite Espargaro getting off the line well. A seamless gearbox would have been a major help, but that was unlikely to appear until after the summer break.

There had been an undercurrent of discontented muttering about how the soft tyres helped the Ducatis and distorted the grid, and it now grew more audible as the Suzukis joined in. But as Valentino Rossi observed, speaking from the third row, Jorge was on the same bike as him and sat on the front row.

Marc Marquez started from the second row with a new exhaust system designed to try to take the edge off his engine's difficult power delivery. There were also rumours of any available space on the clutch basket receiving tungsten inserts – consistent with the story that the problem originated with a low-inertia crankshaft. Of course it would have been much more useful to put the weight on the crank spinning about two and a half times faster, but there was no way of getting to it without breaking Race Direction's seals. Did it work? Marquez reported that corner entry was slightly improved, but still said only positive things about the bike's behaviour on new tyres. He could stay with Lorenzo, he reckoned, for five laps. As it turned out, he couldn't.

Lorenzo outgunned the Suzukis into the first corner and was never headed. Marquez did latch on to him but on the third lap he was out. Coming to the left-hander at the end of the back straight, he appeared to brake far too

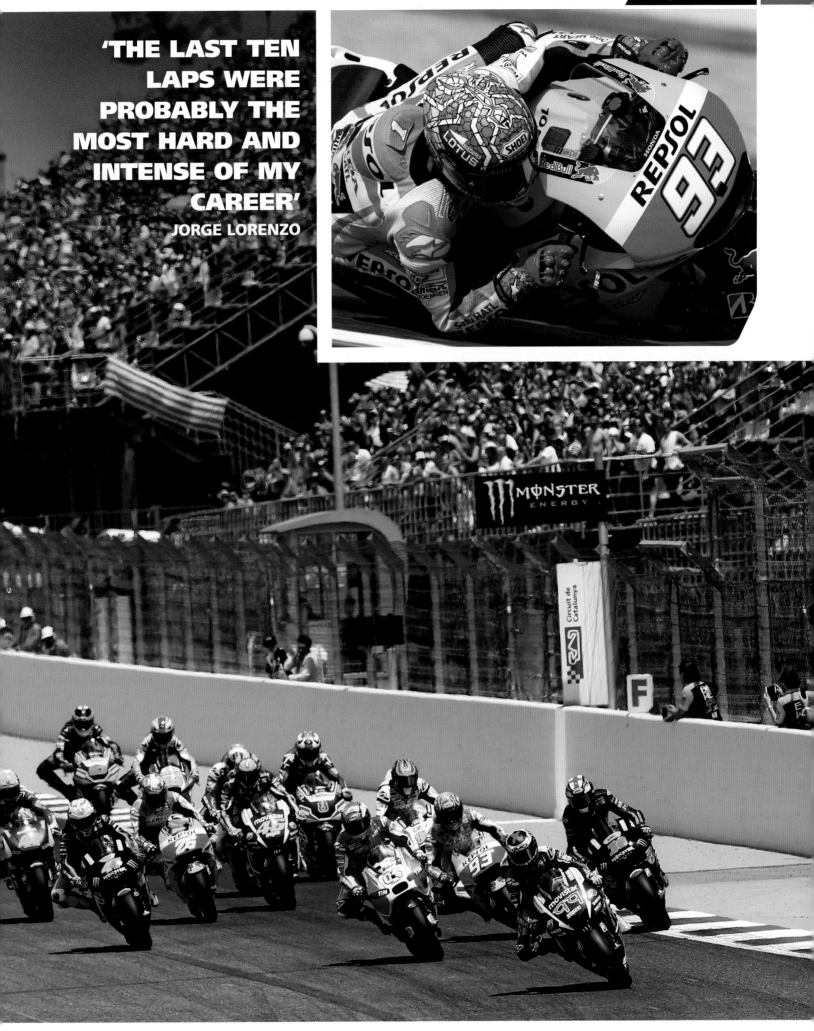

'THE LAST TEN LAPS WERE PROBABLY THE MOST HARD AND INTENSE OF MY CAREER'

JORGE LORENZO

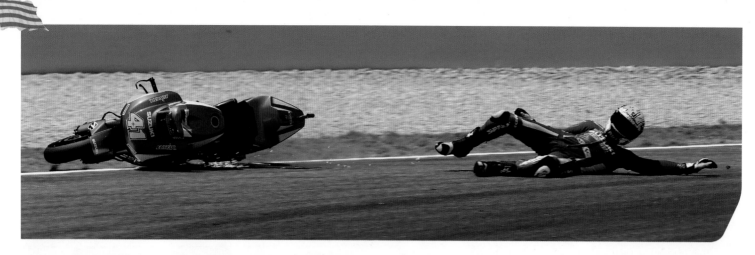

ABOVE Almost inevitably Aleix Espargaro pushed hard trying to make up for the Suzuki's poor start and paid the price

BELOW Andrea Dovizioso's superb start to the season receded into memory as he failed to finish for the second race in a row

late – or maybe the bike had one of those vicious twitches – and Marc squeezed down the outside of the Yamaha and ended up in the gravel trap with a broken gear lever. Marquez said he didn't touch Lorenzo, but Jorge said he felt the Honda graze his leathers. Frankly, it looked like a desperate move. Marc had been dropping hints about having no interest in riding for a safe second place and this looked like the move of a man who didn't care what happened. The two-day test the following week suddenly looked very important indeed.

Jorge did face some pressure, however, and it came from his team-mate. Valentino Rossi was up to second place by lap four, around one and a half seconds in arrears, and was able to match Lorenzo's lap times mid-race, and then better them in the closing stages. Valentino knew from early in practice that he'd be using the hard rear tyre and also adopted a narrower front rim – 3.5 inches as opposed to 4 – but was only too well aware

that you cannot give Lorenzo a start. Jorge had now led 103 consecutive MotoGP laps – a record – and won four consecutive races for the first time in his career. However, the Valentino who finished second this time was a much happier individual than the one on the rostrum in the previous three races. He believed he and his crew had turned a corner with set-up. Now it was simply a matter of sorting out qualifying.

Behind the two Yamahas, at a respectable distance, came perhaps the happiest man on the rostrum. Dani Pedrosa scored his first top-three finish of the year in only his third race after a highly speculative last-chance operation to cure his arm pump. Many people thought we'd never see him race again, but here he was easing through the field, looking more and more like his old self.

As did Rossi. His championship lead may have been whittled down to just one point, but for the first time since the return to Europe he didn't look worried about it.

RCV FOR THE ROAD

Casey Stoner rode an RCV Honda again at Barcelona – but this was a road-going version. This ultimate street bike, which will be going on sale to the public for €188,000, will be built at the rate of just one a day for as long as it takes to fulfil orders, which Honda expects will total between 200 and 250.

The RCV213R-S, to give it its full name, is very close in specification to the Open Class RCV1000R of 2014, so it doesn't have a seamless gearbox or pneumatic valves. The chassis and swinging arm are straight from HRC, as are the sandcast cases, titanium con rods, Ohlins suspension and Brembo brakes. It has a ride-by-wire throttle and other electronics that Honda hasn't previously put on any of its street bikes. In 'regular' trim the engine produces just 156bhp, but a sports kit bumps that up to over 212bhp at a cost of €12,000. It includes a new ECU, different intake ducting, exhaust and quick-shifter, and various changes to electronics, all of which turn the RCV into a projectile.

The visual clues that tell you this is the S-model, not the factory racer, are the 17-inch wheels (although, like the

16-inch race equipment, they're from Marchesini), the cleverly integrated lights, and the mirrors on the end of the bar protectors.

But the street accoutrements are irrelevant. Honda will sell RCVs because affluent fans want to own a piece of

MotoGP technology. Previous experience with such bikes as the Honda NR750 and Ducati's Desmosedici RR suggests that not only will owners get to live with and pore over the latest GP technology, but they'll also have an appreciating asset.

RIGHT Dani Pedrosa returned to the rostrum for the first time since his arm-pump surgery

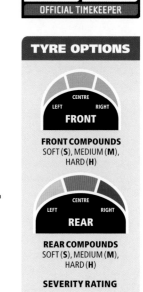

GP MONSTER ENERGY DE CATALUNYA
CIRCUIT DE CATALUNYA
ROUND 7
JUNE 14

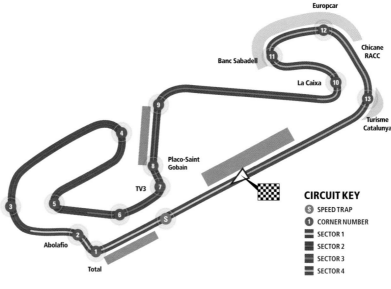

RACE RESULTS

CIRCUIT LENGTH 2.937 miles

NO. OF LAPS 25

RACE DISTANCE 73.431 miles

WEATHER Dry, 28°C

TRACK TEMPERATURE 49°C

WINNER Jorge Lorenzo

FASTEST LAP 1m 42.219s, 103.396mph, Marc Marquez

LAP RECORD 1m 42.182s, 103.458mph, Marc Marquez (2014)

TYRE OPTIONS

FRONT

CENTRE
LEFT   RIGHT

FRONT COMPOUNDS
SOFT (**S**), MEDIUM (**M**), HARD (**H**)

REAR

CENTRE
LEFT   RIGHT

REAR COMPOUNDS
SOFT (**S**), MEDIUM (**M**), HARD (**H**)

SEVERITY RATING

<MILD   SEVERE>

BRIDGESTONE

CIRCUIT KEY
- **S** SPEED TRAP
- **1** CORNER NUMBER
- SECTOR 1
- SECTOR 2
- SECTOR 3
- SECTOR 4

QUALIFYING

	Rider	Nation	Motorcycle	Team	Time	Pole +
1	Espargaro A	SPA	Suzuki	Team Suzuki ECSTAR	1m 40.546s	
2	Viñales	SPA	Suzuki	Team Suzuki ECSTAR	1m 40.629s	0.083s
3	Lorenzo	SPA	Yamaha	Movistar Yamaha MotoGP	1m 40.646s	0.100s
4	Marquez	SPA	Honda	Repsol Honda Team	1m 40.754s	0.208s
5	Dovizioso	ITA	Ducati	Ducati Team	1m 40.907s	0.361s
6	Pedrosa	SPA	Honda	Repsol Honda Team	1m 40.928s	0.382s
7	Rossi	ITA	Yamaha	Movistar Yamaha MotoGP	1m 41.058s	0.512s
8	Smith	GBR	Yamaha	Monster Yamaha Tech 3	1m 41.068s	0.522s
9	Crutchlow	GBR	Honda	CWM LCR Honda	1m 41.195s	0.649s
10	Hernandez	COL	Ducati	Octo Pramac Racing	1m 41.333s	0.787s
11	Espargaro P	SPA	Yamaha	Monster Yamaha Tech 3	1m 41.385s	0.839s
12	Iannone	ITA	Ducati	Ducati Team	1m 41.524s	0.978s
13	Barbera	SPA	Ducati	Avintia Racing	1m 42.003s	Q1
14	Redding	GBR	Honda	EG 0,0 Marc VDS	1m 42.029s	Q1
15	Bradl	GER	Yamaha	Athinà Forward Racing	1m 42.053s	Q1
16	Petrucci	ITA	Ducati	Octo Pramac Racing	1m 42.155s	Q1
17	Di Meglio	FRA	Ducati	Avintia Racing	1m 42.273s	Q1
18	Hayden	USA	Honda	Aspar MotoGP Team	1m 42.485s	Q1
19	Baz	FRA	Yamaha	Athinà Forward Racing	1m 42.592s	Q1
20	Bautista	SPA	Aprilia	Aprilia Racing Team Gresini	1m 42.600s	Q1
21	Miller	AUS	Honda	CWM LCR Honda	1m 42.928s	Q1
22	Laverty E	IRL	Honda	Aspar MotoGP Team	1m 42.971s	Q1
23	De Angelis	RSM	ART	E-Motion IodaRacing Team	1m 42.601s	Q1
24	Melandri	ITA	Aprilia	Aprilia Racing Team Gresini	1m 42.345s	Q1
25	Abraham	CZE	Honda	AB Motoracing	1m 43.008s	Q1

1 JORGE LORENZO
Another race that went according to plan – almost. He got the holeshot from the front row but never opened up a decisive gap, and then Rossi closed him down. Jorge used the hard rear tyre and suffered in the higher temperatures, but by the end of the race he had led 103 consecutive laps.

2 VALENTINO ROSSI
Knew from early on that he'd race with the extra-hard rear and that he'd be quick in the closing laps. But his race was again compromised by qualifying on the third row. Vale was happy, though, that his pace was the equal of Jorge's.

3 DANI PEDROSA
Managed not to go straight to Q2 but again put together good race pace. Although the gap to the leaders was substantial, he got a solid rostrum finish.

4 ANDREA IANNONE
A great result from 12th on the grid, but it was very hard work. Just happy to retake third position in the championship.

5 BRADLEY SMITH
Went for a set-up that gave him front feel at the expense of lap times. Another good race helped by another good start again made him first satellite bike.

6 MAVERICK VIÑALES
His best result so far in qualifying and the race, but Maverick was more interested in the fact that he'd lapped at the same sort of pace as other factory bikes – but, like his team-mate, he lost out at the start on the run to Turn 1.

7 SCOTT REDDING
Season's best result that equalled his career-best MotoGP finish in the trickiest of conditions, exceeding his team's expectations. After 15 laps he had trouble with arm pump, which made it difficult for him to release the brake progressively. Competitive all weekend.

8 STEFAN BRADL
Stefan's second points-scoring round of the year and his first Open Class win.

9 DANILO PETRUCCI
A second top-ten finish after the same difficult weekend experienced by the other Ducati riders. The problems got worse with the heat on Sunday, and he was convinced he couldn't have done better.

10 ALVARO BAUTISTA
The Aprilia's first top-ten finish. Ran with the main pack, avoided all the incidents and had an entertaining dice with Miller before pulling away in the final laps.

11 JACK MILLER
After crashing out of the previous two races, happy to finish despite struggling with the front all weekend.

12 EUGENE LAVERTY
A good Friday, then two crashes on Saturday, and another points-scoring ride on Sunday. Much happier with the bike's ability to find grip at the end of the race.

13 LORIS BAZ
Struggled with chatter but closed to within three points of Open Class leader Barbera.

LAP CHART

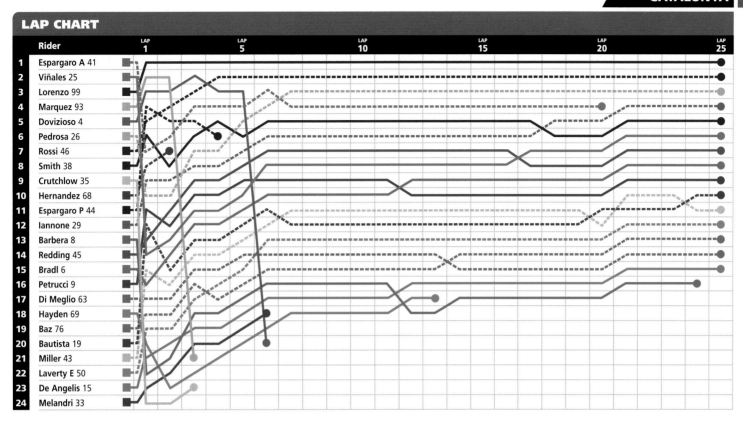

	Rider	LAP 1	LAP 5	LAP 10	LAP 15	LAP 20	LAP 25
1	Espargaro A 41						
2	Viñales 25						
3	Lorenzo 99						
4	Marquez 93						
5	Dovizioso 4						
6	Pedrosa 26						
7	Rossi 46						
8	Smith 38						
9	Crutchlow 35						
10	Hernandez 68						
11	Espargaro P 44						
12	Iannone 29						
13	Barbera 8						
14	Redding 45						
15	Bradl 6						
16	Petrucci 9						
17	Di Meglio 63						
18	Hayden 69						
19	Baz 76						
20	Bautista 19						
21	Miller 43						
22	Laverty E 50						
23	De Angelis 15						
24	Melandri 33						

RACE

	Rider	Motorcycle	Race time	Time +	Fastest lap	Avg. speed	🅱
1	Lorenzo	Yamaha	42m 53.208s		1m 42.225s	102.7mph	M/M
2	Rossi	Yamaha	42m 54.093s	0.885s	1m 42.356s	102.7mph	M/M
3	Pedrosa	Honda	43m 12.663s	19.455s	1m 42.855s	101.9mph	M/M
4	Iannone	Ducati	43m 18.133s	24.925s	1m 42.979s	101.7mph	H/M
5	Smith	Yamaha	43m 20.990s	27.782s	1m 42.818s	101.6mph	M/M
6	Viñales	Suzuki	43m 22.767s	29.559s	1m 43.268s	101.5mph	M/M
7	Redding	Honda	43m 29.632s	36.424s	1m 42.672s	101.3mph	M/M
8	Bradl	Yamaha	43m 35.311s	42.103s	1m 43.535s	101.0mph	M/S
9	Petrucci	Ducati	43m 42.558s	49.350s	1m 43.512s	100.8mph	H/M
10	Bautista	Aprilia	43m 45.777s	52.569s	1m 44.028s	100.7mph	M/S
11	Miller	Honda	43m 46.874s	53.666s	1m 43.929s	100.6mph	M/S
12	Laverty E	Honda	43m 48.973s	55.765s	1m 44.178s	100.5mph	M/S
13	Baz	Yamaha	43m 49.040s	55.832s	1m 44.486s	100.5mph	M/S
14	Di Meglio	Ducati	44m 02.245s	1m 09.037s	1m 44.517s	100.0mph	M/S
15	De Angelis	ART	44m 18.471s	1m 25.263s	1m 44.850s	99.4mph	M/M
16	Barbera	Ducati	43m 35.670s	1 lap	1m 44.277s	97.0mph	M/S
NC	Espargaro A	Suzuki	34m 37.015s	5 laps	1m 42.692s	101.8mph	M/M
NC	Hayden	Honda	23m 20.849s	12 laps	1m 43.905s	98.1mph	M/S
NC	Melandri	Aprilia	10m 58.022s	19 laps	1m 45.936s	96.4mph	M/S
NC	Dovizioso	Ducati	11m 39.502s	19 laps	1m 42.527s	90.7mph	H/M
NC	Espargaro P	Yamaha	6m 57.659s	21 laps	1m 43.166s	101.2mph	M/M
NC	Marquez	Honda	5m 55.818s	22 laps	1m 42.219s	89.1mph	M/M
NC	Crutchlow	Honda	7m 12.563s	22 laps	1m 53.571s	73.3mph	M/M
NC	Hernandez	Ducati	3m 30.978s	23 laps	1m 42.977s	100.2mph	H/M

CHAMPIONSHIP

	Rider	Nation	Team	Points
1	Rossi	ITA	Movistar Yamaha MotoGP	138
2	Lorenzo	SPA	Movistar Yamaha MotoGP	137
3	Iannone	ITA	Ducati Team	94
4	Dovizioso	ITA	Ducati Team	83
5	Marquez	SPA	Repsol Honda Team	69
6	Smith	GBR	Monster Yamaha Tech 3	68
7	Crutchlow	GBR	CWM LCR Honda	47
8	Viñales	SPA	Team Suzuki ECSTAR	46
9	Espargaro P	SPA	Monster Yamaha Tech 3	45
10	Pedrosa	SPA	Repsol Honda Team	39
	Petrucci	ITA	Octo Pramac Racing	39
12	Espargaro A	SPA	Team Suzuki ECSTAR	31
13	Redding	GBR	EG 0,0 Marc VDS	27
14	Hernandez	COL	Octo Pramac Racing	26
15	Barbera	SPA	Avintia Racing	16
16	Baz	FRA	Athinà Forward Racing	13
17	Bautista	SPA	Aprilia Racing Team Gresini	11
	Miller	AUS	CWM LCR Honda	11
19	Bradl	GER	Athinà Forward Racing	9
20	Pirro	ITA	Ducati Team	8
	Hayden	USA	Aspar MotoGP Team	8
22	Laverty E	IRL	Aspar MotoGP Team	7
23	Aoyama	JPN	Repsol Honda Team	5
24	Di Meglio	FRA	Avintia Racing	2
25	De Angelis	RSM	E-Motion IodaRacing Team	1

14 MIKE DI MEGLIO
His first points of the year came thanks to much-improved feel for the first half of the race.

15 ALEX DE ANGELIS
His first point of the year. Alex was able to stay with the top Open Class bikes for seven laps before having to focus on tyres that were going off.

16 HECTOR BARBERA
Made a fantastic start only to find he couldn't stop the bike at Turn 1. Pitted and fixed the problem but missed out on another Open Class victory.

DID NOT FINISH

ALEIX ESPARGARO
Blazingly fast all weekend and gave Suzuki its first pole for eight years, but he was swamped on the run to the first corner. Fought back to the top five but crashed when he ran wide thanks to a combination of worn tyre and bumps.

NICKY HAYDEN
Ran off-track on the first lap avoiding two riders, then his engine stopped. He rejoined the race only to crash at Turn 5.

MARCO MELANDRI
Tried some different chassis settings, but his race was curtailed by a gearbox problem.

ANDREA DOVIZIOSO
Like the other factory Ducati riders, he used the hard front tyre. It didn't help: he crashed early on when he lost the rear while trying to stay with the leaders.

POL ESPARGARO
Got a brilliant start after very average qualifying but was caught out by the track conditions. Lost the front at Turn 3.

MARC MARQUEZ
Said he wasn't interested in following Lorenzo and would rather crash trying to beat him – which is exactly what happened on the third lap at Turn 10.

CAL CRUTCHLOW
Unlucky to be barged wide by Aleix Espargaro but refused to blame him.

YONNY HERNANDEZ
The first of eight crashers. Had a storming first lap and was up to seventh, but lost the front at Turn 10 on the third lap.

DID NOT RACE

KAREL ABRAHAM
Dislocated a toe in a big qualifying crash and had general anaesthesia less than 24 hours before the race, so couldn't have ridden even if he'd been able to.

MOTUL TT ASSEN
TT CIRCUIT ASSEN

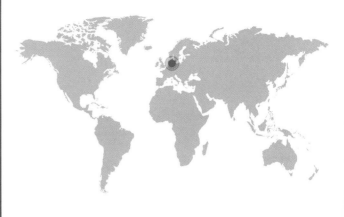

FIGHT CLUB

Marc Marquez was fast again but Valentino Rossi beat him in a dramatic last-corner showdown

The last Saturday running of the Dutch TT will be talked about for a long time, and not because commercial pressures have finally outweighed tradition. Any last inklings Marc Marquez may have had that Valentino Rossi was his friend were dispelled after one of those last-corner dramas in which Rossi specialises. Most of Marc's warm feelings towards Valentino had disappeared in Argentina when, with no justification, he thought he'd been badly done by, but he was sensible enough to keep his opinions to himself, other than a veiled comment about 'Valentino being his reference'.

After Assen, the situation became open hostility, with Valentino playing the innocent party wonderfully well, as he has done so many times in the past. It's worth reviewing that last corner and the events preceding it in detail, concentrating on the top two as frankly no-one else was in the hunt.

Vale started the last lap with a lead of nearly half a second that he'd opened up over the previous two laps after retaking the lead. Marquez closed the gap over the final corners to put himself in a position for a lunge up the inside at the chicane. Rossi took the normal racing line rather than go defensive, and Marquez skittered up the inside on maximum lean. He nudged the Yamaha and Rossi picked the bike up, ran across the gravel trap and won. Marquez also cut the course, on the inside, and finished over a second in arrears. Helicopter shots show definitively that Rossi was always in front.

Both men claimed the moral high ground; Rossi because he was on the classic line and had made the corner, Marc because he thought he had made the pass. Like Rossi's infamous incidents with Sete Gibernau at Jerez and Casey Stoner at Laguna Seca, this one will be

ABOVE The last corner: Marquez charges up the inside and shoves Rossi wide. Then the arguments started

RIGHT This is what dismayed Marquez – Rossi's blast across the gravel trap

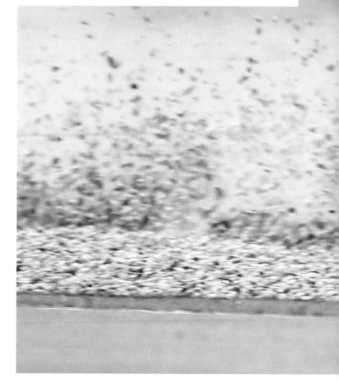

picked over for many years. There are several questions here, most of them unanswerable, but nevertheless there are conclusions that can be drawn.

My colleague Neil Hodgson believes that Valentino, having seen something like +0.4 on his pitboard and then done a near-perfect lap, wasn't expecting a pass, and then had milliseconds to react as Marquez made contact. On the other hand, is it fanciful to believe that Rossi had planned this so he could take advantage by straight-lining the last part of the chicane? Most probably, but even so there were a fair few very experienced professional racers who took to social media to support this theory.

What we do know is that Marquez was on the very outer edge of adhesion when he touched the Yamaha. He was risking all for the win when many racers, even champions, would have been happy to rediscover their confidence with a second place. He has precisely zero interest in second place, as his casually crazy crash in Catalunya showed. He's also young, used to getting his own way, and having difficulty dealing with situations when that doesn't happen. There was more than a touch of petulance about his post-race performance, although he got in one good line when asked what he'd learned from Rossi this time – 'Motocross'.

'I DON'T WANT
TO SAY I DID A
PERFECT RACE,
BUT IT WAS
CLOSE'
VALENTINO ROSSI

As for The Doctor, he's still prepared to lay it on the line in pursuit of victory. His pole position was a thing of wonder. He led Marquez for much of the race in a display not just of speed but also concentration. In the final corner he showed his talent for doing the right thing under the severest pressure. And then there was the press conference alongside his adversary – another exhibition of clinical detachment under pressure. He never misses any opportunity to take an advantage over a competitor.

He may need that ability again this year. Marquez tested a 2014 chassis after the Catalan GP and used it at Assen, albeit with the 2015 swinging arm and suspension linkage. Marc said it allowed him to make mistakes and

get away with them again, although there was no sign of his preferred style of braking into a corner with the rear wheel flapping in the air. Marc was the only rider to use the harder option front tyre, presumably for the support it offered under braking, although it should be mentioned that Assen only has two hard-braking efforts.

The other man who was unhappy with his kit was Jorge Lorenzo, whose record-breaking run of 103 laps in the lead came to an abrupt halt. His problem was the Bridgestone tyre allocation, which didn't offer the softer-edge rubber on which his style depends. This is really because the bike spends so little time upright at Assen that harder edges are necessary, as they are at Sachsenring. Confusingly, the hard edges were in use at Mugello as well, a race where Jorge led every lap. After his worst qualifying of the year, eighth, Jorge made a great start and got into third place, where he remained for the rest of the race.

Andrea Iannone overcame Ducati's problems for a well-deserved fourth and fifth-placed Pol Espargaro won a multi-bike brawl that lasted all race. Stefan Bradl, the one rider who openly admits that he really dislikes Assen, crashed out of the dice and broke his scaphoid, thus bolstering his prejudice. Dani Pedrosa's lowly finishing position was due to a massive crash in warm-up that meant he had to use his spare bike.

There was no doubt that Marquez rediscovered his confidence in his Honda and would now challenge for wins. He also had a little extra motivation: he's merciless anyway but with an imagined injustice burning away he was going to be very difficult to beat. Rossi might have cause to be grateful for his 74-point cushion over the reigning champion at this stage of the season.

ABOVE This turned out to be Stefan Bradl's last race on the Forward Yamaha

OPPOSITE Cal Crutchlow put an end to a run of three non-finishes with a solid sixth place

BELOW Events on the last lap left Marc Marquez with a sense of grievance to add to the one from Argentina

GoPro MOTORRAD GRAND PRIX DEUTSCHLAND
SACHSENRING

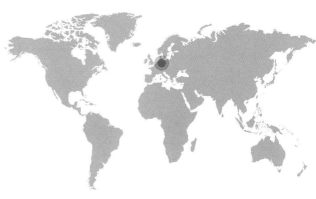

GOOD IN PARTS

Marc Marquez won for the first time in 2015, but Valentino Rossi extended his championship lead

If there's one race track that would let the Hondas off the hook, it was always going to be Sachsenring. After all, Marc Marquez had won here for the past five years, and Dani Pedrosa's record in Germany is also pretty impressive. As Marc himself said, the circuit suits both his style and his bike – although his bike was substantially altered from the previous race.

In what had looked like a move rooted in desperation, Marquez had reverted to his 2014 chassis after the post-Barcelona tests. Going back to known and trusted equipment isn't necessarily a bad thing (except for the egos of HRC engineers), but this decision was made after just a couple of laps because testing was seriously curtailed by heavy rain. The bikes Marc rode in Germany appeared to be the same as those at Assen – the 2014 chassis but with the 2015 swinging arm and suspension linkage.

Was this really the cure for Honda's ailments? If you judge purely on the fact that the Repsol team-mates finished first and second, you'd be tempted to say 'yes'. However, there are only two corners on the Sachsenring that would expose the bike's faults and, given his advantages on the rest of the circuit, Marc didn't need to push his luck on them. It all looked good, but he was understandably cautious about the immediate future, not least because the factory Yamahas also had new frames that the riders both agreed were an improvement.

Jorge Lorenzo was still in a strop about tyres, the same hard-edged design as used at Assen, but put up a fight. He was first into the first corner with a daring move on the outside and led a couple of laps before the inevitable happened. Rear grip dropped off that quickly, although Jorge did set the fastest lap of the race second time around. Marquez was the first to go past, followed by

'IN ASSEN WE BEGAN TO SEE LIGHT AT THE END OF THE TUNNEL; AFTER BARCELONA I FELT GOOD ON THE BIKE AGAIN'
MARC MARQUEZ

Rossi. Jorge couldn't do anything about the Honda but went straight back past his team-mate. Rossi repeated his move a lap later and this time made it stick. That was all Jorge had; he was closed down and passed by Pedrosa and consigned to a lonely fourth place.

Both Yamaha men said later that they'd known from the outset that they wouldn't be able to match the Hondas, and in a sense it didn't matter given the state of the championship. What most certainly did matter was the relative finishing positions of Rossi and Lorenzo. When Pedrosa caught and passed Rossi, the Italian used the speed of the Honda to tow him away from Lorenzo and ensure his championship lead would be increased to a comparably comfortable 13 points. Well, comfortable compared with the single point it had been going into the race.

If the Honda rider who won was ambivalent about his victory, the one in second place saw only progress and vindication. Dani Pedrosa came from second on the grid and was always with the leaders, although he did drop back behind both Yamahas at the start. That ended his chances of a win but he proved to himself that his speculative arm-pump operation after Qatar had worked. He was almost back to full fitness and while he had problems with the bike, his style was very different from that of Marquez and didn't give rise to quite the same problems. There was optimism in the camp, cautious maybe, but optimism nonetheless.

Optimism was in short supply at Ducati and Suzuki, both factories that started the year impressively but faded once the European season got going. Many observers thought the Suzukis would be up with the other factories

OPPOSITE Michael Laverty rode the Aprilia after Marco Melandri finally decided he'd had enough

ABOVE The other Laverty brother, Eugene, rode wearing the helmet design of Ulster racing medic Dr John Hines as a tribute

LEFT Lorenzo goes around the outside at Turn One to give himself a chance of escaping from the Hondas

ABOVE Valentino
Rossi couldn't catch the
Hondas but, vitally, he
beat Jorge Lorenzo

BELOW Aoyama became
the first of several stand-
ins to ride the injured
Karel Abraham's Honda

OPPOSITE Suzuki (in
livery marking the 30th
anniversary of the GSX-R)
and Ducati didn't do well

on the Sachsenring where their excellent handling and grip would outweigh their lack of grunt. It didn't work out that way: one rider couldn't feel the front and the other was spinning the rear continuously. They ended up knocking lumps off each other while dicing for tenth place. At least they looked good. The team ran a superb retro livery to celebrate 30 years of the GSX-R, Suzuki's flagship sports model, much to the delight of fans of a certain age.

Ducati had one of those weekends, as their people knew they would at the tight German track. Andrea Dovizioso added to his recent mechanical problems with that rarest of things, a crash due to rider error. Andrea Iannone, on the other hand, continued to impersonate the early-season version of Dovi, again bringing home the Desmosedici in what, frankly, was the best position it was likely to achieve. Maniac Joe? More like Steady Eddie.

Over at Aprilia, Marco Melandri finally escaped his personal purgatory to be replaced by the factory's test rider, Michael Laverty. Marco's inability to score a point had overshadowed some significant progress with the V4.

Alvaro Bautista finished 14th in Germany, making it five points-scoring races out of the past six, including a remarkable tenth place at the crash-strewn Catalan race, putting him 17th in the championship ahead of all the customer Hondas – not a bad situation to be in at the halfway point of the season.

At the top of the table it looked as if the second half of the year would be a shoot-out for the title between the factory Yamahas. Maybe. After Catalunya, Marc Marquez said that his championship chances were gone. Now he wasn't quite so sure.

LEVELLING THE PLAYING FIELD

At the end of June, after the Dutch TT and before the German GP, software development was officially frozen. This is the first step towards having one type of MotoGP machine on the grid next season with all of them using identical electronics. Next year's 'spec' software, called 'unified' by those who are working on it, will be based on this year's Open programming. There will be no Factory Option or Open Class bikes, and the only differences will be for factories running with concessions because they haven't won races – Suzuki and Aprilia. Ducati has scored enough rostrum finishes to ensure it loses its concessions.

The new unified software can be updated by any factory that chooses to submit its suggestion and coding to MotoGP's Director of Technology, Corrado Cecchinelli, on a closed file-sharing website. A small, set number of people from Honda, Yamaha and Ducati will be allowed to assess the suggestion and all three factories will need to approve it before the new coding is added to the unified system's programming. Dorna may also put forward suggestions, but for them to be accepted will require the approval of all the factories racing in MotoGP – the three who have a say about their competitors' improvements plus Suzuki and Aprilia. This is in line with Motorcycle Sport Manufacturers' Association (MSMA) voting procedures where factories in their first year of racing don't get a vote.

It was accepted by everyone that very little effect would be felt in 2015, and that in 2016 the change in tyre supplier from Bridgestone to Michelin would overshadow any noticeable effect.

The new policy was the result of serious negotiation between the factories and Dorna/IRTA. The software is more complicated than the non-factory teams would have liked, but that was the price of keeping the factories on board. Will it have a massive effect? On the track in terms of results, probably not. In saving private teams serious money, hopefully.

GoPro MOTORRAD GRAND PRIX DEUTSCHLAND
SACHSENRING
ROUND **9**
JULY 12

RACE RESULTS

CIRCUIT LENGTH 2.281 miles

NO. OF LAPS 30

RACE DISTANCE 68.432 miles

WEATHER Dry, 27°C

TRACK TEMPERATURE 42°C

WINNER Marc Marquez

FASTEST LAP 1m 21.530s, 100.662mph, Marc Marquez (record)

PREVOUS LAP RECORD 1m 21.846s, 100.351mph, Dani Pedrosa (2011)

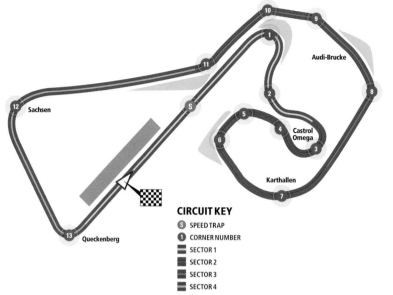

CIRCUIT KEY
- **S** SPEED TRAP
- **1** CORNER NUMBER
- SECTOR 1
- SECTOR 2
- SECTOR 3
- SECTOR 4

TYRE OPTIONS

FRONT

FRONT COMPOUNDS
ASYMMETRIC (**A**), SOFT (**S**), MEDIUM (**M**), HARD (**H**)

REAR

REAR COMPOUNDS
SOFT (**S**), MEDIUM (**M**), HARD (**H**)

SEVERITY RATING

<MILD   SEVERE>

BRIDGESTONE

QUALIFYING

	Rider	Nation	Motorcycle	Team	Time	Pole +
1	Marquez	SPA	Honda	Repsol Honda Team	1m 20.336s	
2	Pedrosa	SPA	Honda	Repsol Honda Team	1m 20.628s	0.292s
3	Lorenzo	SPA	Yamaha	Movistar Yamaha MotoGP	1m 20.921s	0.585s
4	Iannone	ITA	Ducati	Ducati Team	1m 21.029s	0.693s
5	Hernandez	COL	Ducati	Octo Pramac Racing	1m 21.115s	0.779s
6	Rossi	ITA	Yamaha	Movistar Yamaha MotoGP	1m 21.220s	0.884s
7	Espargaro A	SPA	Suzuki	Team Suzuki ECSTAR	1m 21.239s	0.903s
8	Espargaro P	SPA	Yamaha	Monster Yamaha Tech 3	1m 21.274s	0.938s
9	Smith	GBR	Yamaha	Monster Yamaha Tech 3	1m 21.329s	0.993s
10	Crutchlow	GBR	Honda	CWM LCR Honda	1m 21.409s	1.073s
11	Dovizioso	ITA	Ducati	Ducati Team	1m 21.503s	1.167s
12	Viñales	SPA	Suzuki	Team Suzuki ECSTAR	1m 21.796s	1.460s
13	Barbera	SPA	Ducati	Avintia Racing	1m 21.628s	Q1
14	Redding	GBR	Honda	EG 0,0 Marc VDS	1m 21.632s	Q1
15	Petrucci	ITA	Ducati	Octo Pramac Racing	1m 21.760s	Q1
16	Bautista	SPA	Aprilia	Aprilia Racing Team Gresini	1m 22.049s	Q1
17	De Angelis	RSM	ART	E-Motion IodaRacing Team	1m 22.195s	Q1
18	Miller	AUS	Honda	CWM LCR Honda	1m 22.225s	Q1
19	Hayden	USA	Honda	Aspar MotoGP Team	1m 22.362s	Q1
20	Baz	FRA	Yamaha	Athinà Forward Racing	1m 22.394s	Q1
21	Di Meglio	FRA	Ducati	Avintia Racing	1m 22.441s	Q1
22	Aoyama	JPN	Honda	AB Motoracing	1m 22.543s	Q1
23	Laverty E	IRL	Honda	Aspar MotoGP Team	1m 22.693s	Q1
24	Laverty M	GBR	Aprilia	Aprilia Racing Team Gresini	1m 22.947s	Q1
25	Corti	ITA	Yamaha	Athinà Forward Racing	1m 23.374s	Q1

1 MARC MARQUEZ
Led every session and set a new lap record. However, Marc was careful not to get too excited as the track has always been good to both Honda and himself.

2 DANI PEDROSA
Delighted to finish strongly for the first time this year. Gave the team it's first one-two finish since the same race exactly 12 months previously.

3 VALENTINO ROSSI
Happy to extend his championship lead over Lorenzo but described his race as 'I tried to beat Dani.' Although the Honda man was too strong in the closing stages, Valentino used the Honda's speed to help him move away from his team-mate.

4 JORGE LORENZO
Put his well-documented dislike of the tyres behind him to rip round the outside at the first corner and lead the first four laps. Two laps later Rossi was past and just before half-distance Pedrosa also came by, leaving Jorge to a lonely fourth place.

5 ANDREA IANNONE
Lost a lot of time to the other factory bikes in the middle two sectors, so set his own pace and controlled the gap to Smith.

6 BRADLEY SMITH
Managed to qualify badly after being very fast all through free practice. Rescued the situation with another brave start then got held up fighting with Hernandez.

7 CAL CRUTCHLOW
A big crash in qualifying cracked bones in a leg and an arm; Cal thought he was wrong not to chose the hard front tyre like the factory riders.

8 POL ESPARGARO
Dropped back to 12th but then came back strongly, passing his brother and both Pramac Ducatis.

9 DANILO PETRUCCI
Couldn't take advantage of the soft tyre in qualifying but had a great race. Took risks, and was especially strong on the brakes.

10 ALEIX ESPARGARO
Never found a set-up on a track where the Suzuki team hoped the strengths of its bike would come to the fore. Took risks right from the start to make up places and ended the race in a dice with Viñales.

11 MAVERICK VIÑALES
Had the same problems as his team-mate: lots of spinning compromised acceleration – not good on such a tight track.

12 YONNY HERNANDEZ
Qualified and started brilliantly only to find himself unable to replicate his practice times.

13 HECTOR BARBERA
Unhappy with Miller again after a first-lap collision. Stalked Miller and Bautista before making his move to finish top Open bike.

14 ALVARO BAUTISTA
Got away with the second group and only lost them when rear-tyre grip reduced. However, the team's new electronics strategy enabled Alvaro to finish safely and in front of the customer Hondas.

LAP CHART

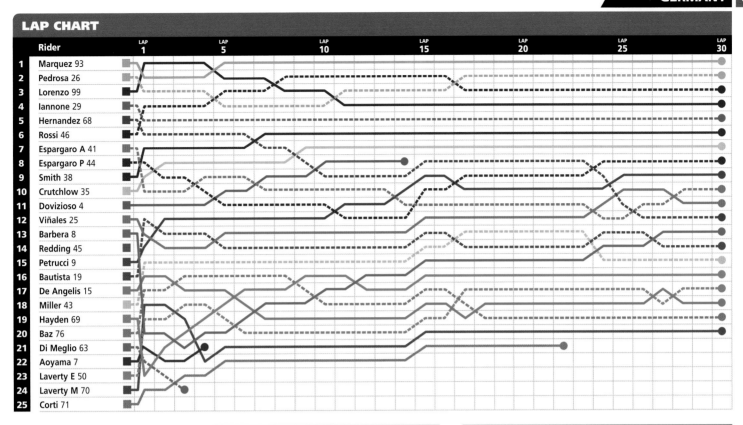

	Rider	LAP 1	LAP 5	LAP 10	LAP 15	LAP 20	LAP 25	LAP 30
1	Marquez 93							
2	Pedrosa 26							
3	Lorenzo 99							
4	Iannone 29							
5	Hernandez 68							
6	Rossi 46							
7	Espargaro A 41							
8	Espargaro P 44							
9	Smith 38							
10	Crutchlow 35							
11	Dovizioso 4							
12	Viñales 25							
13	Barbera 8							
14	Redding 45							
15	Petrucci 9							
16	Bautista 19							
17	De Angelis 15							
18	Miller 43							
19	Hayden 69							
20	Baz 76							
21	Di Meglio 63							
22	Aoyama 7							
23	Laverty E 50							
24	Laverty M 70							
25	Corti 71							

RACE

	Rider	Motorcycle	Race time	Time +	Fastest lap	Avg. speed	🅱
1	Marquez	Honda	41m 01.087s		1m 21.530s	100.0mph	H/M
2	Pedrosa	Honda	41m 03.313s	2.226s	1m 21.714s	100.0mph	H/M
3	Rossi	Yamaha	41m 06.695s	5.608s	1m 21.641s	99.9mph	A/M
4	Lorenzo	Yamaha	41m 11.015s	9.928s	1m 21.811s	99.7mph	A/M
5	Iannone	Ducati	41m 21.872s	20.785s	1m 22.024s	99.2mph	A/M
6	Smith	Yamaha	41m 24.302s	23.215s	1m 22.403s	99.1mph	A/M
7	Crutchlow	Honda	41m 30.968s	29.881s	1m 22.319s	98.9mph	M/M
8	Espargaro P	Yamaha	41m 36.040s	34.953s	1m 22.743s	98.7mph	A/M
9	Petrucci	Ducati	41m 36.962s	35.875s	1m 22.595s	98.6mph	A/M
10	Espargaro A	Suzuki	41m 38.340s	37.253s	1m 22.763s	98.5mph	A/M
11	Viñales	Suzuki	41m 38.361s	37.274s	1m 22.940s	98.5mph	A/M
12	Hernandez	Ducati	41m 43.168s	42.081s	1m 22.502s	98.4mph	M/M
13	Barbera	Ducati	41m 49.698s	48.611s	1m 22.880s	98.1mph	A/S
14	Bautista	Aprilia	41m 51.774s	50.687s	1m 23.086s	98.1mph	A/S
15	Miller	Honda	41m 54.856s	53.769s	1m 22.963s	97.9mph	M/S
16	Hayden	Honda	42m 00.008s	58.921s	1m 22.305s	97.7mph	A/S
17	Laverty E	Honda	42m 03.825s	1m 02.738s	1m 23.405s	97.6mph	A/S
18	De Angelis	ART	42m 04.209s	1m 03.122s	1m 23.405s	97.6mph	A/S
19	Baz	Yamaha	42m 12.249s	1m 11.162s	1m 23.449s	97.2mph	A/S
20	Laverty M	Aprilia	42m 16.997s	1m 15.910s	1m 23.895s	97.1mph	A/S
NC	Corti	Yamaha	36m 51.914s	8 laps	1m 25.036s	81.6mph	A/S
NC	Dovizioso	Ducati	19m 20.973s	16 laps	1m 22.395s	99.0mph	A/M
NC	Aoyama	Honda	5m 39.886s	26 laps	1m 23.556s	96.6mph	A/S
NC	Di Meglio	Ducati	4m 59.748s	27 laps	1m 24.036s	82.1mph	A/S
NC	Redding	Honda	–	–	–	–	M/M

CHAMPIONSHIP

	Rider	Nation	Team	Points
1	Rossi	ITA	Movistar Yamaha MotoGP	179
2	Lorenzo	SPA	Movistar Yamaha MotoGP	166
3	Iannone	ITA	Ducati Team	118
4	Marquez	SPA	Repsol Honda Team	114
5	Dovizioso	ITA	Ducati Team	87
6	Smith	GBR	Monster Yamaha Tech 3	87
7	Pedrosa	SPA	Repsol Honda Team	67
8	Crutchlow	GBR	CWM LCR Honda	66
9	Espargaro P	SPA	Monster Yamaha Tech 3	64
10	Viñales	SPA	Team Suzuki ECSTAR	57
11	Petrucci	ITA	Octo Pramac Racing	51
12	Espargaro A	SPA	Team Suzuki ECSTAR	44
13	Hernandez	COL	Octo Pramac Racing	32
14	Redding	GBR	EG 0,0 Marc VDS	30
15	Barbera	SPA	Avintia Racing	19
16	Baz	FRA	Athinà Forward Racing	14
17	Bautista	SPA	Aprilia Racing Team Gresini	13
18	Miller	AUS	CWM LCR Honda	12
19	Bradl	GER	Athinà Forward Racing	9
20	Pirro	ITA	Ducati Team	8
	Hayden	USA	Aspar MotoGP Team	8
22	Laverty E	IRL	Aspar MotoGP Team	7
23	Aoyama	JPN	Repsol Honda Team	5
24	Di Meglio	FRA	Avintia Racing	2
25	De Angelis	RSM	E-Motion IodaRacing Team	1

15 JACK MILLER
Started strongly but at two-thirds distance had a major moment on the fastest part of the track that let Bautista and Barbera through.

16 NICKY HAYDEN
Again the victim of a first-turn collision that put him off-track. Got back up to Barbera but then lost rear grip.

17 EUGENE LAVERTY
Had no rear grip at the start of the race but the tyres hooked up at half-distance and Eugene was faster at the end of the race than on new rubber.

18 ALEX DE ANGELIS
Happy to race with the customer Hondas for the first time but rear-grip problems meant there was no chance of fighting for a point.

19 LORIS BAZ
Lost confidence with the front after a few laps, then tweaked his back saving a slide, after which he was unable to defend his position.

20 MICHAEL LAVERTY
Replaced Marco Melandri and, like his team-mate, had a good first half of the race but lost ground when the tyre dropped off.

DID NOT FINISH

CLAUDIO CORTI
Replaced Bradl having not raced for eight months. Hit front-end problems in the race and pitted to change tyres. Retired when the problems recurred.

ANDREA DOVIZIOSO
Qualified badly and therefore was pushing hard early on. Made a mistake while behind Crutchlow and crashed out.

MIKE DI MEGLIO
Crashed on the fourth lap after getting on a white line in Turn 4.

HIROSHI AOYAMA
Replaced Abraham to try to help the team with its direction. Found the bike very nervous in the first part of the track and slid off without injury.

SCOTT REDDING
Some very encouraging performances in practice but had a first-lap crash in the race – lost the front when he came off the brake in the final corner.

DID NOT RACE

KAREL ABRAHAM
Still not fit after his accident in Cataluyna qualifying. Replaced by Hiro Aoyama.

STEFAN BRADL
Missed his home race after breaking right scaphoid at Assen. Replaced by Claudio Corti.

RED BULL
INDIANAPOLIS GRAND PRIX
INDIANAPOLIS MOTOR SPEEDWAY

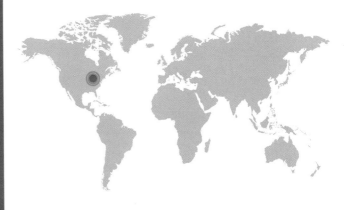

AMERICAN BEAUTY

Marc Marquez continued his winning streak and Jorge Lorenzo closed the gap to Valentino Rossi

Things always seem clearer after a holiday, and MotoGP is no exception. After three weekends off, it seemed obvious that Marc Marquez would extend his run of nine victories in the USA – five of them achieved at The Brickyard. It also seemed obvious that Valentino Rossi's chances of defending his championship lead depended absolutely on improving his qualifying performance. Everyone else could settle in behind these major payers and sort out the minor issues. Could Ducati – or rather could Dovizioso – get back to that early-season form? Could Suzuki continue its progress? Could anyone, even Marquez, ride the Honda the way he wanted to?

Qualifying did nothing to dispel the notion that this was a track for Marquez and Honda. The Repsol Hondas qualified first and second, with Lorenzo third. Rossi could only manage the third row – again – well behind a delighted Danilo Petrucci, who was top Ducati rider in a career-best fifth place. There was no evidence to suggest anything other than a runaway win by Marquez and that's what the man himself planned – open up a gap and then control it.

Sunday surprised Marc and indeed everyone else. Lorenzo got off the line and lapped at a pace significantly faster then his qualifying form had suggested. Marquez went with him. Now the question was how long could Marc stay with the Yamaha? The answer turned out to be a lot longer than anyone thought.

Behind the leading pair, who circulated never more than half a second apart, Rossi made a good start and got into another private dice with Dani Pedrosa after crossing a gap of nearly two seconds.

The two fights were resolved in very different ways. Marquez made his move on the 25th lap of 27 in the

ABOVE Stefan Bradl
returned from injury as
an Aprilia rider, replacing
Marco Melandri in the
factory team

OPPOSITE Andrea
Dovizioso could see no
end to his run of bad form

RIGHT Jorge Lorenzo
tried to escape but Marc
Marquez went with
him and pounced in
the closing stages

form of the classic Indy run into Turn 1 – very fast and
very brave. Lorenzo, mentally exhausted from trying to
make a break, had no answer. His pace had been such
that Marquez had had doubts of his own at mid-distance
but was able to push after he'd made the pass and
opened the gap to over half a second at the flag. The
Rossi/Pedrosa dice was considerably more action-packed:
Rossi closed in at around half distance and there was a
flurry of passing and repassing in the final few laps before
Valentino made a successful last-lap move at Turn 2.

Those two late changes of position put a much rosier
hue on the weekend than Rossi might have expected. His
closest championship rival took only four points out of his
lead, reducing it to nine; it could have been a lot worse.
Marquez moved past Andrea Iannone into third place but
still 56 points in arrears, a big number but somehow not
a comfortable margin from Yamaha's point of view.

Further down the field, Iannone finished fifth, just
holding off a charging Bradley Smith. Both men – like
Maverick Viñales at Suzuki – illustrated another clear
trend, that of shifts of power within teams.

At Ducati, Andrea Dovizioso hadn't had a sniff of the
rostrum since Le Mans, while the rider previously known
as Maniac Joe appeared to have abandoned his wild ways
and was now doing a good impersonation of the old,
consistent, reliable Dovi.

Yamaha, meanwhile, announced that it had re-signed
Pol Espargaro to continue with the Tech 3 team; the
Catalan is a factory employee whereas Smith is contracted
to the team. Having consistently outperformed his
team-mate, Bradley was now getting very disgruntled
and made his feelings known at the pre-event press

'WE WERE PRETTY
MUCH ON THE
LIMIT; THE TRUTH
IS THAT JORGE
IMPROVED A LOT
DURING THE RACE'
MARC MARQUEZ

conference. After winning the Suzuka Eight Hours with Espargaro, he felt he wasn't getting the treatment he deserved regarding machinery updates. In defence of the team, it's difficult to know how Tech 3 could guarantee anything of the sort. Despite this storm in a teacup, it was expected that Smith would soon re-sign as well.

Suzuki's remarkable rookie, Viñales, both out-qualified and out-raced his more experienced team-mate, Aleix Espargaro, for the first time. This was down to a new approach; think only of race set-up in free practice and desist from testing at the races.

There was also a newly competitive atmosphere at Aprilia. Alvaro Bautista had put in sterling work and scored points no fewer than six times, but Marco Melandri was way off the pace. Now Alvaro had a permanent new team-mate, Stefan Bradl, who promptly out-qualified him. The German had disentangled himself from the troubled Forward Racing operation (see facing page) and despite still suffering the effects of his Assen injury he impressed his new team. Alvaro restored what he would regard as normal order in the race and welcomed the fact that he now had a team-mate who would push him on.

Back at Honda, there was muted celebration over its 700th win in GP racing – forced grins and T-shirts on the rostrum. No one was counting Marquez out of the title chase, even if the gap was more than significant, but in the Constructors' Championship Honda was still 43 points behind Yamaha and in range of Ducati. In the Teams' Championship, Repsol Honda took back second place from Ducati, but remained embarrassingly far behind Movistar Yamaha – over three races' worth of points. Perhaps a landmark like your 700th win suddenly seems very important when that's all you have to shout about.

ABOVE Scott Redding's problems were put in perspective by the woes of other Honda riders

BELOW Three laps to go and Marc Marquez has pulled the pin; Jorge Lorenzo had no answer

OPPOSITE Familiar face – Colin Edwards was on hand to help celebrate Yamaha's 60th anniversary

FORWARD RACING

After the German GP the owner of Forward Racing, Giovanni Cuzari, was arrested and held in jail on a variety of charges related to financial irregularities in the Swiss canton of Lugano. Not surprisingly, this led to problems for the team. Sponsors left or didn't make payments, leaving the team unable to compete at Indianapolis.

IRTA and Dorna gave leave to the team, which competes in Moto2 as well as MotoGP, to miss the trip to the USA and concentrate on trying to get back on the grid in Europe and save the 40 jobs involved. The plan was to try to keep going and sell the team's MotoGP grid slots, the two obvious candidates being Ajo Motorsport's Aki Ajo and Leopard Racing's Flavio Becca.

Forward's managing director, Marco Curioni, managed to persuade the authorities to give him access to some of the team's assets and, with IRTA's help, it was confirmed that the team would be at the next round in the Czech Republic with all four bikes. Keeping the team on track for three races – up to and including Misano – seemed a distinct possibility but beyond

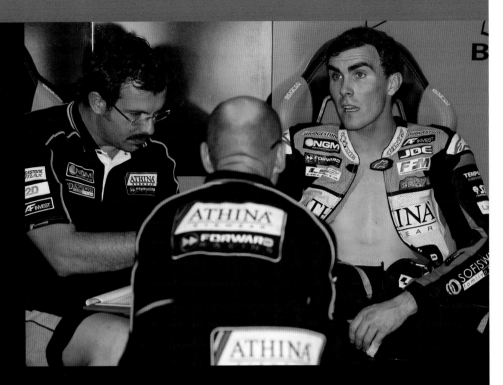

that some serious money would be needed, not least for the three October races outside Europe.

Missing a race was particularly hard on Loris Baz, who was only five points behind Hector Barbera in the Open Class

standings but had to sit and watch the Spaniard score another point. That might seem insignificant, but winning the class usually yields only one or two points – or none at all! – so a small gap is hard to bridge.

OFFICIAL TIMEKEEPER

RACE RESULTS

CIRCUIT LENGTH 2.591 miles

NO. OF LAPS 27

RACE DISTANCE 69.957 miles

WEATHER Dry, 28°C

TRACK TEMPERATURE 35°C

WINNER Marc Marquez

FASTEST LAP 1m 32.625s, 100.662mph, Marc Marquez (record)

PREVIOUS LAP RECORD 1m 32.831s, 100.476mph, Marc Marquez (2014)

CIRCUIT KEY
- **S** SPEED TRAP
- **1** CORNER NUMBER
- SECTOR 1
- SECTOR 2
- SECTOR 3
- SECTOR 4

TYRE OPTIONS

FRONT

FRONT COMPOUNDS
SOFT (**S**), MEDIUM (**M**), HARD (**H**)

REAR

REAR COMPOUNDS
SOFT (**S**), MEDIUM (**M**), HARD (**H**)

SEVERITY RATING

<MILD   SEVERE>

BRIDGESTONE

QUALIFYING

	Rider	Nation	Motorcycle	Team	Time	Pole +
1	Marquez	SPA	Honda	Repsol Honda Team	1m 31.884s	
2	Pedrosa	SPA	Honda	Repsol Honda Team	1m 32.005s	0.171s
3	Lorenzo	SPA	Yamaha	Movistar Yamaha MotoGP	1m 32.186s	0.302s
4	Crutchlow	GBR	Honda	CWM LCR Honda	1m 32.208s	0.324s
5	Petrucci	ITA	Ducati	Octo Pramac Racing	1m 32.243s	0.359s
6	Smith	GBR	Yamaha	Monster Yamaha Tech 3	1m 32.269s	0.385s
7	Iannone	ITA	Ducati	Ducati Team	1m 32.468s	0.584s
8	Rossi	ITA	Yamaha	Movistar Yamaha MotoGP	1m 32.511s	0.627s
9	Viñales	SPA	Suzuki	Team Suzuki ECSTAR	1m 32.571s	0.687s
10	Dovizioso	ITA	Ducati	Ducati Team	1m 32.636s	0.752s
11	Espargaro P	SPA	Yamaha	Monster Yamaha Tech 3	1m 32.670s	0.786s
12	Espargaro A	SPA	Suzuki	Team Suzuki ECSTAR	1m 32.814s	0.930s
13	Redding	GBR	Honda	EG 0,0 Marc VDS	1m 33.170s	Q1
14	Barbera	SPA	Ducati	Avintia Racing	1m 33.190s	Q1
15	Hernandez	COL	Ducati	Octo Pramac Racing	1m 33.278s	Q1
16	Miller	AUS	Honda	CWM LCR Honda	1m 33.381s	Q1
17	Bradl	GER	Aprilia	Aprilia Racing Team Gresini	1m 33.822s	Q1
18	Bautista	SPA	Aprilia	Aprilia Racing Team Gresini	1m 33.839s	Q1
19	Laverty E	IRL	Honda	Aspar MotoGP Team	1m 33.978s	Q1
20	Hayden	USA	Honda	Aspar MotoGP Team	1m 34.030s	Q1
21	De Angelis	RSM	ART	E-Motion IodaRacing Team	1m 34.226s	Q1
22	Di Meglio	FRA	Ducati	Avintia Racing	1m 34.322s	Q1
23	Elias	SPA	Honda	AB Motoracing	1m 35.167s	Q1

1 MARC MARQUEZ

Marc's fifth consecutive win at The Brickyard and another win in the USA, where he hasn't been beaten on a MotoGP bike. Tailed Lorenzo at lap-record speed until passing three laps from home.

2 JORGE LORENZO

Got the holeshot from third on the grid and set an astonishing pace in the 1min 32sec bracket for most of the race. Marquez followed closely and three laps from home made his move. Jorge didn't have the energy to respond but was happy to reduce Rossi's championship lead by four points.

3 VALENTINO ROSSI

Another third-row start, but he was up to fourth in a couple of laps, after which he crossed a significant gap to Pedrosa. The Honda man fought back but Valentino was able to secure a rostrum finish with a last-lap pass and, more importantly, limit the damage to his championship lead.

4 DANI PEDROSA

Came under criticism from team management for not hanging on to third place, which Rossi took off him on the final lap after they'd swapped positions several times.

5 ANDREA IANNONE

Had a good start and got up to fourth but was quickly deposed by Rossi. After that, he knew he didn't have the pace to go with the top four and concentrated on keeping Smith at bay.

6 BRADLEY SMITH

Qualified respectably in sixth but started with no launch control selected and lost a place to his team-mate on the first lap. Bradley got sixth back on lap two and started to hunt down Iannone's Ducati. By the flag he was with him but disappointed not to be able to make a pass.

7 POL ESPARGARO

Started well, but again suffered from his now usual problems with new tyres and a full tank. Crutchlow came through when Pol ran wide, but he was able to fight back and retake the place.

8 CAL CRUTCHLOW

Lost a lot of time at Turn 2 when he found his brakes weren't up to temperature and ran on. Fought back and had an entertaining fight with Pol Espargaro.

9 ANDREA DOVIZIOSO

Ended up dead last when he was victim of the domino effect at the second corner.

Finished the lap in 21st place, so his result was pretty impressive given that Indianapolis is a difficult place to pass.

10 DANILO PETRUCCI

Started from the second row having gone direct to Q2, then finished in the top ten and so considered it a good weekend: 'I'm living a very beautiful moment.'

11 MAVERICK VIÑALES

Changed the way he worked in practice and concentrated throughout on race set-up. Not his most successful weekend, but Mack beat his team-mate in both qualifying and the race for the first time.

LAP CHART

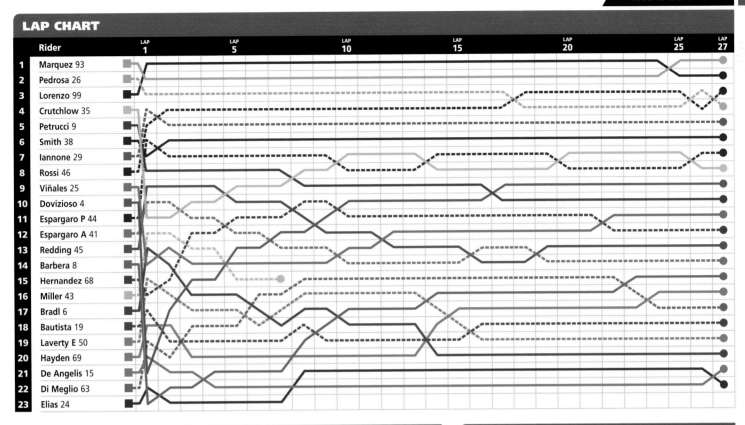

	Rider	LAP 1	LAP 5	LAP 10	LAP 15	LAP 20	LAP 25	LAP 27
1	Marquez 93							
2	Pedrosa 26							
3	Lorenzo 99							
4	Crutchlow 35							
5	Petrucci 9							
6	Smith 38							
7	Iannone 29							
8	Rossi 46							
9	Viñales 25							
10	Dovizioso 4							
11	Espargaro P 44							
12	Espargaro A 41							
13	Redding 45							
14	Barbera 8							
15	Hernandez 68							
16	Miller 43							
17	Bradl 6							
18	Bautista 19							
19	Laverty E 50							
20	Hayden 69							
21	De Angelis 15							
22	Di Meglio 63							
23	Elias 24							

RACE

	Rider	Motorcycle	Race time	Time +	Fastest lap	Avg. speed	
1	Marquez	Honda	41m 55.371s		1m 32.625s	100.1mph	H/H
2	Lorenzo	Yamaha	41m 56.059s	0.688s	1m 32.652s	100.0mph	H/H
3	Rossi	Yamaha	42m 01.337s	5.966s	1m 32.847s	99.9mph	H/H
4	Pedrosa	Honda	42m 01.518s	6.147s	1m 32.829s	99.9mph	H/H
5	Iannone	Ducati	42m 16.899s	21.528s	1m 33.492s	99.2mph	H/M
6	Smith	Yamaha	42m 17.122s	21.751s	1m 33.301s	99.2mph	H/H
7	Espargaro P	Yamaha	42m 25.749s	30.378s	1m 33.539s	98.9mph	H/H
8	Crutchlow	Honda	42m 26.978s	31.607s	1m 33.437s	98.9mph	H/H
9	Dovizioso	Ducati	42m 28.192s	32.821s	1m 33.684s	98.8mph	H/M
10	Petrucci	Ducati	42m 29.888s	34.517s	1m 33.671s	98.7mph	H/M
11	Viñales	Suzuki	42m 34.381s	38.010s	1m 33.673s	98.5mph	H/M
12	Hernandez	Ducati	42m 37.186s	41.815s	1m 33.782s	98.5mph	H/M
13	Redding	Honda	42m 45.580s	50.209s	1m 34.030s	98.1mph	H/H
14	Espargaro A	Suzuki	42m 55.836s	1m 00.465s	1m 34.237s	97.7mph	H/M
15	Barbera	Ducati	42m 59.518s	1m 04.147s	1m 34.573s	97.6mph	H/S
16	Hayden	Honda	43m 00.437s	1m 05.066s	1m 34.607s	97.6mph	H/S
17	Di Meglio	Ducati	43m 02.312s	1m 06.941s	1m 34.593s	97.5mph	M/S
18	Bautista	Aprilia	43m 09.233s	1m 13.862s	1m 34.534s	97.2mph	H/S
19	Laverty E	Honda	43m 14.077s	1m 18.706s	1m 34.782s	97.1mph	H/S
20	Bradl	Aprilia	43m 15.101s	1m 19.730s	1m 34.702s	97.0mph	H/S
21	De Angelis	ART	43m 15.253s	1m 19.882s	1m 34.957s	97.0mph	H/S
22	Elias	Honda	43m 15.305s	1m 19.934s	1m 35.239s	97.0mph	M/S
NC	Miller	Honda	11m 09.915s	20 laps	1m 34.503s	97.4mph	H/S

CHAMPIONSHIP

	Rider	Nation	Team	Points
1	Rossi	ITA	Movistar Yamaha MotoGP	195
2	Lorenzo	SPA	Movistar Yamaha MotoGP	186
3	Marquez	SPA	Repsol Honda Team	139
4	Iannone	ITA	Ducati Team	129
5	Smith	GBR	Monster Yamaha Tech 3	97
6	Dovizioso	ITA	Ducati Team	94
7	Pedrosa	SPA	Repsol Honda Team	80
8	Crutchlow	GBR	CWM LCR Honda	74
9	Espargaro P	SPA	Monster Yamaha Tech 3	73
10	Viñales	SPA	Team Suzuki ECSTAR	62
11	Petrucci	ITA	Octo Pramac Racing	57
12	Espargaro A	SPA	Team Suzuki ECSTAR	46
13	Hernandez	COL	Octo Pramac Racing	36
14	Redding	GBR	EG 0,0 Marc VDS	33
15	Barbera	SPA	Avintia Racing	20
16	Baz	FRA	Athinà Forward Racing	14
17	Bautista	SPA	Aprilia Racing Team Gresini	13
18	Miller	AUS	CWM LCR Honda	12
19	Bradl	GER	Athinà Forward Racing	9
20	Pirro	ITA	Ducati Team	8
	Hayden	USA	Aspar MotoGP Team	8
22	Laverty E	IRL	Aspar MotoGP Team	7
23	Aoyama	JPN	Repsol Honda Team	5
24	Di Meglio	FRA	Avintia Racing	2
25	De Angelis	RSM	E-Motion IodaRacing Team	1

12 YONNY HERNANDEZ
His only mistake was bad qualifying, which meant he was caught up in the first-lap fracas. Finished the first lap 19th, then got up to tenth only to be passed by Viñales and Dovizioso in the closing laps.

13 SCOTT REDDING
Made a very good start and battled with Crutchlow in the early laps. However, once the tyres' performance dropped, Scott had his usual crop of problems.

14 ALEIX ESPARGARO
Hit problems after three laps with the rear locking on corner entry. Turned engine braking right down but that didn't help, and he finished the race with a destroyed rear tyre.

15 HECTOR BARBERA
Top Open rider again despite being pushed off track at the second corner and having to work his way back through the field.

16 NICKY HAYDEN
Much happier in the race than in qualifying, but was caught up in the first-lap mêlée. Got in front of Barbera a couple of times but couldn't finish as top Open rider in what may have been his last American GP.

17 MIKE DI MEGLIO
A good race given his qualifying position, and Mike ran in a points-scoring position for a good while only to fade due to the heat and the effects of a Saturday crash.

18 ALVARO BAUTISTA
Serious problems with the right side of the rear tyre towards the end of the race kept Alvaro out of the points.

19 EUGENE LAVERTY
Hopeful of being able to fight for top Open rider. Unfortunately, he suffered severe pain in his left arm for reasons unknown and rode the race 'one-armed'.

20 STEFAN BRADL
First ride for Aprilia having jumped ship from the Forward Racing team. The effects of the scaphoid he broke at the Dutch TT made the last part of the race very difficult.

21 ALEX DE ANGELIS
Started well but the usual chatter and lack of top speed saw Alex quickly relegated to the rear of the field.

22 TONI ELIAS
Replaced Abraham, having competed this year only in the Suzuka Eight Hours, where he had a good race with Moriwaki. Not surprisingly, he was off the pace.

DID NOT FINISH

JACK MILLER
He said the bike felt great at the start but started sliding and tucking the front; he folded the front as he was backing the bike into Turn 6.

DID NOT RACE

KAREL ABRAHAM
Absent due to the foot injury received in Catalunya. Replaced by Toni Elias.

bwin GRAND PRIX CESKÉ REPUBLIKY
AUTOMOTODROM BRNO

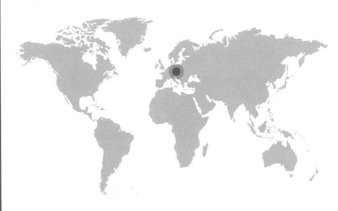

PERFECTION IN MOTION

Jorge Lorenzo won again and this time he didn't give the rest any hope at all

This was the fifth time in the season that Jorge Lorenzo led a race from start to finish without being headed. This victory put him level on points with Valentino Rossi but in the lead of the championship on count-back. Most importantly, though, this was the first time that Rossi appeared to have no answer to his team-mate's speed. Previously, Valentino had been able to console himself with his race pace, or the fact that he'd closed a gap, or his speed at the end of a race on hard tyres. This time his race had no redeeming feature, no excuse. All of a sudden Valentino looked like a 36-year-old champion who was having to work very hard to keep up with the young pretenders. For once, the pressure was showing.

For once, too, Rossi gave himself every chance of running with Lorenzo and the inevitable Marc Marquez. He was on the front row of the grid for only the second time this year, although the two Spaniards dominated practice and looked to have far superior race pace. Rossi and his crew chief, Silvano Galbusera, have made a habit of throwing in the sort of Sunday night fix that enables Valentino to be more competitive than expected on race day, but this wasn't one of those days.

The real question was how long Marquez would be able to run at Lorenzo's pace. Were we in for a rerun of the previous race, Indianapolis, where Lorenzo couldn't get rid of Marquez? Or would the Honda refuse to co-operate? The answer was very much the latter.

Marquez chased Lorenzo from the start but by the seventh lap he knew the game was up. He stopped looking ahead and started to look behind in order to control the gap to Rossi. It was a big gap, and Marc kept it that way. If Valentino took back so much as a tenth of

ABOVE Maverick Viñales had the most impressive race so far of a stellar rookie season

OPPOSITE Dani Pedrosa found yet another way to get injured in free practice

RIGHT The Ducatis had a strong race, with Andrea Dovizioso showing signs of a return to form

a second, Marquez upped his pace to keep the gap at an unbridgeable five seconds.

Having managed to get himself on the front row, the prerequisite to being competitive, Valentino didn't get a good start and spent the first couple of laps tangled up with the factory Ducatis, themselves looking more competitive than in recent weeks. When he did get through to third place, Lorenzo was already over two and a half seconds up the road. Rossi's hope was that his hard tyres, front and rear, would come to him later in the race – Lorenzo had gone for mediums. That didn't happen and neither was there a repeat of Argentina, where Rossi closed down Marquez hand over fist thanks to a similar tyre choice. In short, Valentino didn't lay a glove on either of them.

While the three riders on the podium acted out their races almost perfectly in line with a script that could have been written after practice, you couldn't say the same about the man who provided most of the entertainment on race day – Dani Pedrosa.

Just when we thought Dani had recovered fully from his radical arm-pump operation and was ready to challenge for victory again, he was floored by a ridiculous accident. In free practice he had a front-fork failure that sprayed oil on his tyres, causing a nasty crash going into the final esses. Dani was stretchered off with what looked like serious damage to his left foot and the Repsol team played down his chances of riding on Saturday. Fortunately, he was fit to ride but clearly struggling.

Come race day, Dani spent most of his time in combat with a Ducati. First he tangled with both

'I COULD HAVE
BEEN A LITTLE
BIT FASTER.
I HAD A MARGIN,
NOT ENOUGH TO
BE COMFORTABLE
BUT ENOUGH
TO RISK LESS'
JORGE LORENZO

ABOVE Hector Barbera and Loris Baz renewed their battle for Open Class honours

BELOW Two great champions greet each other on the grid: Niki Lauda and Angel Nieto

OPPOSITE Viñales raced with the Tech 3 Yamahas before crashing – his best MotoGP showing so far

Yonny Hernandez and Danilo Petrucci in the first corner and dropped to 12th place. Then in the closing stages he had to pass both factory Ducatis. Iannone didn't prove to be too big a problem, but Dovizioso most certainly did. The Ducati is fast, and Dovi is a demon on the brakes and very difficult to pass. Pedrosa probed at nearly every corner, only to be expertly repulsed. He found a way past on the penultimate lap only to be immediately repassed, then finally found a way to make a pass stick on the last lap. For a man with a nasty injury and no grip, it was a pretty impressive race, even if Dani didn't think so.

The other seriously impressive if unheralded race performance came from Maverick Viñales. It's true that he did crash his Suzuki late on, but look at where he was: fighting with both Tech 3 Yamahas less than 20 seconds from the winner and over 10 seconds in front of his team-mate. It was another remarkable effort from a remarkable rookie.

This was one of those weekends when Jorge Lorenzo was absolutely unbeatable. He was quickest in all but one of the sessions – by over half a second in the vital third free practice – and rode as perfectly as anyone has any right to. He claimed that it wasn't a perfect race for him, that he was slower than expected at the start and that he didn't have to push hard at the end. The one thing he did say was that he was proud to have taken the championship lead because he had been 29 points in arrears after the third race of the year. Now the question was this: could anyone take the fight back to Jorge on the remaining tracks in the calendar?

BACK TO BRNO

It's a strange thing to say about the best-attended event of the year, but the Czech GP is safe. This was far from sure in the run-up to the 2015 event. Strong rumours that the race wouldn't happen were confirmed by the fact that Dorna had to hold emergency meetings with circuit management and the official website stopped selling tickets two weeks before the event.

Despite weekend attendances totalling more than 250,000, sanctioning fees hadn't been fully paid and there had been regular disputes with local government, which not unreasonably wondered why such a popular event needed public subsidy.

Thankfully for the future of an event that the paddock enjoys as much as the spectators, Dorna announced that it will now work with a new public body formed by the Central Moravian Government and the City of Brno authorities, which will act as promoter of the event and work alongside Dorna. The importance to the local economy of the GP was underlined by the presence of the Czech Republic's Minister of Education, Youth & Sports, Katerina

Valachová, who appeared on the podium to hand out trophies and made an official statement welcoming the formation of the new body.

The first Czechoslovakian Grand Prix was held at Brno in 1965, on the original 8.66-mile road course. The current 3.36-mile circuit was first used in 1987 and

hosted the Czechoslovakian GP until 1991. Brno didn't appear on the calendar in 1992, but the event was revived in 1993 as the Grand Prix of the Czech Republic and has taken place every year since. This year was the 50th running of the Czech GP and thankfully it won't be the last.

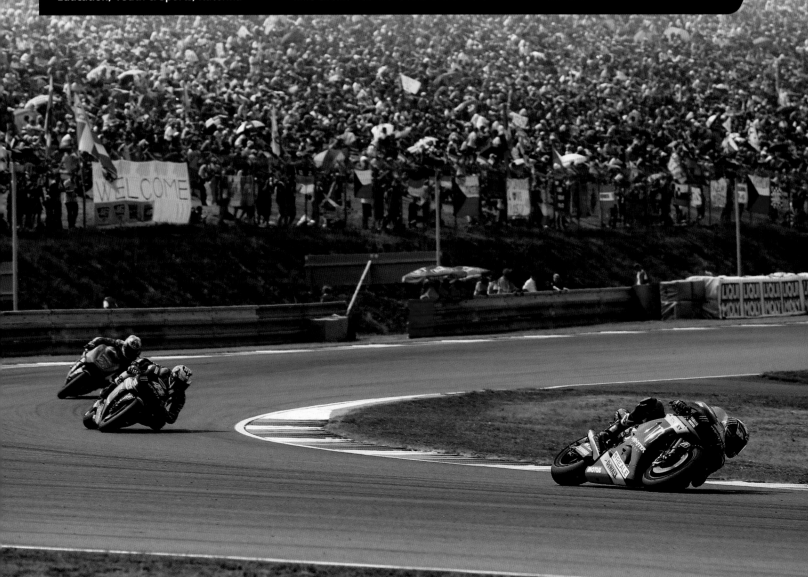

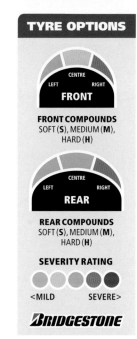

bwin GRAND PRIX ČESKÉ REPUBLIKY
AUTOMOTODROM BRNO
ROUND **11**
AUGUST 16

RACE RESULTS

CIRCUIT LENGTH 3.357 miles

NO. OF LAPS 22

RACE DISTANCE 73.860 miles

WEATHER Dry, 26°C

TRACK TEMPERATURE 39°C

WINNER Jorge Lorenzo

FASTEST LAP 1m 56.048s, 104.142 mph, Marc Marquez

LAP RECORD 1m 56.027s, 104.141 mph, Dani Pedrosa (2014)

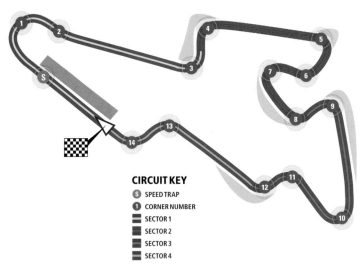

CIRCUIT KEY
- **S** SPEED TRAP
- **1** CORNER NUMBER
- SECTOR 1
- SECTOR 2
- SECTOR 3
- SECTOR 4

TYRE OPTIONS

FRONT
CENTRE / LEFT / RIGHT

FRONT COMPOUNDS
SOFT (**S**), MEDIUM (**M**), HARD (**H**)

REAR
CENTRE / LEFT / RIGHT

REAR COMPOUNDS
SOFT (**S**), MEDIUM (**M**), HARD (**H**)

SEVERITY RATING
<MILD   SEVERE>

BRIDGESTONE

QUALIFYING

	Rider	Nation	Motorcycle	Team	Time	Pole +
1	Lorenzo	SPA	Yamaha	Movistar Yamaha MotoGP	1m 54.989s	
2	Marquez	SPA	Honda	Repsol Honda Team	1m 55.063s	0.074s
3	Rossi	ITA	Yamaha	Movistar Yamaha MotoGP	1m 55.353s	0.364s
4	Iannone	ITA	Ducati	Ducati Team	1m 55.390s	0.401s
5	Smith	GBR	Yamaha	Monster Yamaha Tech 3	1m 55.460s	0.471s
6	Dovizioso	ITA	Ducati	Ducati Team	1m 55.935s	0.946s
7	Viñales	SPA	Suzuki	Team Suzuki ECSTAR	1m 55.954s	0.965s
8	Espargaro P	SPA	Yamaha	Monster Yamaha Tech 3	1m 55.955s	0.966s
9	Pedrosa	SPA	Honda	Repsol Honda Team	1m 55.969s	0.980s
10	Crutchlow	GBR	Honda	CWM LCR Honda	1m 56.192s	1.203s
11	Barbera	SPA	Ducati	Avintia Racing	1m 56.399s	1.410s
12	Hernandez	COL	Ducati	Octo Pramac Racing	1m 56.739s	1.750s
13	Petrucci	ITA	Ducati	Octo Pramac Racing	1m 56.713s	Q1
14	Redding	GBR	Honda	EG 0,0 Marc VDS	1m 56.765s	Q1
15	Espargaro A	SPA	Suzuki	Team Suzuki ECSTAR	1m 56.806s	Q1
16	Bradl	GER	Aprilia	Aprilia Racing Team Gresini	1m 57.133s	Q1
17	Di Meglio	FRA	Ducati	Avintia Racing	1m 57.215s	Q1
18	Baz	FRA	Yamaha	Forward Racing	1m 57.540s	Q1
19	Bautista	SPA	Aprilia	Aprilia Racing Team Gresini	1m 57.552s	Q1
20	Laverty E	IRL	Honda	Aspar MotoGP Team	1m 57.634s	Q1
21	Hayden	USA	Honda	Aspar MotoGP Team	1m 57.645s	Q1
22	Miller	AUS	Honda	CWM LCR Honda	1m 57.855s	Q1
23	De Angelis	RSM	ART	E-Motion IodaRacing Team	1m 58.599s	Q1
24	Corti	ITA	Yamaha	Forward Racing	1m 59.145s	Q1
25	Abraham	CZE	Honda	AB Motoracing	1m 59.903s	Q1

1 JORGE LORENZO
Pole, holeshot, never headed – just like his four other wins so far. Marquez hung on for as long as he could until Jorge opened an unbridgeable gap.

2 MARC MARQUEZ
Stuck with Lorenzo for as long as he could, which was six or seven laps, before giving up watching the gap to the leader and instead concentrating on managing the gap to Rossi in third.

3 VALENTINO ROSSI
Another rostrum in the run that stretched back nearly a year, but not happy as he could find no redeeming features in the weekend. Yes, Valentino had a bad start off the front row, but he never had the pace to challenge his team-mate.

4 ANDREA IANNONE
Much more competitive than at the previous few races but the engine's variable-length inlet trumpets stuck in one position, which the factory calculated lost Iannone two tenths of a second per lap.

5 DANI PEDROSA
Victim of a strange Friday accident caused by fork failure that badly hurt his left foot. Got sideswiped by both Pramac Ducatis in the first corners and then found he had front-end troubles. Caught Dovi in the closing stages.

6 ANDREA DOVIZIOSO
Happier than in previous races and able to hold third place early on, but difficulties in turning saw him passed by Rossi and his team-mate.

7 BRADLEY SMITH
Top satellite rider again but the distance to the winner, over 20 seconds, annoyed him. His frustration about the absence of a new contract was expressed as disappointment at the lack of machinery updates.

8 POL ESPARGARO
Happy to get across a gap to his team-mate and ride with better corner entry than Bradley, but still confused as to why he was the only Yamaha rider with rear grip issues.

9 ALEIX ESPARGARO
As at Indy, never fully comfortable with the bike. Unable to keep corner speed when tyres dropped off after six or seven laps.

10 DANILO PETRUCCI
Made up places off the start but started to lose rear grip and couldn't hold on to ninth place. Closed down on Espargaro but decided trying a pass would be too risky.

11 YONNY HERNANDEZ
Never had the feeling with the front in the race that he'd found in warm-up. Managed to fend off Redding's last-lap attack.

12 SCOTT REDDING
Spent most of the race with Hernandez and passed him on the penultimate lap only to make a mistake and allow the Colombian back through.

13 ALVARO BAUTISTA
Lost a lot of time after being shoved out on the first lap. Thereafter showed great pace that could have seen him with the satellite Ducatis. Passed his team-mate in final laps.

LAP CHART

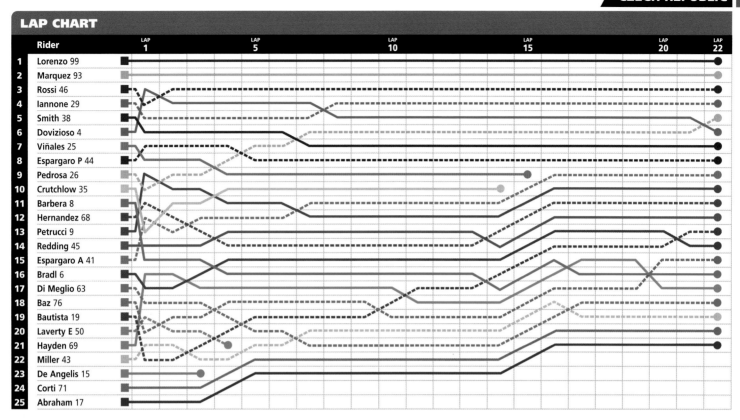

	Rider	LAP 1	LAP 5	LAP 10	LAP 15	LAP 20	LAP 22
1	Lorenzo 99						
2	Marquez 93						
3	Rossi 46						
4	Iannone 29						
5	Smith 38						
6	Dovizioso 4						
7	Viñales 25						
8	Espargaro P 44						
9	Pedrosa 26						
10	Crutchlow 35						
11	Barbera 8						
12	Hernandez 68						
13	Petrucci 9						
14	Redding 45						
15	Espargaro A 41						
16	Bradl 6						
17	Di Meglio 63						
18	Baz 76						
19	Bautista 19						
20	Laverty E 50						
21	Hayden 69						
22	Miller 43						
23	De Angelis 15						
24	Corti 71						
25	Abraham 17						

RACE

	Rider	Motorcycle	Race time	Time +	Fastest lap	Avg. speed	🅱
1	Lorenzo	Yamaha	42m 53.042s		1m 56.169s	103.3mph	M/M
2	Marquez	Honda	42m 57.504s	4.462s	1m 56.048s	103.1mph	M/H
3	Rossi	Yamaha	43m 03.439s	10.397s	1m 56.747s	102.9mph	H/H
4	Iannone	Ducati	43m 06.113s	13.071s	1m 56.860s	102.7mph	M/M
5	Pedrosa	Honda	43m 08.692s	15.650s	1m 56.975s	102.7mph	M/M
6	Dovizioso	Ducati	43m 08.767s	15.725s	1m 56.943s	102.6mph	M/M
7	Smith	Yamaha	43m 14.863s	21.821s	1m 57.250s	102.4mph	M/M
8	Espargaro P	Yamaha	43m 16.282s	23.240s	1m 57.454s	102.4mph	H/M
9	Espargaro A	Suzuki	43m 36.826s	43.784s	1m 57.844s	101.6mph	H/M
10	Petrucci	Ducati	43m 38.303s	45.261s	1m 58.121s	101.5mph	H/M
11	Hernandez	Ducati	43m 43.015s	49.973s	1m 58.530s	101.3mph	M/M
12	Redding	Honda	43m 43.216s	50.174s	1m 57.976s	101.3mph	M/M
13	Bautista	Aprilia	43m 47.479s	54.437s	1m 58.710s	101.2mph	M/S
14	Bradl	Aprilia	43m 47.666s	54.624s	1m 58.380s	101.2mph	M/S
15	Baz	Yamaha	43m 53.358s	1m 00.316s	1m 58.679s	100.9mph	M/S
16	Barbera	Ducati	43m 54.637s	1m 01.595s	1m 58.405s	100.9mph	M/S
17	Hayden	Honda	43m 55.430s	1m 02.388s	1m 58.338s	100.8mph	M/S
18	Di Meglio	Ducati	43m 58.986s	1m 05.944s	1m 58.943s	100.7mph	M/S
19	Miller	Honda	44m 04.449s	1m 11.407s	1m 59.007s	100.5mph	M/S
20	Corti	Yamaha	44m 43.075s	1m 50.033s	2m 00.377s	99.0mph	M/S
21	Abraham	Honda	44m 55.697s	2m 02.655s	2m 01.716s	98.6mph	M/S
NC	Viñales	Suzuki	29m 31.557s	7 laps	1m 57.436s	102.3mph	M/M
NC	Crutchlow	Honda	27m 38.315s	8 laps	1m 57.652s	102.0mph	M/H
NC	Laverty E	Honda	8m 04.096s	18 laps	1m 58.977s	99.9mph	M/S
NC	De Angelis	ART	6m 05.782s	19 laps	1m 59.257s	99.1mph	M/S

CHAMPIONSHIP

	Rider	Nation	Team	Points
1	Lorenzo	SPA	Movistar Yamaha MotoGP	211
	Rossi	ITA	Movistar Yamaha MotoGP	211
3	Marquez	SPA	Repsol Honda Team	159
4	Iannone	ITA	Ducati Team	142
5	Smith	GBR	Monster Yamaha Tech 3	106
6	Dovizioso	ITA	Ducati Team	104
7	Pedrosa	SPA	Repsol Honda Team	91
8	Espargaro P	SPA	Monster Yamaha Tech 3	81
9	Crutchlow	GBR	CWM LCR Honda	74
10	Petrucci	ITA	Octo Pramac Racing	63
11	Viñales	SPA	Team Suzuki ECSTAR	62
12	Espargaro A	SPA	Team Suzuki ECSTAR	53
13	Hernandez	COL	Octo Pramac Racing	41
14	Redding	GBR	EG 0,0 Marc VDS	37
15	Barbera	SPA	Avintia Racing	20
16	Bautista	SPA	Aprilia Racing Team Gresini	16
17	Baz	FRA	Forward Racing	15
18	Miller	AUS	CWM LCR Honda	12
19	Bradl	GER	Forward Racing	11
20	Pirro	ITA	Ducati Team	8
	Hayden	USA	Aspar MotoGP Team	8
22	Laverty E	IRL	Aspar MotoGP Team	7
23	Aoyama	JPN	Repsol Honda Team	5
24	Di Meglio	FRA	Avintia Racing	2
25	De Angelis	RSM	E-Motion IodaRacing Team	1

14 STEFAN BRADL
Followed his team-mate home for the team's first double points-scoring race of the year. His recently repaired wrist only made itself felt over the last two laps.

15 LORIS BAZ
Top Open Class finisher, giving the beleaguered Forward team reason to smile. Won a good dice with Hayden and Barbera to reduce the gap to the Spaniard at the top of the class to five points.

16 HECTOR BARBERA
With his team-mate, dominated qualifying but ran out of tyre in the race and had problems going into and coming out of corners. Couldn't hold off Baz and lost one point from his lead in the Open Class.

17 NICKY HAYDEN
His best start of the year but suffered from poor grip. Passed Barbera to lead the Open Class but then made a mistake, ran wide and let him and Baz through.

18 MIKE DI MEGLIO
Lost time in the first half of the race with a bike that felt totally different from any other time over the weekend. Much happier when the fuel load went down and was able to catch Miller.

19 JACK MILLER
Ran off-track avoiding Laverty's crash early on, then caught up to Baz but started getting a lot of spin. When it found grip, the bike wheelied. Glad to get it home.

21 CLAUDIO CORTI
Finished his second race for the Forward team after retiring from his first, at Indianapolis.

22 KAREL ABRAHAM
Rode his home race with his foot injury far from healed. It was an achievement to get to the flag.

DID NOT FINISH

MAVERICK VIÑALES
Crashed six laps from home while only 20 seconds adrift of the leader and dicing with other factory bikes. A major step forward despite the crash.

CAL CRUTCHLOW
Never happy with his set-up and had to push to maintain the sort of pace he needed. Crashed at the penultimate esses and apologised to the team.

EUGENE LAVERTY
Much happier with the bike over the last two races but crashed on lap five due to a tyre not behaving as expected. Lucky to avoid injury when clipped by Miller.

ALEX DE ANGELIS
Fell because of chatter – the perennial problem exacerbated by the Brno tarmac – after being passed by four bikes in a straight line and trying to stay with them.

OCTO BRITISH GRAND PRIX
SILVERSTONE

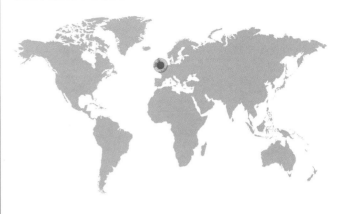

THE WEATHER MAN

Rossi seized the opportunity and put clear water between himself and Lorenzo, while Ducati returned to form

The contrast between the Valentino Rossi who won the British Grand Prix and the one who finished third two weeks earlier in the Czech Republic couldn't have been more marked. Thirty-six years old? At Brno he'd looked much, much older. At Silverstone he looked ten years younger. No wonder. Jorge Lorenzo had been keen to tell us after Brno how proud he was to have jumped a 29-point gap at the top of the championship in seven races, and here was Valentino regaining the championship lead and opening up a 12-point lead in one fell swoop.

And all on a circuit where he'd never won and that the man himself regarded as a place where his championship aspirations could be damaged.

Yes, the conditions played to Valentino's strengths, but it wasn't as if Lorenzo and Marquez have never won in the wet – and Valentino, indeed, reckoned that this was his first wet-weather win in a decade. It came after the sort of qualifying that we'd become used to; Marquez on pole and Lorenzo right behind him, with Valentino nearly three-quarters of a second slower than Marc, on the second row. Yet again, the question on everyone's lips was how long Marquez could keep up with Lorenzo. The familiar assumption – that Jorge would get the holeshot and that Marc would pursue him closely for as long as it took to find out whether or not he could win – was now our default setting. The only question over third place was whether Rossi would be able to maintain his run of rostrum finishes.

That all changed with the weather. After two fine days, race day dawned wet and got wetter. Rossi was quickest in warm-up, which made everyone sit up and take notice, although the sight of Danilo Petrucci in

'I THINK THE LAST RACE I WON IN THE WET WAS TEN YEARS AGO'

VALENTINO ROSSI

second didn't really register. It should have done. The race very nearly started on slicks but a further shower sent the entire field into pitlane at the end of the warm-up lap. By the letter of the law, the whole field then should have started from pitlane in an orderly queue, but Race Direction wisely chose to red-flag procedings and start again – this time with the grid forming up on the unanimous choice of wet-weather tyres. It's worth noting that if some gambler had gone to the grid on wet tyres at the first time of asking, the race would have been deemed to have started.

Lorenzo didn't seem to notice the change in conditions and led off the line only to be quickly passed by Rossi and Marquez. Jorge was then nearly punted out of the race by Pol Espargaro but regained the track. Cal Crutchlow wasn't so lucky, and to add insult to injury it was his team-mate Jack Miller who knocked him down. The Aussie had been trying to hold off Pol on the brakes but got it all wrong. Silverstone has never been kind to Crutchlow but this episode of friendly fire ruined a very good chance of a rostrum finish.

While the midfield runners pushed and shoved, Rossi pulled away with Marquez in his wake, but that ended on lap 16 when Marc highsided out of the race at Copse. It looked like an off-throttle crash, so was it another symptom of the Honda's engine-braking woes or just a standard wet-weather incident? Certainly the man himself was pushing, only too well aware that any hopes he retained of the championship depended on winning races or at least taking points off the Yamahas in front of him. He did admit that he never had a

ABOVE Cal Crutchlow looked to be heading for the podium until his team-mate Jack Miller had a rush of blood

LEFT Scott Redding yet again responded superbly to the pressure of his home race

ABOVE In the wet conditions Valentino Rossi harried Marc Marquez before passing him and towing him into a mistake

BELOW Nicky Hayden always goes well in the wet; he finished top of the Open Class

OPPOSITE Danilo Petrucci was the hero of Silverstone with his second place after giving Rossi a severe fright

good feeling with the bike in the wet and that he now considered his title chances to have disappeared.

Rossi saw Marquez's crash on a big screen and momentarily relaxed, allowing the Ducatis of Dovizioso and Petrucci to close the gap from six seconds to 1.6 seconds. But he was able to focus his concentration once more and get to the flag safely. It wasn't really a surprise to see two Ducati riders on the rostrum, but to have Petrucci in second place was most definitely unexpected. Danilo has always been a good wet-weather rider and the 14.1 Ducati was much better in the wet than in the dry, but this result was beyond all expectations. He admitted to some trepidation in passing Pedrosa and Lorenzo but then engaged in a ferocious battle with Dovizioso. Andrea said later that he was convinced Danilo was going to crash at every corner, so extreme was his braking. For his part, Petrucci tried to ignore his old friend on the factory bike and focus on Rossi in front of him. Going into the last lap he thought, 'If I crash now I'm going straight to the airport, not back to the pits.' He didn't, and joined an all-Italian rostrum, the second of the year, where the others seemed almost as pleased to see Danilo as he was to be there.

The big loser was the man Rossi later said he wouldn't have beaten in the dry – Jorge Lorenzo. He pointed to his visor when he walked back into his pit. It had misted up. It was the second time this year that his helmet had cost him points.

Was Rossi lucky? Only in that Jorge had an avoidable problem. Everything else was down to his experience and ability to adapt to the unexpected.

THE BRITISH ARE COMING

British fans are enjoying a golden era, the like of which they haven't seen in Grand Prix racing since the days of Barry Sheene. They can enjoy watching Danny Kent and Sam Lowes win in Moto3 and Moto2, and Cal Crutchlow knocking on the door of a MotoGP victory while Bradley Smith (pictured below) gets better and better.

Scott Redding's sixth place gave a damp but large crowd reasons to be cheerful in the MotoGP race. For the first time in the class, he was able to outshine Smith and Crutchlow. Scott may have been helped by the announcement that in 2016 he will be riding a Ducati for Pramac. Scott tested a Desmosedici two years ago and got on with it famously, which is more than can be said for the Honda. There was more good news for British fans before the event when Smith announced he had signed for another year with Tech 3 and Crutchlow said that he would stay

with LCR Honda. That puts them in sync with all the big players and guarantees a frenetic rider market in 2016.

Sam Lowes (pictured above) was also due to join MotoGP with the factory Aprilia team, but the testing abilities of new recruit Stefan Bradl caused a rethink. Instead of being bad news for the Brit, this may turn out to be a blessing. Aprilia will employ him as test rider while he will race for team manager Fausto Gresini's Moto2 team. Instead of having to choose between staying in Moto2 and making the leap to MotoGP, he'll now get the best of both worlds.

OCTO BRITISH GRAND PRIX
SILVERSTONE
ROUND 12
AUGUST 30

OFFICIAL TIMEKEEPER

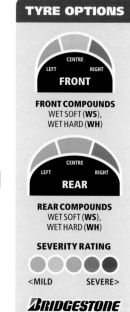

TYRE OPTIONS

FRONT

FRONT COMPOUNDS
WET SOFT (**WS**),
WET HARD (**WH**)

REAR

REAR COMPOUNDS
WET SOFT (**WS**),
WET HARD (**WH**)

SEVERITY RATING

<MILD   SEVERE>

BRIDGESTONE

RACE RESULTS

CIRCUIT LENGTH 3.666 miles

NO. OF LAPS 20

RACE DISTANCE 73.322 miles

WEATHER Wet, 16°C

TRACK TEMPERATURE 18°C

WINNER Valentino Rossi

FASTEST LAP 2m 16.486s,
96.685mph, Valentino Rossi

LAP RECORD 2m 01.941s,
108.181mph, Dani Pedrosa (2013)

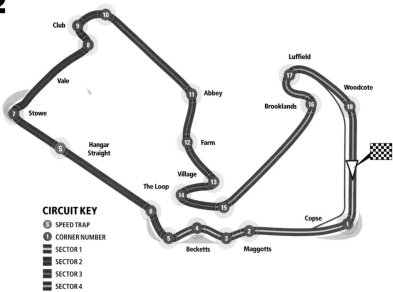

CIRCUIT KEY
- **S** SPEED TRAP
- **1** CORNER NUMBER
- SECTOR 1
- SECTOR 2
- SECTOR 3
- SECTOR 4

QUALIFYING

	Rider	Nation	Motorcycle	Team	Time	Pole +
1	Marquez	SPA	Honda	Repsol Honda Team	2m 00.234s	
2	Lorenzo	SPA	Yamaha	Movistar Yamaha MotoGP	2m 00.522s	0.288s
3	Pedrosa	SPA	Honda	Repsol Honda Team	2m 00.716s	0.482s
4	Rossi	ITA	Yamaha	Movistar Yamaha MotoGP	2m 00.947s	0.713s
5	Espargaro P	SPA	Yamaha	Monster Yamaha Tech 3	2m 01.031s	0.797s
6	Smith	GBR	Yamaha	Monster Yamaha Tech 3	2m 01.140s	0.906s
7	Redding	GBR	Honda	EG 0,0 Marc VDS	2m 01.329s	1.095s
8	Crutchlow	GBR	Honda	LCR Honda	2m 01.376s	1.142s
9	Iannone	ITA	Ducati	Ducati Team	2m 01.874s	1.640s
10	Espargaro A	SPA	Suzuki	Team Suzuki ECSTAR	2m 01.880s	1.646s
11	Hernandez	COL	Ducati	Octo Pramac Racing	2m 01.894s	1.660s
12	Dovizioso	ITA	Ducati	Ducati Team	2m 01.979s	1.745s
13	Viñales	SPA	Suzuki	Team Suzuki ECSTAR	2m 02.016s	Q1
14	Bradl	GER	Aprilia	Aprilia Racing Team Gresini	2m 02.657s	Q1
15	Baz	FRA	Yamaha	Forward Racing	2m 02.677s	Q1
16	Miller	AUS	Honda	LCR Honda	2m 02.697s	Q1
17	Barbera	SPA	Ducati	Avintia Racing	2m 02.784s	Q1
18	Petrucci	ITA	Ducati	Octo Pramac Racing	2m 02.800s	Q1
19	Laverty E	IRL	Honda	Aspar MotoGP Team	2m 02.894s	Q1
20	Bautista	SPA	Aprilia	Aprilia Racing Team Gresini	2m 02.908s	Q1
21	Hayden	USA	Honda	Aspar MotoGP Team	2m 02.946s	Q1
22	Di Meglio	FRA	Ducati	Avintia Racing	2m 03.641s	Q1
23	Corti	ITA	Yamaha	Forward Racing	2m 03.789s	Q1
24	Abraham	CZE	Honda	AB Motoracing	2m 04.133s	Q1
25	De Angelis	RSM	ART	E-Motion IodaRacing Team	2m 04.304s	Q1

1 VALENTINO ROSSI
His first wet-weather win in ten years underpinned by decent qualifying (fourth) and being fastest in wet warm-up. Tried to break Marquez but couldn't open a gap. When Marc crashed, Valentino relaxed and allowed Petrucci to close rapidly, so had to push again. Most significantly, he retook the championship lead with a 12-point advantage.

2 DANILO PETRUCCI
Made up 16 places for his career-best finish. Both bike and rider were known to be good in the wet, but this was still some achievement. Dovizioso gave him a hard time and for a lap or two it looked as if Danilo would catch Rossi. A universally popular rostrum finish.

3 ANDREA DOVIZIOSO
Back on the rostrum for the first time since Le Mans despite poor qualifying and a worse start. Worked his way back from 11th place at the end of the first lap. Followed Petrucci and then swapped places with him several times before deciding to settle for third.

4 JORGE LORENZO
Lost his championship lead, but the damage was compounded by his visor misting up – not the first time he's had a problem with his crash helmet.

5 DANI PEDROSA
Top Honda rider, but never happy with the way the bike felt or with his performance. This on top of a run of results that Dani has been unhappy with.

6 SCOTT REDDING
His best MotoGP result so far, and typical of a rider who seems to thrive on the pressure of a home race. Slow off the start but got back to and past the group containing Smith and the Espargaro brothers.

7 BRADLEY SMITH
Damage limitation in front of his home crowd. Showed well in the dry – third fastest on Friday – but couldn't stay with the factory bikes in the wet.

8 ANDREA IANNONE
Like his team-mate, Andrea started badly and also struggled all weekend with the bumpy parts of the track. Rear grip on corner entry was the problem.

9 ALEIX ESPARGARO
Hit by Hernandez in the first corner and lost time. Noticed some noises from the back of the bike and had his rear tyre performance drop off. As he had a good gap on the following group, Aleix backed off to ensure the team got maximum data from its first wet race.

10 ALVARO BAUTISTA
Equalled his best finish of the year in his first wet race on the bike. Understood the tyres very early and set his rhythm accordingly – an intelligent race.

11 MAVERICK VIÑALES
Dropped to last place on the first lap as he avoided the fallen Hernandez. His race pace was consistent so his first wet MotoGP race was deemed satisfactory.

LAP CHART

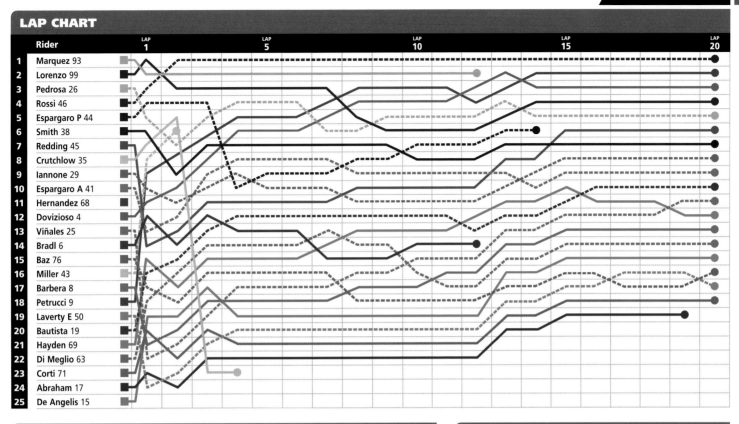

	Rider					
		LAP 1	LAP 5	LAP 10	LAP 15	LAP 20
1	Marquez 93					
2	Lorenzo 99					
3	Pedrosa 26					
4	Rossi 46					
5	Espargaro P 44					
6	Smith 38					
7	Redding 45					
8	Crutchlow 35					
9	Iannone 29					
10	Espargaro A 41					
11	Hernandez 68					
12	Dovizioso 4					
13	Viñales 25					
14	Bradl 6					
15	Baz 76					
16	Miller 43					
17	Barbera 8					
18	Petrucci 9					
19	Laverty E 50					
20	Bautista 19					
21	Hayden 69					
22	Di Meglio 63					
23	Corti 71					
24	Abraham 17					
25	De Angelis 15					

RACE

	Rider	Motorcycle	Race time	Time +	Fastest lap	Avg. speed	
1	Rossi	Yamaha	46m 15.617s		2m 16.486s	95.1mph	WS/WS
2	Petrucci	Ducati	46m 18.627s	3.010s	2m 16.995s	94.9mph	WS/WS
3	Dovizioso	Ducati	46m 19.734s	4.117s	2m 16.971s	94.9mph	WS/WS
4	Lorenzo	Yamaha	46m 21.343s	5.726s	2m 16.916s	94.9mph	WS/WS
5	Pedrosa	Honda	46m 26.749s	11.132s	2m 17.195s	94.7mph	WS/WS
6	Redding	Honda	46m 41.084s	25.467s	2m 17.951s	94.2mph	WS/WS
7	Smith	Yamaha	46m 42.334s	26.717s	2m 18.534s	94.1mph	WS/WS
8	Iannone	Ducati	46m 45.010s	29.393s	2m 17.809s	94.1mph	WS/WS
9	Espargaro A	Suzuki	46m 54.432s	38.815s	2m 18.563s	93.8mph	WS/WS
10	Bautista	Aprilia	46m 57.329s	41.712s	2m 18.942s	93.6mph	WS/WS
11	Viñales	Suzuki	47m 00.393s	44.776s	2m 18.542s	93.6mph	WS/WS
12	Hayden	Honda	47m 08.106s	52.489s	2m 18.452s	93.3mph	WS/WS
13	Barbera	Ducati	47m 26.828s	1m 11.211s	2m 18.811s	92.7mph	WS/WS
14	Di Meglio	Ducati	47m 30.909s	1m 15.292s	2m 19.044s	92.6mph	WS/WS
15	De Angelis	ART	47m 33.480s	1m 17.863s	2m 20.437s	92.4mph	WS/WS
16	Baz	Yamaha	47m 34.927s	1m 19.310s	2m 20.095s	92.4mph	WS/WS
17	Laverty E	Honda	47m 35.352s	1m 19.735s	2m 20.964s	92.4mph	WS/WS
18	Corti	Yamaha	48m 13.703s	1m 58.086s	2m 22.277s	91.2mph	WS/WS
19	Abraham	Honda	48m 20.040s	1 lap	2m 23.339s	86.4mph	WS/WS
NC	Espargaro P	Yamaha	32m 41.904s	6 laps	2m 18.058s	94.1mph	WS/WS
NC	Marquez	Honda	27m 48.613s	8 laps	2m 16.569s	94.9mph	WS/WS
NC	Bradl	Aprilia	28m 16.151s	8 laps	2m 18.536s	93.3mph	WS/WS
NC	Crutchlow	Honda	13m 08.693s	16 laps	2m 21.957s	66.9mph	WS/WS
NC	Miller	Honda	4m 50.258s	18 laps	2m 22.096s	90.9mph	WS/WS
NC	Hernandez	Ducati	–	–	–	–	WS/WS

CHAMPIONSHIP

	Rider	Nation	Team	Points
1	Rossi	SPA	Movistar Yamaha MotoGP	236
2	Lorenzo	ITA	Movistar Yamaha MotoGP	224
3	Marquez	SPA	Repsol Honda Team	159
4	Iannone	ITA	Ducati Team	150
5	Dovizioso	ITA	Ducati Team	120
6	Smith	GBR	Monster Yamaha Tech 3	115
7	Pedrosa	SPA	Repsol Honda Team	102
8	Petrucci	ITA	Octo Pramac Racing	83
9	Espargaro P	SPA	Monster Yamaha Tech 3	81
10	Crutchlow	GBR	LCR Honda	74
11	Viñales	SPA	Team Suzuki ECSTAR	67
12	Espargaro A	SPA	Team Suzuki ECSTAR	60
13	Redding	GBR	EG 0,0 Marc VDS	47
14	Hernandez	COL	Octo Pramac Racing	41
15	Barbera	SPA	Avintia Racing	23
16	Bautista	SPA	Aprilia Racing Team Gresini	22
17	Baz	FRA	Forward Racing	15
18	Hayden	USA	Aspar MotoGP Team	12
19	Miller	AUS	LCR Honda	12
20	Bradl	GER	Forward Racing	11
21	Pirro	ITA	Ducati Team	8
22	Laverty E	IRL	Aspar MotoGP Team	7
23	Aoyama	JPN	Repsol Honda Team	5
24	Di Meglio	FRA	Avintia Racing	4
25	De Angelis	RSM	E-Motion IodaRacing Team	2

12 NICKY HAYDEN
Top of the Open Class for only the second time. Looked to be heading for a finish well inside the top ten but was taken by two factory bikes in the final laps. Seriously fast in the middle of the race but electronics made life difficult in the closing stages.

13 HECTOR BARBERA
Didn't win but scored three points to increase his Open Class lead over Baz.

14 MIKE DI MEGLIO
Looked like he could give Hayden a race for victory in the Open Class until his visor misted up.

15 ALEX DE ANGELIS
His second bike wasn't set up for fully wet conditions so he had some hard work on his hands in the early laps. Happy to score points for the second time this season.

16 LORIS BAZ
Fastest Open rider in qualifying, and started the race well. That changed when rear tyre grip diminished.

17 EUGENE LAVERTY
Pushed hard – as hard as he's ever done in the wet – but had no grip coming out of corners. Didn't find any feeling in wet warm-up or for the race. Really unhappy to ride so hard and not score points.

18 CLAUDIO CORTI
No experience at all with the Yamaha in the wet. Not surprisingly, his main problem was a lack of rear grip.

19 KAREL ABRAHAM
Happy to finish but not about anything else. The bike was nervous and unstable at the rear, with no grip out of corners and vibration that hurt his still-healing foot.

DID NOT FINISH

POL ESPARGARO
Blazingly fast start then ran off-track. Passed his brother and his team-mate only to lose the rear going into Turn 3.

MARC MARQUEZ
Crashed out as he shadowed Rossi. Marc was in no mood to settle for anything other than a win.

STEFAN BRADL
Had trouble with cold tyres at the start, then closed up to his team-mate only to loose the front when braking for Vale.

CAL CRUTCHLOW
Looked fast and comfortable in warm-up and the race, and on for a rostrum at least, only to be taken out by his crashing team-mate on lap 2.

JACK MILLER
Was trying to hold off Pol Espargaro on the brakes when he lost the front and scooped up his team-mate.

YONNY HERNANDEZ
A victim of first-corner bunching; fell after a collision with Aleix Espargaro.

GP TIM DI SAN MARINO
E DELLA RIVIERA DI RIMINI
MISANO WORLD CIRCUIT MARCO SIMONCELLI

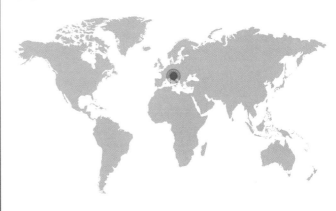

OUTLOOK UNCERTAIN

The weather intervened again and this time Marquez won with British riders either side of him on the rostrum

Valentino Rossi's now customary special helmet design for a home race featured a little fish being pursued by a large shark. To make sure we got the point, the fish was yellow and had a number 46 on its head. The large predator wasn't one particular opponent, we were told, but represented all of his rivals. It harked back to a remark he made a few years ago, about getting older and being surrounded by 'young sharks' who smelled blood in the water.

Before the race, all the attention was on Misano's new surface, a much-overdue upgrade that had exhibited stupendous grip levels in summer testing. The new tarmac had obviously mellowed a little in the intervening months, and while everyone agreed that a good job had been done in flattening out the bumps, the grip turned out to be merely the usual level to be expected from an international circuit. As it turned out, in a remarkable race in which every rider but one swapped bikes twice, the tiddler wasn't caught by that big shark but did get nibbled by a couple of smaller predators. Yes, Valentino did extend his championship lead to a very handy 23 points, but it could have been better.

It was dry when the race started but heavy rain arrived after six laps, sending most of the field into the pits for their 'wet' bikes. Dovizioso and Crutchlow stayed out for an extra lap and lost their chances of a rostrum finish, and for a while it looked like Bradley Smith had done the same. The second bike change was even more crucial. Those who got back on slicks quickly took enormous chunks of time out of the others. There were a few laps when Smith, the one man who didn't change bikes, was at least ten seconds a lap quicker than Rossi, who was in the lead but yet to revert to his dry bike.

'THE TEAM
INFORMED ME
OF THE SITUATION
AND HELPED ME
DECIDE WHEN
TO COME IN'
MARC MARQUEZ

It was like watching last year's Aragón race all over again. Back then, the Repsol Hondas stayed out too long on slicks when the rains came and Marquez and Pedrosa crashed when their tyres cooled below normal operating temperatures. This time, the Movistar Yamahas stayed out too long on wets as the slick guys closed them down hand over fist. On both occasions, the team-mates were more concerned with watching each other than seeing the bigger picture. The Yamaha men, after all, were more worried about their title fight than the victory. When they did finally get back on slicks, Lorenzo, spooked by the pace of Scott Redding going past him, promptly crashed hard on his out lap, having asked too much of the left side of his tyre after the run of four right-handers that starts at the fearsome Turn 11. Rossi stayed out on treaded rubber a lap longer and only had time left to get up to fifth place. Both Yamaha riders were outwitted by Marquez, who made his second stop four laps before Rossi and had time to rejoin in fifth and take the lead three laps later.

The old chestnut of whether or not to introduce bike-to-pits radio arose afterwards, but as Lorenzo spent several laps ignoring the word BOX in very large letters on his pit board, it's doubtful if more modern technology would have conveyed the message any better. In these situations the crux of the argument, of course, is that you need to know the crossover point – when the men on new tyres begin to go faster than the guys on the tyres they started with. Trouble is, once a team knows where the crossover point is, it's too late to tell its riders so that they can take advantage. Marquez did hint that his team kept him informed of times but emphasised that he

OPPOSITE The rain flags got a good work-out. Scott Redding's crash early on turned out to be a blessing as it dictated his bike-change times – which proved to be ideal

ABOVE Rossi's helmet design said it all – little yellow number 46 being pursued by a big shark

LEFT Two British racers on a top-class podium for the first time since the 1970s

made the decisions about when to come in. Clearly he had learned from Aragón last year.

Bradley Smith made a mistake followed by a brave decision. He realised that he'd stayed out on slicks too long so stuck with them. He dealt with seeing some big numbers on his pitboard and then, in a brilliant display of concentration, surged up the order to second place, reaping some reward for his superbly consistent season. 'Luck favours the brave,' he said, summing it up nicely.

Scott Redding was forced into his decision to change, first by crashing early on slicks and then being so seriously uncomfortable on wets that he changed back at the first opportunity. When the swapping was over he found himself fourth and set about hunting down Loris Baz. To the delight of his team, Scott made the podium for the first time in his MotoGP career. Baz also deserved serious praise after the season he and his Forward Racing team-mates had had: the lanky Frenchman was one of the first to change to wets and made a similarly clever judgement when changing back. His fourth place put him back to the top of the Open Class, despite the team having had to miss Indy, and he was also pleased to prove that he isn't too tall for MotoGP.

It's difficult to argue that Rossi was wrong to concentrate on what Lorenzo was doing, and it's always very unwise to do something radically different tactically from your championship rivals. From that perspective, increasing his championship lead from 12 to 23 points meant that Valentino had a very good weekend. Marquez, by contrast, was free to follow his instincts and go for the win, even if it meant taking considerably more risks. And he's never been averse to that, has he?

ABOVE Tech 3's Hervé Poncharal and Guy Coulon wonder how long Bradley Smith can last on slicks

BELOW Miller was 12th – and would have been higher had the factory bikes not come by in the last few laps

OPPOSITE Marquez shadows the factory Yamahas; it was Marc who out-thought them and timed his bike changes best

WINGS OVER MISANO

When technical regulations specifically forbid any engine development, engineers will seek out advantages in less obvious areas. Hence Ducati's season-long experimentation with aerofoils on the fairing and the new biplane design that appeared at Misano. Yamaha also joined in and resurrected its 1999 experiment.

Valentino Rossi and Jorge Lorenzo tried Yamaha's winglets in practice and Rossi went to the line for the first, dry part of the race with them. The decision was made because 'they can't do any harm' and because there had been a 1kph increase in top speed with them fitted. In this championship, any advantage, however tiny, has to be seized. Yamaha did state that a downforce improvement could be detected by the front-fork telemetry, but also added that there had been absolutely no effect on lap time. How much downforce? Well, the fact that Yamaha's wings were fixed to the fairing with four pop rivets suggests the answer was 'not a lot'.

As usual, the factories wouldn't reveal what they were trying to achieve, but the obvious answer was 'anti-wheelie'. Yamaha's riders said they couldn't detect any difference with winglets fitted, but Andrea Iannone was sure that Ducati's wings helped stability in long, fast corners.

The only visible difference has been in photos of bikes over the crest at the end of Mugello's front straight. Where others were trying to aviate the front wheel, the Ducati was flying straight and level. As downforce is proportional to speed squared, and the speed there is well over 200mph, perhaps this isn't surprising. Whether such aerodynamic devices can have a noticeable or useful effect at even slightly lower speeds remains open to question.

GP TIM DI SAN MARINO
E DELLA RIVIERA DI RIMINI
MISANO WORLD CIRCUIT MARCO SIMONCELLI

ROUND **13**
SEPTEMBER 13

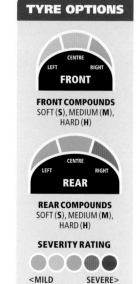

OFFICIAL TIMEKEEPER

RACE RESULTS

CIRCUIT LENGTH 2.626 miles

NO. OF LAPS 28

RACE DISTANCE 73.528 miles

WEATHER Dry, 25°C

TRACK TEMPERATURE 31°C

WINNER Marc Marquez

FASTEST LAP 1m 33.273s, 101.345mph, Jorge Lorenzo (record)

PREVIOUS LAP RECORD 1m 33.906s, 100.662mph, Jorge Lorenzo (2011)

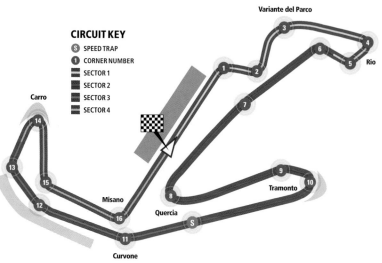

CIRCUIT KEY
- S SPEED TRAP
- 1 CORNER NUMBER
- SECTOR 1
- SECTOR 2
- SECTOR 3
- SECTOR 4

TYRE OPTIONS

FRONT

FRONT COMPOUNDS
SOFT (**S**), MEDIUM (**M**), HARD (**H**)

REAR

REAR COMPOUNDS
SOFT (**S**), MEDIUM (**M**), HARD (**H**)

SEVERITY RATING

<MILD   SEVERE>

BRIDGESTONE

QUALIFYING

	Rider	Nation	Motorcycle	Team	Time	Pole +
1	Lorenzo	SPA	Yamaha	Movistar Yamaha MotoGP	1m 32.146s	
2	Marquez	SPA	Honda	Repsol Honda Team	1m 32.252s	0.106s
3	Rossi	ITA	Yamaha	Movistar Yamaha MotoGP	1m 32.358s	0.212s
4	Pedrosa	SPA	Honda	Repsol Honda Team	1m 32.434s	0.288s
5	Pirro	ITA	Ducati	Ducati Team	1m 32.736s	0.590s
6	Smith	GBR	Yamaha	Monster Yamaha Tech 3	1m 32.801s	0.655s
7	Iannone	ITA	Ducati	Ducati Team	1m 32.821s	0.675s
8	Dovizioso	ITA	Ducati	Ducati Team	1m 32.934s	0.788s
9	Petrucci	ITA	Ducati	Octo Pramac Racing	1m 33.169s	1.023s
10	Espargaro A	SPA	Suzuki	Team Suzuki ECSTAR	1m 33.187s	1.041s
11	Crutchlow	GBR	Honda	LCR Honda	1m 33.220s	1.074s
12	Espargaro P	SPA	Yamaha	Monster Yamaha Tech 3	1m 33.222s	1.076s
13	Redding	GBR	Honda	EG 0,0 Marc VDS	1m 33.340s	Q1
14	Viñales	SPA	Suzuki	Team Suzuki ECSTAR	1m 33.439s	Q1
15	Hernandez	COL	Ducati	Octo Pramac Racing	1m 33.710s	Q1
16	Baz	FRA	Yamaha	Forward Racing	1m 34.093s	Q1
17	Miller	AUS	Honda	LCR Honda	1m 34.137s	Q1
18	Barbera	SPA	Ducati	Avintia Racing	1m 34.296s	Q1
19	Bradl	GER	Aprilia	Aprilia Racing Team Gresini	1m 34.333s	Q1
20	Bautista	SPA	Aprilia	Aprilia Racing Team Gresini	1m 34.368s	Q1
21	Laverty E	IRL	Honda	Aspar MotoGP Team	1m 34.468s	Q1
22	Di Meglio	FRA	Ducati	Avintia Racing	1m 34.722s	Q1
23	Hayden	USA	Honda	Aspar MotoGP Team	1m 34.732s	Q1
24	Corti	ITA	Yamaha	Forward Racing	1m 35.385s	Q1
25	Abraham	CZE	Honda	AB Motoracing	1m 35.406s	Q1
26	De Angelis	RSM	ART	E-Motion IodaRacing Team	1m 35.684s	Q1

1 MARC MARQUEZ
Pitted to go back to his dry bike two laps before Lorenzo and Pedrosa, and four before Rossi. That was the vital decision that allowed Marc to take his first win at Misano. Made the point that he took his team's advice on when to change bikes.

2 BRADLEY SMITH
Stayed out too long on slicks, so decided to stick with them. Despite his lap times going well over two minutes, he persevered and got to the flag without changing bikes. This was his career-best MotoGP finish.

3 SCOTT REDDING
His first rostrum in the MotoGP class, despite crashing shortly after it started raining. That incident sent him in for his wet bike early, and he also timed his switch back perfectly. He found himself in fourth place but had time to hunt down Baz.

4 LORIS BAZ
The new leader of the Open Class. Made both bike changes early, which proved to be the best strategy in this race. Only did six laps on the wet tyres. Couldn't fend off Redding in the final laps.

5 VALENTINO ROSSI
Didn't make the best decision on when to change bikes and ended his run of 16 podium finishes. In particular, he was the last rider to change back to slicks.

6 DANILO PETRUCCI
Best Ducati for the second race running, this time after tricky practice and qualifying. Spent second dry spell trying to catch Rossi, which he found was easier said than done.

7 ANDREA IANNONE
Yet another who delayed returning to slicks and paid the price, even though he had destroyed his wets very quickly.

8 ANDREA DOVIZIOSO
Led the race after most of the field went in to change to wet bikes after six laps. In seventh when he changed back, but did so too late. Came out of pits 13th and could only improve to eighth before the flag. Accepted responsibility for the timings.

9 DANI PEDROSA
Missed his pit board more than once for the critical change back to slicks and then got stuck in traffic when he did make the swap.

10 ALEIX ESPARGARO
The team was caught out by the difference in the track surface from the July test and

by the conditions on the day. Aleix was only really happy in the first dry phase of the race.

11 CAL CRUTCHLOW
A poor result after not changing bikes at optimum times; for the dry stint at the end he was on a used tyre.

12 JACK MILLER
Looked on for his first top-ten finish of the year when the field shook out after the final bike changes, but then he hit electrical problems. The bike wouldn't make power or go into any gear below fourth.

LAP CHART

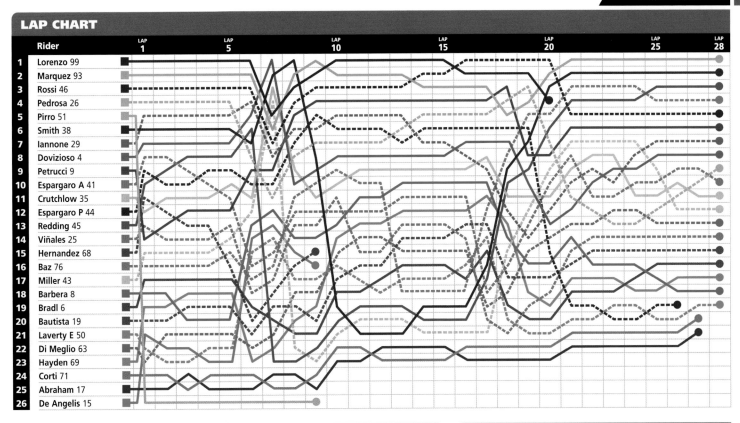

	Rider						
		LAP 1	LAP 5	LAP 10	LAP 15	LAP 20	LAP 25 / LAP 28
1	Lorenzo 99						
2	Marquez 93						
3	Rossi 46						
4	Pedrosa 26						
5	Pirro 51						
6	Smith 38						
7	Iannone 29						
8	Dovizioso 4						
9	Petrucci 9						
10	Espargaro A 41						
11	Crutchlow 35						
12	Espargaro P 44						
13	Redding 45						
14	Viñales 25						
15	Hernandez 68						
16	Baz 76						
17	Miller 43						
18	Barbera 8						
19	Bradl 6						
20	Bautista 19						
21	Laverty E 50						
22	Di Meglio 63						
23	Hayden 69						
24	Corti 71						
25	Abraham 17						
26	De Angelis 15						

RACE

	Rider	Motorcycle	Race time	Time +	Fastest lap	Avg. speed	
1	Marquez	Honda	48m 23.819s		1m 33.396s	91.1mph	M/M
2	Smith	Yamaha	48m 31.107s	7.288s	1m 34.105s	90.9mph	H/M
3	Redding	Honda	48m 42.612s	18.793s	1m 34.042s	90.5mph	H/M
4	Baz	Yamaha	48m 50.246s	26.427s	1m 35.138s	90.3mph	M/S
5	Rossi	Yamaha	48m 57.015s	33.196s	1m 33.833s	90.1mph	H/M
6	Petrucci	Ducati	48m 58.906s	35.087s	1m 34.949s	90.0mph	M/M
7	Iannone	Ducati	49m 00.346s	36.527s	1m 33.800s	90.0mph	M/M
8	Dovizioso	Ducati	49m 01.253s	37.434s	1m 34.041s	90.0mph	H/M
9	Pedrosa	Honda	49m 03.335s	39.516s	1m 33.636s	89.9mph	H/M
10	Espargaro A	Suzuki	49m 03.511s	39.692s	1m 35.027s	89.9mph	H/S
11	Crutchlow	Honda	49m 05.814s	41.995s	1m 34.399s	89.9mph	H/M
12	Miller	Honda	49m 09.894s	46.075s	1m 35.218s	89.7mph	M/M
13	Di Meglio	Ducati	49m 12.200s	48.381s	1m 35.684s	89.6mph	M/S
14	Viñales	Suzuki	49m 16.144s	52.325s	1m 35.189s	89.5mph	H/M
15	Bautista	Aprilia	49m 17.176s	53.348s	1m 35.524s	89.5mph	M/S
16	Bradl	Aprilia	49m 22.647s	58.828s	1m 35.508s	89.3mph	M/S
17	Hayden	Honda	49m 26.468s	1m 02.649s	1m 35.680s	89.2mph	M/S
18	Barbera	Ducati	49m 28.587s	1m 04.768s	1m 35.686s	89.1mph	H/M
19	Laverty E	Honda	49m 29.496s	1m 05.677s	1m 35.406s	89.1mph	M/S
20	Corti	Yamaha	49m 17.998s	1 lap	1m 38.268s	86.2mph	M/S
21	Abraham	Honda	49m 47.935s	1 lap	1m 37.725s	85.4mph	M/S
NC	Espargaro P	Yamaha	46m 17.620s	2 laps	1m 34.606s	88.5mph	M/M
NC	Lorenzo	Yamaha	35m 49.666s	8 laps	1m 33.273s	87.9mph	H/M
NC	Hernandez	Ducati	15m 59.360s	19 laps	1m 35.362s	88.7mph	M/M
NC	De Angelis	ART	15m 59.710s	19 laps	1m 36.393s	88.6mph	M/M
NC	Pirro	Ducati	23m 05.901s	19 laps	1m 47.946s	61.3mph	M/M

CHAMPIONSHIP

	Rider	Nation	Team	Points
1	Rossi	SPA	Movistar Yamaha MotoGP	247
2	Lorenzo	ITA	Movistar Yamaha MotoGP	224
3	Marquez	SPA	Repsol Honda Team	184
4	Iannone	ITA	Ducati Team	159
5	Smith	GBR	Monster Yamaha Tech 3	135
6	Dovizioso	ITA	Ducati Team	128
7	Pedrosa	SPA	Repsol Honda Team	109
8	Petrucci	ITA	Octo Pramac Racing	93
9	Espargaro P	SPA	Monster Yamaha Tech 3	81
10	Crutchlow	GBR	LCR Honda	79
11	Viñales	SPA	Team Suzuki ECSTAR	69
12	Espargaro A	SPA	Team Suzuki ECSTAR	66
13	Redding	GBR	EG 0,0 Marc VDS	63
14	Hernandez	COL	Octo Pramac Racing	41
15	Baz	FRA	Forward Racing	28
16	Bautista	SPA	Aprilia Racing Team Gresini	23
	Barbera	SPA	Avintia Racing	23
18	Miller	AUS	LCR Honda	16
19	Hayden	USA	Aspar MotoGP Team	12
20	Bradl	GER	Forward Racing	11
21	Pirro	ITA	Ducati Team	8
22	Laverty E	IRL	Aspar MotoGP Team	7
	Di Meglio	FRA	Avintia Racing	7
24	Aoyama	JPN	Repsol Honda Team	5
25	De Angelis	RSM	E-Motion IodaRacing Team	2

13 MIKE DI MEGLIO
His best result of the year. Could have been better if he'd known when his dry bike was ready. Another one who stayed out longer than was ideal on wets.

14 MAVERICK VIÑALES
Struggled all weekend, but refused to blame the very different track conditions from the test – after which Maverick and Aleix had been very confident.

15 ALVARO BAUTISTA
Lost four places when he changed from the wet bike back to the dry one, but got two of them back to grab the last point.

16 STEFAN BRADL
Waited at least a lap too long to change back to slicks because there was still rain on his screen even though the track seemed dry.

17 NICKY HAYDEN
Unlike his team-mate, Nicky felt best on the wet bike, which explains the late change back to slicks.

18 HECTOR BARBERA
Lost the lead of the Open Class to Baz. Changed to the wet bike in a good position but stayed out too long before changing back.

19 EUGENE LAVERTY
The only time he had front grip was on Friday and after the second bike change on race day.

20 CLAUDIO CORTI
He was too late going in to make the first bike change after losing positions early on.

21 KAREL ABRAHAM
Still seriously handicapped by his foot injury from Barcelona; it was stopping him riding as he wants, particularly when accelerating. His wet set-up was also far from ideal.

DID NOT FINISH

POL ESPARGARO
Retired due to technical problems on the last lap. The difficulties started when he got back on his dry bike having run sixth for much of the race.

JORGE LORENZO
Crashed hard on his first lap back on slicks. The left side of the tyre wasn't up to temperature after five right-handers and he went down at Turn 15.

YONNY HERNANDEZ
Crashed after swapping to his wet bike, bringing de Angelis down in the process.

ALEX DE ANGELIS
Innocent victim of Hernandez's crash, scooped up by the crashing Ducati.

MICHELE PIRRO
Qualified fifth as a wild-card entry then suffered a fuel-pump problem on the grid and started from pitlane on his wet bike. Retired when his tyres were destroyed after nine laps.

GRAN PREMIO MOVISTAR DE ARAGÓN
MOTORLAND ARAGÓN

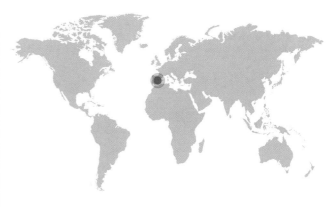

ANOTHER BRICK IN THE WALL

Lorenzo won and took nine points out of Rossi's lead, mainly thanks to a rejuvenated Pedrosa

Jorge Lorenzo put together yet another faultless lights-to-flag win, but the image that will dominate memories of this GP is that of Marc Marquez. Specifically, Marquez halfway round the second lap, just after he'd crashed his Honda while closing on Jorge. He was shouting and pointing at the fallen machine in a manner reminiscent of Basil Fawlty giving his recalcitrant Austin a good thrashing. Along with everyone else watching, Marc was only too well aware of what happens if you give Jorge a clear track and a start. The front end of the Honda slid away as Marc was pressing and although he later said it was his mistake, his reaction in the immediate aftermath of the crash suggested that he may have had a different opinion at the time.

The second memory of Aragón 2015 will be of the other Repsol Honda rider, Dani Pedrosa. He turned in his most aggressive ride for years to win a fabulous battle for second place during the last five laps of the race. Pedrosa had been running in second place around three seconds behind Lorenzo but with Rossi shadowing him. If Valentino stayed in third place, his lead in the championship would be reduced by nine points; if he took second, the damage would be limited to just five points. As he had only 23 to play with, with four races to come, you can appreciate that third wasn't an option. After all, if there's one aspect of racing where Valentino is a past master, it's the art of winning the last-lap duel. The exceptions to that rule are so rare that they're easy to recall: Ukawa in South Africa, Barros in Valencia, Gibernau in Germany.

So when, with five laps to go, Rossi slipped past Pedrosa, the crowd cheered and assumed that was

'THIS RACE WAS VERY
IMPORTANT TO FORGET
ABOUT THE LAST TWO RACES'
JORGE LORENZO

job done. Then Dani went straight back past. The cheering only abated slightly; after all we'd seen this on many occasions. What has always, and I mean *always*, happened before is that Valentino makes the same move again next time round, this time making sure there's no way back for his victim. Sure enough, he made the same move but this time the unthinkable happened; Dani repassed in exactly the same way as he had the previous lap. The cheering ceased as if it had been switched off at the mains.

Rossi's next pass was at Turn 1, but he ran a little wide and Pedrosa forced his way back in front at Turn 2. It went to the last lap. Sure enough, Rossi made another pass only for Dani to force his way back inside at Turn 5 and push Valentino out to the edge of the track. That really was job done, although Valentino tried a Hail Mary lunge at Turn 14, a move that ensured he couldn't carry any speed onto the back straight.

As Valentino sat in *parc fermé* shaking his head before warmly embracing Dani, Jorge was gleefully celebrating. He had an artist's easel set up and dashed off a sketch of the giant wall with the caption 'Yes we can!' This was a reminder that he'd had a hand in designing the trophies, which were admittedly rather pleasing replicas of the wall. Then he rode back into *parc fermé* with his hand upright on top of his helmet, like a shark's fin, a reference to Valentino's crash helmet design at Misano.

It was easy to overlook the achievement of Andrea Iannone in fourth place, just 11 days after re-dislocating his shoulder when he fell while out jogging. Way behind Iannone there was a great fight for fifth and Andrea

ABOVE Rossi and Lorenzo nearly had a calamitous coming-together in pitlane while rehearsing bike swaps

LEFT The field streams through in front of Motorland Aragón's outsize brick wall

LEFT TOP Aleix Espargaro gave Suzuki its best result so far – sixth place

Dovizoso didn't know whether to laugh or cry about winning it as he was over 15 seconds behind his team-mate. As well as Dovi's Ducati, the group contained a Suzuki (Aleix Espargaro with an impressive return to form), the Tech 3 Yamahas and Cal Crutchlow's Honda. Each bike had a slight advantage somewhere on the track, but the result was near-identical lap times. One mistake, as Bradley Smith and Pol Espargaro found, put a rider at the back of the group with time to make up.

A similarly entertaining group fought for victory in the Open Class and featured Nicky Hayden, Eugene Laverty, Loris Baz, Hector Barbera, Jack Miller and Mike di Meglio. Laverty emerged to claim his first Open 'win' after starting the race with his first Open 'pole'. The Northern Irishman had been riding well in the previous few races and finally found a set-up that got him to the flag without significant problems.

The reaction of the top three riders in *parc fermé* was instructive. Pedrosa, on the podium for the first time since the summer break, was delighted. Lorenzo was ecstatic. Rossi was thoughtful. Valentino wasn't quite as despondent as in Brno, but he was well aware that he'd played all his cards – 'including one I didn't know I had' – and come up short. He'd arrived at Aragón with a 23-point lead, almost a race win's worth, and he was leaving with an advantage of 14, not even a third-place haul. Admittedly, Aragón was one of the tracks where Rossi had expected to suffer – but so was Silverstone.

Things now looked to have swung in Lorenzo's favour, but Rossi's experience could still give him the advantage should conditions change or the unexpected happen, as both Silverstone and Misano had shown. Only a brave man would bet on the final outcome.

ABOVE Eugene Laverty celebrates 14th place and his first victory in the Open Class

BELOW The number of times Rossi has lost a last-lap showdown can be counted on the fingers of one hand; Pedrosa added to that total

STEALTH FIGHTER

Quietly and efficiently, the Aprilia factory team has been making serious progress. Aprilia wasn't due to return to MotoGP until 2016, when its new bike will be ready, but decided to race this year as part of the development programme. So the team started with its old superbike-based ART and did its development work in public.

Against most people's expectations, Alvaro Bautista only failed to score points in four of the races up to and including Aragón, with best results of tenth places at Catalunya and Silverstone. Marco Melandri started the year as the other rider but it feels kindest to draw a veil over his personal nightmare.

After the summer break Melandri was replaced by Stefan Bradl, who'd jumped ship from Forward Racing, and the German introduced a new element to the team. Bradl promptly started out-qualifying Bautista, although by Aragón he hadn't yet beaten the Spaniard in a race. The team was impressed. It reported a new level of technical feedback and precision, and promptly secured Bradl's signature for 2016.

The Aprilia was massively overweight but was equipped through the season with various upgrades, including a seamless gearbox – which came very soon after the arrival of a dry clutch. A new, longer swinging arm was introduced for the Aragón race.

British Moto2 charger Sam Lowes had been due to join the team but will now act as test rider in 2016 before joining the racing team for 2017 and 2018. In the meantime he will ride for the Gresini team, which runs the Aprilias in Moto2.

RIGHT Lorenzo reduced Rossi's championship lead to 14 points

GRAN PREMIO MOVISTAR DE ARAGÓN
MOTORLAND ARAGÓN
ROUND **14**
SEPTEMBER 27

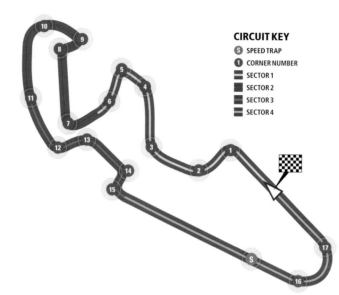

CIRCUIT KEY
- **S** SPEED TRAP
- **1** CORNER NUMBER
- ▬ SECTOR 1
- ▬ SECTOR 2
- ▬ SECTOR 3
- ▬ SECTOR 4

RACE RESULTS

CIRCUIT LENGTH 3.155 miles

NO. OF LAPS 23

RACE DISTANCE 72.572 miles

WEATHER Dry, 23°C

TRACK TEMPERATURE 39°C

WINNER Jorge Lorenzo

FASTEST LAP 1m 48.120s, 105.012mph, Jorge Lorenzo (record)

PREVIOUS LAP RECORD 1m 48.565s, 104.577mph, Dani Pedrosa (2013)

TYRE OPTIONS

FRONT

FRONT COMPOUNDS
SOFT (**S**), MEDIUM (**M**), HARD (**H**)

REAR

REAR COMPOUNDS
SOFT (**S**), MEDIUM (**M**), HARD (**H**)

SEVERITY RATING

<MILD   SEVERE>

BRIDGESTONE

QUALIFYING

	Rider	Nation	Motorcycle	Team	Time	Pole +
1	Marquez	SPA	Honda	Repsol Honda Team	1m 46.635s	
2	Lorenzo	SPA	Yamaha	Movistar Yamaha MotoGP	1m 46.743s	0.108s
3	Iannone	ITA	Ducati	Ducati Team	1m 47.178s	0.543s
4	Espargaro P	SPA	Yamaha	Monster Yamaha Tech 3	1m 47.334s	0.699s
5	Pedrosa	SPA	Honda	Repsol Honda Team	1m 47.357s	0.722s
6	Rossi	ITA	Yamaha	Movistar Yamaha MotoGP	1m 47.492s	0.857s
7	Espargaro A	SPA	Suzuki	Team Suzuki ECSTAR	1m 47.573s	0.938s
8	Crutchlow	GBR	Honda	LCR Honda	1m 47.574s	0.939s
9	Petrucci	ITA	Ducati	Octo Pramac Racing	1m 47.775s	1.140s
10	Smith	GBR	Yamaha	Monster Yamaha Tech 3	1m 47.830s	1.195s
11	Hernandez	COL	Ducati	Octo Pramac Racing	1m 48.556s	1.921s
12	Viñales	SPA	Suzuki	Team Suzuki ECSTAR	1m 48.648s	2.013s
13	Dovizioso	ITA	Ducati	Ducati Team	1m 48.294s	Q1
14	Redding	GBR	Honda	EG 0,0 Marc VDS	1m 48.674s	Q1
15	Laverty E	IRL	Honda	Aspar MotoGP Team	1m 49.035s	Q1
16	Hayden	USA	Honda	Aspar MotoGP Team	1m 49.102s	Q1
17	Bradl	GER	Aprilia	Aprilia Racing Team Gresini	1m 49.109s	Q1
18	Di Meglio	FRA	Ducati	Avintia Racing	1m 49.253s	Q1
19	Barbera	SPA	Ducati	Avintia Racing	1m 49.426s	Q1
20	Miller	AUS	Honda	LCR Honda	1m 49.436s	Q1
21	Bautista	SPA	Aprilia	Aprilia Racing Team Gresini	1m 49.437s	Q1
22	Baz	FRA	Yamaha	Forward Racing	1m 49.496s	Q1
23	Abraham	CZE	Honda	AB Motoracing	1m 49.761s	Q1
24	De Angelis	RSM	ART	E-Motion IodaRacing Team	1m 50.134s	Q1
25	Elias	SPA	Yamaha	Forward Racing	1m 50.755s	Q1

1 JORGE LORENZO
Like his five previous victories, this was a lights-out-to-chequered-flag demonstration of how to ride the Yamaha at lap-record speed. Never headed and never looked like he could be caught.

2 DANI PEDROSA
The surprise of the GP, and combative from the first free practice. Achieved that rarest of things – beating Valentino Rossi in a hand-to-hand fight over the final laps.

3 VALENTINO ROSSI
Gave up nine points of his championship lead to Lorenzo, partly down to Pedrosa's fighting spirit and not helped by average qualifying – but still his best result at Motorland.

4 ANDREA IANNONE
Given that he re-dislocated his shoulder 11 days before the race, a front-row start and fourth place were little short of heroic. By far the best Ducati rider.

5 ANDREA DOVIZIOSO
Pleased to finish fifth having started 13th, but very unhappy to be 16 seconds behind his team-mate. Got his usual blazing start and made up a lot of places on the first lap to head a group.

6 ALEIX ESPARGARO
A season-best finish after a run of disappointing races. Now, he just needed to find out why it happened.

7 CAL CRUTCHLOW
Slow off the mark thanks to a slipping clutch but finished well despite rear-grip problems that limited what he could do in the group battle for fifth place.

8 BRADLEY SMITH
He was part of the fine dice for fifth when he ran wide while following Dovizioso; that cost him two places and a second in time, which took ten laps to claw back.

9 POL ESPARGARO
He finished less than two seconds behind fifth place but was ninth – that's a statistic that demonstrates how closely the group was matched. Pol's problem was losing the rubber off his gear lever, leaving him to shift with bare, slippery metal.

10 YONNY HERNANDEZ
This result restored Yonny's confidence after a fallow period. The Colombian started well but couldn't push as he wanted to, so after the first five laps he looked to keep a good, constant pace – which he did.

11 MAVERICK VIÑALES
Not a stellar result, but a lot better for him than it looked on Friday. Still displeased with his Suzuki's rear grip, but rode away from a group of riders on softer tyres towards the end of the race.

12 SCOTT REDDING
Another difficult race after the joy of Misano. The problems were mainly getting the brakes up to temperature and pumping from the rear suspension. Lap times deteriorated dramatically towards the end of the race due to the rear tyre moving on its rim.

LAP CHART

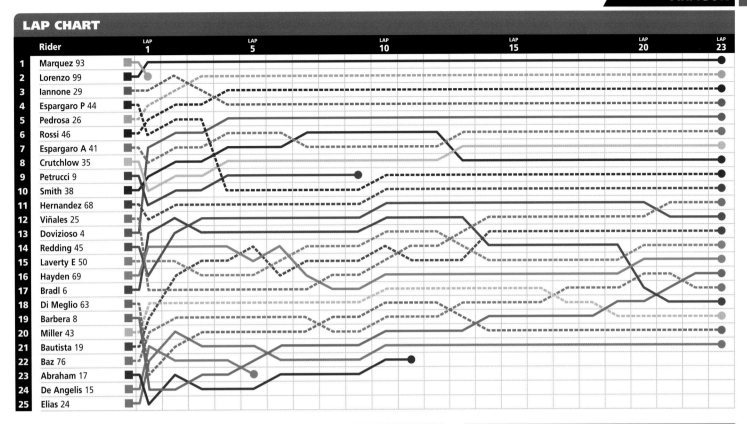

	Rider	LAP 1	LAP 5	LAP 10	LAP 15	LAP 20	LAP 23
1	Marquez 93						
2	Lorenzo 99						
3	Iannone 29						
4	Espargaro P 44						
5	Pedrosa 26						
6	Rossi 46						
7	Espargaro A 41						
8	Crutchlow 35						
9	Petrucci 9						
10	Smith 38						
11	Hernandez 68						
12	Viñales 25						
13	Dovizioso 4						
14	Redding 45						
15	Laverty E 50						
16	Hayden 69						
17	Bradl 6						
18	Di Meglio 63						
19	Barbera 8						
20	Miller 43						
21	Bautista 19						
22	Baz 76						
23	Abraham 17						
24	De Angelis 15						
25	Elias 24						

RACE

	Rider	Motorcycle	Race time	Time +	Fastest lap	Avg. speed	
1	Lorenzo	Yamaha	41m 44.933s		1m 48.120s	104.3mph	M/M
2	Pedrosa	Honda	41m 47.616s	2.683s	1m 48.451s	104.1mph	M/M
3	Rossi	Yamaha	41m 47.706s	2.773s	1m 48.165s	104.1mph	M/M
4	Iannone	Ducati	41m 52.791s	7.858s	1m 48.581s	104.0mph	M/M
5	Dovizioso	Ducati	42m 09.255s	24.322s	1m 48.986s	103.3mph	M/M
6	Espargaro A	Suzuki	42m 09.762s	24.829s	1m 49.120s	103.3mph	M/M
7	Crutchlow	Honda	42m 10.300s	25.367s	1m 48.980s	103.2mph	M/M
8	Smith	Yamaha	42m 10.436s	25.503s	1m 49.138s	103.2mph	M/M
9	Espargaro P	Yamaha	42m 11.385s	26.452s	1m 49.035s	103.1mph	M/M
10	Hernandez	Ducati	42m 28.822s	43.889s	1m 50.148s	102.4mph	M/M
11	Viñales	Suzuki	42m 29.188s	44.255s	1m 49.879s	102.4mph	M/M
12	Redding	Honda	42m 33.109s	48.176s	1m 50.029s	102.3mph	M/M
13	Bautista	Aprilia	42m 34.688s	49.755s	1m 49.961s	102.2mph	M/S
14	Laverty E	Honda	42m 35.204s	50.271s	1m 50.506s	102.2mph	M/S
15	Hayden	Honda	42m 35.297s	50.364s	1m 50.408s	102.2mph	M/M
16	Barbera	Ducati	42m 35.655s	50.722s	1m 50.139s	102.2mph	M/M
17	Baz	Yamaha	42m 36.930s	51.997s	1m 50.313s	102.2mph	M/S
18	Bradl	Aprilia	42m 38.339s	53.406s	1m 50.406s	102.1mph	M/S
19	Miller	Honda	42m 41.792s	56.859s	1m 50.460s	102.0mph	M/M
20	Di Meglio	Ducati	42m 44.450s	59.607s	1m 50.397s	101.8mph	M/S
21	Elias	Yamaha	43m 00.170s	1m 15.237s	1m 50.909s	101.2mph	S/S
NC	Abraham	Honda	20m 51.886s	12 laps	1m 51.714s	99.8mph	M/S
NC	Petrucci	Ducati	16m 30.763s	14 laps	1m 49.000s	103.1mph	M/M
NC	De Angelis	ART	9m 22.518s	18 laps	1m 51.176s	100.9mph	M/S
NC	Marquez	Honda	1m 50.515s	22 laps	–	–	M/M

CHAMPIONSHIP

	Rider	Nation	Team	Points
1	Rossi	SPA	Movistar Yamaha MotoGP	263
2	Lorenzo	ITA	Movistar Yamaha MotoGP	249
3	Marquez	SPA	Repsol Honda Team	184
4	Iannone	ITA	Ducati Team	172
5	Smith	GBR	Monster Yamaha Tech 3	143
6	Dovizioso	ITA	Ducati Team	139
7	Pedrosa	SPA	Repsol Honda Team	129
8	Petrucci	ITA	Octo Pramac Racing	93
9	Crutchlow	GBR	LCR Honda	88
10	Espargaro P	SPA	Monster Yamaha Tech 3	88
11	Espargaro A	SPA	Team Suzuki ECSTAR	76
12	Viñales	SPA	Team Suzuki ECSTAR	74
13	Redding	GBR	EG 0,0 Marc VDS	67
14	Hernandez	COL	Octo Pramac Racing	47
15	Baz	FRA	Forward Racing	28
16	Bautista	SPA	Aprilia Racing Team Gresini	26
17	Barbera	SPA	Avintia Racing	23
18	Miller	AUS	LCR Honda	16
19	Hayden	USA	Aspar MotoGP Team	13
20	Bradl	GER	Forward Racing	11
21	Laverty E	IRL	Aspar MotoGP Team	9
22	Pirro	ITA	Ducati Team	8
23	Di Meglio	FRA	Avintia Racing	7
24	Aoyama	JPN	Repsol Honda Team	5
25	De Angelis	RSM	E-Motion IodaRacing Team	2

13 ALVARO BAUTISTA
A good start but boxed in on the first corner. Fought first with Laverty and then with his team-mate Bradl, by which point it was too late to follow Viñales up the field.

14 EUGENE LAVERTY
Top Open Class bike in both qualifying and, for the first time, the race – an achievement that had been beckoning for Eugene since the summer break.

15 NICKY HAYDEN
Handicapped by a broken right thumb – the legacy of a training accident – but rode without too much trouble.

16 HECTOR BARBERA
Ran off-track on the second lap, rejoined last, then used up his tyres getting back.

17 LORIS BAZ
Suffered severe neck pains following a crash on Saturday morning. Involved in the group dice for Open victory but neither gained nor lost points in that struggle.

18 STEFAN BRADL
Started really well but hit sudden and severe rear-tyre degradation after half distance, after which a coming-together with Laverty dropped him even further back.

19 JACK MILLER
Involved with the group of Open Class riders until the last five laps, when his front tyre degraded badly.

20 MIKE DI MEGLIO
Had wheelie-control problems from the start of the race and a serious front-end vibration at the end when he was racing with Baz.

21 TONI ELIAS
Replaced Corti at Forward Yamaha for the remaining races of the season. Diced with de Angelis, but then circulated alone after Alex crashed.

DID NOT FINISH

KAREL ABRAHAM
Retired after seven laps when his injured foot couldn't take any more. Fortunately, X-rays suggested nothing appeared to have moved.

DANILO PETRUCCI
His first retirement of the season thanks to a crash on lap 10. It was an incident that surprised Danilo and the team could find no explanation for it in the data.

ALEX DE ANGELIS
Couldn't run with the Open Class group and found himself dicing with Elias. Toni was faster on the straights but Alex got him back in the corners until his rival hit his rear wheel on lap six and he crashed out.

MARC MARQUEZ
Crashed on the second lap as he closed in on fast-starting Lorenzo. Said it was his fault, although his pointing and screaming at the bike as it lay on its side indicated otherwise.

MOTUL GRAND PRIX OF JAPAN
TWIN-RING MOTEGI

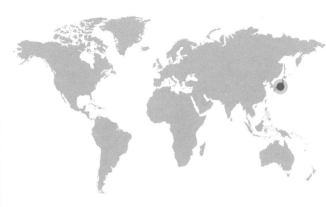

WHAT'S MY LINE?

Dani Pedrosa conserved his tyres best and won on a drying track as Rossi took a crucial second place off Lorenzo

It looked like another runaway win for Jorge Lorenzo. He qualified on pole, got annoyed that Valentino Rossi was quick enough to be second, indulged in some theatrical behaviour to draw attention to his damaged shoulder, then got the holeshot and opened up a gap of two and a half seconds in three laps. Then he added another half second in two laps. Then it stopped raining. At this point Dani Pedrosa was over eight seconds back in fourth place with Andrea Dovizioso and Valentino Rossi between him and Lorenzo.

By the time it became clear that there wasn't going to be enough rain to properly wet the track again (there was a brief sprinkling on lap eight) it was too late to contemplate swapping bikes. Now it was a case of 'run what ya brung', and it turned out that Dani had brought more tyre than the rest. Motegi is the hardest braking circuit of the year, so we had the rather unusual sight of hard-compound rubber on the front and soft on the rear. It's a characteristic of the wet-weather Bridgestones' tread compounds that when they wear or overheat the rubber doesn't ball-up and get thrown off, rather it stays on the carcass as a high-hysteresis layer – in other words a sticky mass that lets the tyre move around alarmingly. Lorenzo's early charge put his front tyre further down this road than those of his opposition.

In contrast, Pedrosa hadn't been comfortable in the opening laps but as the track came to him he surged past first Dovizioso and then up to Rossi. When the Honda caught him, Rossi had been lapping around three and a half seconds behind Lorenzo for a few laps and didn't look like he had the pace to catch his team-mate. Valentino understood that Dani was his ticket to the leader, and latched onto his back wheel.

Dani took the lead on lap 18 of the 24 with an easy outbraking move at the end of the back straight. Valentino went past his team-mate two laps later when Jorge ran wide at Turn 3. On the face of it, this didn't look like a significant move, but it ensured that Rossi's championship lead widened from 14 to 18 points with three races left. This meant that Valentino could now finish behind Jorge in every race and still become champion – a significant milestone.

Jorge arrived in Japan with his left arm in a sling thanks to a minibike accident at a barbecue hosted by Sete Gibernau (yes, really). After setting pole but being severely worried by Rossi's unexpected pace, Jorge turned up to the front-row press conference with his arm supported by a casually tied silk scarf. He discarded it when he sat down, replacing it with an ice pack – not at all theatrical! To be fair to him, Jorge didn't mention his ligament injury after the race, preferring to bemoan his luck with the weather. He thought he'd have won if the rain had stayed; no-one was arguing.

Marc Marquez was also carrying an injury, this time a broken hand that he sustained when he fell off his mountain bike, and it obviously handicapped him throughout the weekend. His fourth-place finish meant the end of his admittedly thin chances of the title, ensuring that one of the factory Yamaha men would become champion.

In the Open Class, Hector Barbera finished ninth and jumped back to the top of that table. In a class where it's difficult to score more than a point or two, overcoming Loris Baz's five-point lead in one hit was a major achievement.

ABOVE Well-worn rear tyres in *parc fermé*, but front tyre wear was the critical factor

RIGHT The start was wet but the rain had already stopped – note eventual winner Pedrosa dropping back in the centre of the photo

OPPOSITE Honda gave multiple eight-hour winner Takumi Takahashi his first MotoGP race as a wild card

'AT FIRST I TOOK
THINGS CALMLY
AND LOST TOO
MUCH TIME, BUT
THE STRATEGY
WORKED'
DANI PEDROSA

ABOVE Cal Crutchlow won the battle for top satellite bike honours with a last-lap pass on Bradley Smith

BELOW Valentino Rossi warmly congratulates Dani Pedrosa in *parc fermé*

A scan of the tyres on the top three bikes in *parc fermé* showed that their finishing order had been determined at least in part by how their riders had used their front tyres. Pedrosa's was worn but not badly so, Lorenzo's was a mess, and Rossi's was somewhere in between. Dani's rear tyre was also well worn in the centre, but this wasn't as big a problem as it looked. Bridgestone manufactures its wets with a good amount of rubber below the tread sipes (the valleys that allow water to escape to the shoulder) so Dani still had a

decently functioning slick even though he'd worn all the grooves off the centre section.

We were lucky to be talking about tyres and titles. After Alex de Angelis's crash in FP4 it looked as if the subject would be a lot more sombre. Alex effectively turned left coming out of Turn 10 and slammed into unprotected barriers. The red flag came out and, after lengthy treatment, de Angelis was taken to hospital by helicopter. He suffered fractures to five vertebrae, broken ribs, a broken collarbone, a broken shoulder blade, bruised lungs and concussion. Thankfully, news of him on Sunday morning was encouraging: there was no neurological damage and there were no complications, so it looked as if he would make a good recovery.

Sunday morning warm-up was delayed but went ahead without medical helicopter cover due to low cloud, to the shock and surprise of most of the paddock. The Chief Medical Officer made the call after deciding that the upgraded facilities at the circuit were adequate for any needs and with police co-operation it would be possible to transfer an injured rider to hospital in 50 minutes. Despite the absence of the helicopter, the mood in the paddock was far lighter on race day than it had been the previous day.

That was especially true for Rossi. He'd been grinning happily since he realised how much his Saturday speed had rattled Lorenzo. As for Pedrosa, he celebrated his 50th career win on the rostrum with Honda Motor's President and CEO, Takahiro Hachigo. There were a few Honda employees who were very pleased to see Hachigo-san smiling broadly. Dani had just saved them a potentially painful Monday morning debrief.

NICKY HAYDEN

The 2006 World Champion announced at Motegi that 2015 was his last year in MotoGP. In 2016 he would be racing for Ten Kate Honda in the World Superbike Championship.

Nicky received a warm and lengthy round of applause from his fellow riders as well as the assembled media at the Thursday press conference, where his answers to questions showed exactly why he's so well regarded: mention of his greatest moment, Valencia 2006, bought a smile, and then he refused to talk about any bad times on the grounds that he'd had years on both a Repsol Honda and a factory Ducati, so a lot of people would happily swap their best days for his bad days. 'I would be a fool to complain about anything.'

Going to Superbike now was a 'good fit', after two tough years on the customer Honda. Nicky wouldn't say that the prospect of being the first man to win both titles was a motivation but he did admit the thought had crossed his mind – as had the idea of becoming the oldest AMA champ as well as the youngest.

The old dream of going back to the dirt and winning a mile is, he said, receding into the distance. But he added, 'I am a lifer in this sport', so rider management in the future is another possibility for him.

'My sport, my family; that's all I know.'

Shortly after Nicky announced his retirement, Dorna revealed that he would be inducted as a MotoGP Legend at Valencia, the scene of his greatest triumph. He is the 22nd Legend, and the one with the fewest GP victories, just three. His award is for the length of his career – he was the only man to beat Rossi in the 990cc era – and recognition of his universal popularity.

RIGHT Yamaha entered Katsuyuki Nakasuga on what looked to be a prototype of the 2016 M-1

MOTUL GRAND PRIX OF JAPAN
TWIN-RING MOTEGI
ROUND **15**
OCTOBER 11

OFFICIAL TIMEKEEPER

RACE RESULTS

CIRCUIT LENGTH 2.983 miles

NO. OF LAPS 24

RACE DISTANCE 71.597 miles

WEATHER Wet, 19°C

TRACK TEMPERATURE 21°C

WINNER Dani Pedrosa

FASTEST LAP 1m 54.867s, 93.454mph, Jorge Lorenzo

LAP RECORD 1m 45.350s, 101.905mph, Jorge Lorenzo (2014)

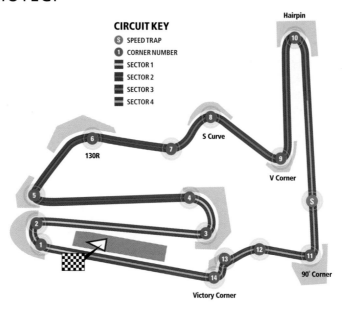

CIRCUIT KEY

- **S** SPEED TRAP
- **1** CORNER NUMBER
- SECTOR 1
- SECTOR 2
- SECTOR 3
- SECTOR 4

Hairpin · 130R · S Curve · V Corner · 90° Corner · Victory Corner

TYRE OPTIONS

FRONT
CENTRE · LEFT · RIGHT

FRONT COMPOUNDS
SOFT (**S**), HARD (**H**)

REAR
CENTRE · LEFT · RIGHT

REAR COMPOUNDS
SOFT (**S**), HARD (**H**)

SEVERITY RATING
<MILD   SEVERE>

BRIDGESTONE

QUALIFYING

	Rider	Nation	Motorcycle	Team	Time	Pole +
1	Lorenzo	SPA	Yamaha	Movistar Yamaha MotoGP	1m 43.790s	
2	Rossi	ITA	Yamaha	Movistar Yamaha MotoGP	1m 43.871s	0.081s
3	Marquez	SPA	Honda	Repsol Honda Team	1m 44.216s	0.426s
4	Dovizioso	ITA	Ducati	Ducati Team	1m 44.322s	0.532s
5	Iannone	ITA	Ducati	Ducati Team	1m 44.436s	0.646s
6	Pedrosa	SPA	Honda	Repsol Honda Team	1m 44.582s	0.792s
7	Espargaro A	SPA	Suzuki	Team Suzuki ECSTAR	1m 44.809s	1.019s
8	Crutchlow	GBR	Honda	LCR Honda	1m 44.932s	1.142s
9	Smith	GBR	Yamaha	Monster Yamaha Tech 3	1m 45.067s	1.277s
10	Viñales	SPA	Suzuki	Team Suzuki ECSTAR	1m 45.081s	1.291s
11	Espargaro P	SPA	Yamaha	Monster Yamaha Tech 3	1m 45.219s	1.429s
12	Redding	GBR	Honda	EG 0,0 Marc VDS	1m 45.333s	1.543s
13	Bradl	GER	Aprilia	Aprilia Racing Team Gresini	1m 45.432s	Q1
14	Hernandez	COL	Ducati	Octo Pramac Racing	1m 45.438s	Q1
15	Nakasuga	JPN	Yamaha	Yamaha Factory Racing Team	1m 45.496s	Q1
16	Bautista	SPA	Aprilia	Aprilia Racing Team Gresini	1m 45.608s	Q1
17	Petrucci	ITA	Ducati	Octo Pramac Racing	1m 45.691s	Q1
18	Barbera	SPA	Ducati	Avintia Racing	1m 45.724s	Q1
19	Takahashi	JPN	Honda	Team HRC with Nissin	1m 45.743s	Q1
20	Laverty E	IRL	Honda	Aspar MotoGP Team	1m 45.751s	Q1
21	Hayden	USA	Honda	Aspar MotoGP Team	1m 45.843s	Q1
22	Miller	AUS	Honda	LCR Honda	1m 46.039s	Q1
23	Baz	FRA	Yamaha	Forward Racing	1m 46.048s	Q1
24	Di Meglio	FRA	Ducati	Avintia Racing	1m 46.179s	Q1
25	Elias	SPA	Yamaha	Forward Racing	1m 46.256s	Q1
26	Akiyoshi	JPN	Honda	AB Motoracing	1m 47.760s	Q1
27	De Angelis	RSM	ART	E-Motion IodaRacing Team	1m 48.192s	Q1

1 DANI PEDROSA
His 50th win across all classes and his first in over a year. Started slowly but was massively faster than the rest when the track started to dry. Came from eight seconds down to pass Dovizioso and both factory Yamahas.

2 VALENTINO ROSSI
Crucially, Valentino was able to pass Lorenzo late in the race by tagging on to Pedrosa. That opened up his championship lead to 18 points. As his objective for the weekend had been solely to beat Lorenzo, Rossi was happy.

3 JORGE LORENZO
Another stunning start and blazingly quick opening laps had Jorge leading by over three seconds after just five laps. But this charge probably played against him because when the track dried, his front tyre was severely worn and he had no defence against Pedrosa or Rossi.

4 MARC MARQUEZ
His broken hand, suffered in a mountain-bike crash, clearly handicapped him in the dry but Marc said there was no problem in the wet. Like his team-mate, he started badly and was much quicker when the track started to dry.

5 ANDREA DOVIZIOSO
Lost the front end repeatedly in the wet but still found that he had serious front-tyre wear when the track dried.

6 CAL CRUTCHLOW
Took a few laps to get some heat into the rear tyre, after which he came on strong. That ruined the front tyre and the fight with Smith for top Satellite rider reduced the rear wet to a slick.

7 BRADLEY SMITH
Ran a short wheelbase after two Saturday crashes. Made progress in the race but lost out to Crutchlow on the final lap.

8 KATSUYUKI NAKASUGA
Yamaha's tester had a solid wild-card ride on a prototype of next year's M-1 in the Yamaha factory's 60th anniversary colours.

9 HECTOR BARBERA
Regained the lead in the Open Class on a track he has twice left in a helicopter, and all in his 100th MotoGP race.

10 SCOTT REDDING
Went with the hard wet tyres front and rear, unlike the rest who used the softer rear. The set-up came to him late in the race when he made some rapid progress to achieve the team's target of a top-ten finish.

11 ALEIX ESPARGARO
Very quick in the opening laps, dicing with other factory bikes. Pushed the front too hard and ran off track, then reduced his rear tyre to a slick getting some places back. A much better ride than the finishing position suggests.

12 TAKUMI TAKAHASHI
Points from 18th on the grid in the multiple eight-hour winner's first GP as a wild-card rider.

13 NICKY HAYDEN
Expected better than 13th in the wet, but lost out to the opposition on the straights.

LAP CHART

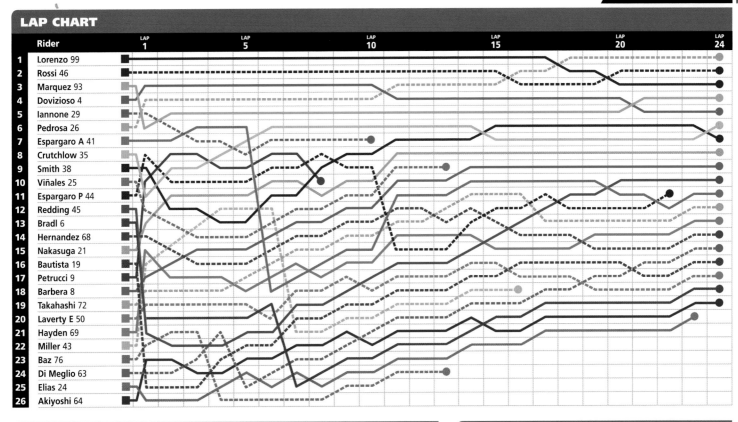

	Rider	LAP 1	LAP 5	LAP 10	LAP 15	LAP 20	LAP 24
1	Lorenzo 99						
2	Rossi 46						
3	Marquez 93						
4	Dovizioso 4						
5	Iannone 29						
6	Pedrosa 26						
7	Espargaro A 41						
8	Crutchlow 35						
9	Smith 38						
10	Viñales 25						
11	Espargaro P 44						
12	Redding 45						
13	Bradl 6						
14	Hernandez 68						
15	Nakasuga 21						
16	Bautista 19						
17	Petrucci 9						
18	Barbera 8						
19	Takahashi 72						
20	Laverty E 50						
21	Hayden 69						
22	Miller 43						
23	Baz 76						
24	Di Meglio 63						
25	Elias 24						
26	Akiyoshi 64						

RACE

	Rider	Motorcycle	Race time	Time +	Fastest lap	Avg. speed	🅱
1	Pedrosa	Honda	46m 50.767s		1m 55.394s	91.7mph	H/S
2	Rossi	Yamaha	46m 59.340s	8.573s	1m 55.221s	91.4mph	H/S
3	Lorenzo	Yamaha	47m 02.894s	12.127s	1m 54.867s	91.3mph	H/S
4	Marquez	Honda	47m 18.608s	27.841s	1m 56.129s	90.8mph	H/S
5	Dovizioso	Ducati	47m 25.852s	35.085s	1m 55.187s	90.5mph	H/S
6	Crutchlow	Honda	47m 28.030s	37.263s	1m 56.412s	90.5mph	H/S
7	Smith	Yamaha	47m 28.434s	37.667s	1m 56.524s	90.5mph	H/S
8	Nakasuga	Yamaha	47m 35.421s	44.654s	1m 56.914s	90.2mph	H/S
9	Barbera	Honda	47m 39.339s	48.572s	1m 56.775s	90.1mph	H/S
10	Redding	Honda	47m 40.888s	50.121s	1m 57.566s	90.0mph	H/H
11	Espargaro A	Suzuki	47m 51.302s	1m 00.535s	1m 56.525s	89.7mph	H/S
12	Takahashi	Honda	47m 51.978s	1m 01.211s	1m 57.419s	89.7mph	H/S
13	Hayden	Honda	48m 02.028s	1m 11.261s	1m 57.479s	89.4mph	H/H
14	Hernandez	Ducati	48m 04.663s	1m 13.896s	1m 57.238s	89.3mph	H/S
15	Di Meglio	Ducati	48m 06.188s	1m 15.421s	1m 58.117s	89.3mph	H/S
16	Bautista	Aprilia	48m 11.274s	1m 20.507s	1m 58.261s	89.1mph	H/S
17	Laverty E	Honda	48m 21.991s	1m 31.224s	1m 57.783s	88.8mph	H/S
18	Bradl	Aprilia	48m 37.600s	1m 46.833s	1m 57.656s	88.3mph	H/S
19	Akiyoshi	Honda	48m 50.839s	2m 00.072s	1m 59.572s	87.9mph	S/S
20	Elias	Yamaha	47m 36.873s	1 lap	2m 01.116s	86.4mph	S/S
NC	Espargaro P	Yamaha	43m 43.391s	2 laps	1m 56.966s	90.0mph	H/S
NC	Miller	Honda	32m 00.359s	8 laps	1m 56.596s	89.5mph	H/S
NC	Viñales	Suzuki	25m 39.571s	11 laps	1m 56.748s	90.1mph	H/S
NC	Baz	Yamaha	26m 50.498s	11 laps	1m 57.752s	86.7mph	H/S
NC	Iannone	Ducati	19m 42.393s	14 laps	1m 57.217s	90.8mph	H/S
NC	Petrucci	Ducati	15m 48.657s	16 laps	1m 56.904s	90.5mph	H/S

CHAMPIONSHIP

	Rider	Nation	Team	Points
1	Rossi	SPA	Movistar Yamaha MotoGP	283
2	Lorenzo	ITA	Movistar Yamaha MotoGP	265
3	Marquez	SPA	Repsol Honda Team	197
4	Iannone	ITA	Ducati Team	172
5	Pedrosa	SPA	Repsol Honda Team	154
6	Smith	GBR	Monster Yamaha Tech 3	152
7	Dovizioso	ITA	Ducati Team	150
8	Crutchlow	GBR	LCR Honda	98
9	Petrucci	ITA	Octo Pramac Racing	93
10	Espargaro P	SPA	Monster Yamaha Tech 3	88
11	Espargaro A	SPA	Team Suzuki ECSTAR	81
12	Viñales	SPA	Team Suzuki ECSTAR	74
13	Redding	GBR	EG 0,0 Marc VDS	73
14	Hernandez	COL	Octo Pramac Racing	49
15	Barbera	SPA	Avintia Racing	30
16	Baz	FRA	Forward Racing	28
17	Bautista	SPA	Aprilia Racing Team Gresini	26
18	Miller	AUS	LCR Honda	16
	Hayden	USA	Aspar MotoGP Team	16
20	Bradl	GER	Forward Racing	11
21	Laverty E	IRL	Aspar MotoGP Team	9
22	Nakasuga	JPN	Yamaha Factory Racing Team	8
	Pirro	ITA	Ducati Team	8
	Di Meglio	FRA	Avintia Racing	8
25	Aoyama	JPN	Repsol Honda Team	5
26	Takahashi	JPN	Team HRC with Nissin	4
27	De Angelis	RSM	E-Motion IodaRacing Team	2

14 YONNY HERNANDEZ
Vibrations at the start and a worn tyre at the end stopped him challenging Hayden.

15 MIKE DI MEGLIO
Scored the last point despite running off-track early on, after which he kept to the wet line to preserve his tyres.

16 ALVARO BAUTISTA
Never able to replicate his dry-weather pace on Sunday.

17 EUGENE LAVERTY
Tyre degradation at both ends slowed him severely towards the finish.

18 STEFAN BRADL
Put himself off track when he hit the pit-lane speed-limiter button while trying to adjust the traction control. Got back on but had lost the advantage of his great qualifying performance.

19 KOUSUKE AKIYOSHI
Honda's veteran replaced Abraham on the AB Cardion customer Honda.

20 TONI ELIAS
His first wet-weather experience of the Yamaha M-1. Not surprisingly, Toni couldn't match the pace of the other Open Class bikes.

DID NOT FINISH

POL ESPARGARO
Fell three laps from the flag braking for Turn 11 while chasing his brother. Banged into the barrier, thankfully without injury.

JACK MILLER
Made a conscious effort to be calmer than in the wet at Silverstone. Nevertheless, lost the front but was able to get going again. Then crashed again when he touched a white line while following Laverty.

ANDREA IANNONE
Put out by an engine problem early on.

MAVERICK VIÑALES
Had gearbox problems before crashing going down to Turn 11.

LORIS BAZ
Never found the feel he needed with the front. It was so bad he pitted early to change bikes before retiring. Lost his Open Class lead to Barbera.

DANILO PETRUCCI
Never happy on the brakes and sure enough lost the front while chasing Iannone early on.

DID NOT RACE

ALEX DE ANGELIS
Suffered a massive crash in FP4 that brought out the red flag. Transported to hospital by helicopter where broken vertebrae, ribs, collarbone and shoulder blade were diagnosed. It could have been worse.

KAREL ABRAHAM
Replaced by Akiyoshi due to his foot injury from Catalunya not healing.

PRAMAC AUSTRALIAN MOTORCYCLE GRAND PRIX
PHILLIP ISLAND

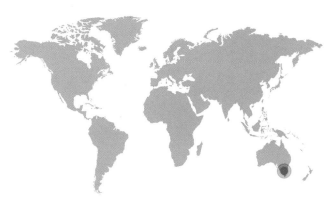

CLASH OF THE TITANS

Marc Marquez won an epic with Jorge Lorenzo second and, crucially, Valentino Rossi back in fourth

No other circuit provides such a high proportion of truly great races. The glorious curves of Phillip Island did it again, this time serving up a four-man dice in which a Honda, two Yamahas and a Ducati used their widely differing strengths to lap within fractions of a second of each other for the entire race – and while doing so the leading four made over 50 passes.

It would have been thrilling at any time of the season, but with the added intrigue of the 18-point gap between Valentino Rossi and Jorge Lorenzo at the top of the table causing feverish recalculations every time there was an overtake, it became totally transfixing. There were at least three times in the race when it looked as if the plot had been resolved and the order decided, only for one of the combatants to make another impossible manoeuvre at the Southern Loop or find a way to pass going up to Lukey Heights to make it 'game on' again.

Two breathtaking moves on the last lap massively altered how the championship contenders felt coming away from Australia.

One of those great last-lap overtakes came from Andrea Iannone. He had been using the Ducati's top-end power to blast past down into Doohan's while the others slipstreamed as if it was a Moto3 race, and he'd also found passing places where you'd have thought only a Yamaha could go. When Rossi and Marquez got in each other's way coming down into MG, Iannone took them both in one move, the best pass of all in a race full of sublime riding. There was also a short cameo appearance for one of Phillip Island's much-feared seagulls: 'It wanted to kiss me,' said Iannone, but the poor bird met its end against his helmet and punched a hole in the Ducati's fairing.

ABOVE Andrea Iannone leads the charge on lap one; the Ducati's top-end pace was stunning

BELOW Aprilia's Alvaro Bautista keeps an eye on lap times with the help of his phone

OPPOSITE Rossi swoops down off Lukey Heights in the best weather for the Australian GP in years

The other memorable last-lap move was by Marquez. As Jerry Burgess always used to say, the thing you must beware of around the Island is burning out your front tyre. Marquez thought he'd done just that after he briefly got the lead off Lorenzo and spent a few laps trying to get away. But as Jorge hadn't been able to escape it was no surprise that neither could Marc, and the Yamaha man was soon in front again. By the last lap Marc was worried that he'd cooled off his tyre too much but, to no one's surprise, he attacked anyway, taking back a big chunk of territory on the brakes at Honda. After that the *coup de grâce* at MG was simple. Marc made the point that he wouldn't have attacked a championship contender in the way he did unless he 'could see it' – and clearly he could.

At this juncture Rossi was third and would have lost only four points from his championship lead. Iannone had other ideas, however, and forced his way inside the Yamaha at MG, then powered into the final long left-hander. There was no way back for Valentino and the damage was now seven points – a much more serious matter.

After qualifying Lorenzo had been very unhappy about providing a tow for Iannone's second place on the grid. The Italian had thanked him and promised payback. When Andrea stormed off the line and out-dragged them all into the first corner, it was tempting to imagine just how angry Jorge was getting – but at the end of the race Jorge was more than pleased to see Andrea on the podium. Although recriminations about this race were to emerge a week later, it's worth

'I DON'T KNOW
WHERE I PULLED
THAT TIME OUT
FROM, BUT IT WAS
WHAT MADE THE
DIFFERENCE!'
MARC MARQUEZ

ABOVE Marc Marquez won the best race of the year with a stunning final lap at Phillip Island

BELOW With good news of Alex de Angelis, the Ioda team fielded Damian Cudlin as a replacement

OPPOSITE Viñales raced with Crutchlow and Pedrosa to sixth, only six seconds behind the winner

remembering that none of them surfaced while the participants were in Australia.

Behind the fab four, there were other notable rides, not least from local hero Jack Miller, who snatched the final point and the Open Class win. But the most impressive supporting actor was Maverick Viñales on the Suzuki. He'd had a sixth place before, at Catalunya, but to dice with Dani Pedrosa and Cal Crutchlow and finish just six seconds behind the winner was a whole new level of competitiveness for bike and rider.

The fact that Pedrosa didn't appear at the front was a surprise given his recent stellar form, but he's the one rider on the grid who has never liked Phillip Island. There's a theory that he doesn't like cold weather, that the breeze on his neck reminds him constantly that his front tyre is cooling rapidly. Hey, this might even explain Silverstone as well as Phillip Island.

The points gap at the top of the table was now 11, which meant that theoretically Valentino could still follow Jorge home in the two remaining races and become champion. The bad news for Rossi, though, was that he had now been beaten on the last lap in two of the past three races, and yet these showdowns always used to be one of his great strengths. This was also only the second time all year he'd finished off the rostrum, and the first time in a dry race.

Phillip Island put the season in crystal-clear focus as well as providing some indelible memories. It showed exactly how hard it has been for Valentino Rossi, at the age of 36, to fight off the young sharks when they smell blood – even on a track where he won five times in a row.

ASYMMETRIC ABSOLUTION

In 2014 Bridgestone introduced its asymmetrical front tyre at Phillip Island. Most riders were suspicious of it and didn't change their minds after plummeting track temperatures resulted in a spate of crashes, one of which robbed Cal Crutchlow of a rostrum finish when he fell while braking with the bike vertical; Cal was so unimpressed that he refused to use the tyre when it appeared again in Germany this year.

For this year's Phillip Island race, everyone – Crutchlow included – used the asymmetrical front tyre. Bridgestone made some significant alterations to it, as Shinji Aoki, Manager of Motorcycle Tyre Development, explained.

'The asymmetric front slick we developed for this year's Australian Grand Prix used the same rubber compounds as last year's version, but this year we changed the areas in which the two compound zones were located on the tyre. Last year's asymmetric front slick had the extra-soft compound rubber located only on the right shoulder of the tyre, while the centre and left shoulders were comprised of the soft-compound rubber. For this year,

the extra-soft rubber was used on the right and centre sections of the tyre, with the soft-compound rubber used only on the left shoulder.

'At the end of last year's race, the track temperature dropped significantly, which resulted in some riders losing control while braking, so we wanted to avoid a repeat of that situation this year. The change ensured better warm-up performance and braking feel than last

year, while still maintaining good cornering stability through the fast left-hand turns.

'This new development was universally praised by the riders and over the whole weekend we only had one crash in MotoGP across all sessions including the race. I believe our new, safer, asymmetric front slick was a major contributor to this reduction in incidents.'

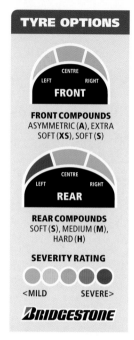

PRAMAC AUSTRALIAN MOTORCYCLE GRAND PRIX

PHILLIP ISLAND

ROUND 16
OCTOBER 18

RACE RESULTS

CIRCUIT LENGTH 2.764 miles

NO. OF LAPS 27

RACE DISTANCE 74.628 miles

WEATHER Dry, 15°C

TRACK TEMPERATURE 42°C

WINNER Marc Marquez

FASTEST LAP 1m 29.280s, 111.412mph, Marc Marquez

LAP RECORD 1m 28.108s, 112.903mph, Marc Marquez (2013)

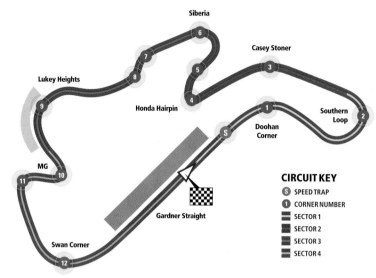

CIRCUIT KEY
- (S) SPEED TRAP
- (1) CORNER NUMBER
- SECTOR 1
- SECTOR 2
- SECTOR 3
- SECTOR 4

QUALIFYING

	Rider	Nation	Motorcycle	Team	Time	Pole +
1	Marquez	SPA	Honda	Repsol Honda Team	1m 28.364s	
2	Iannone	ITA	Ducati	Ducati Team	1m 28.680s	0.316s
3	Lorenzo	SPA	Yamaha	Movistar Yamaha MotoGP	1m 28.680s	0.316s
4	Pedrosa	SPA	Honda	Repsol Honda Team	1m 28.712s	0.348s
5	Crutchlow	GBR	Honda	LCR Honda	1m 28.912s	0.548s
6	Viñales	SPA	Suzuki	Team Suzuki ECSTAR	1m 28.932s	0.568s
7	Rossi	ITA	Yamaha	Movistar Yamaha MotoGP	1m 29.014s	0.650s
8	Espargaro A	SPA	Suzuki	Team Suzuki ECSTAR	1m 29.015s	0.651s
9	Espargaro P	SPA	Yamaha	Monster Yamaha Tech 3	1m 29.222s	0.858s
10	Dovizioso	ITA	Ducati	Ducati Team	1m 29.267s	0.903s
11	Redding	GBR	Honda	EG 0,0 Marc VDS	1m 29.499s	1.135s
12	Smith	GBR	Yamaha	Monster Yamaha Tech 3	1m 29.626s	1.262s
13	Petrucci	ITA	Ducati	Octo Pramac Racing	1m 29.918s	Q1
14	Barbera	SPA	Ducati	Avintia Racing	1m 30.064s	Q1
15	Miller	AUS	Honda	LCR Honda	1m 30.104s	Q1
16	Laverty E	IRL	Honda	Aspar MotoGP Team	1m 30.105s	Q1
17	Hernandez	COL	Ducati	Octo Pramac Racing	1m 30.135s	Q1
18	Bautista	SPA	Aprilia	Aprilia Racing Team Gresini	1m 30.147s	Q1
19	Baz	FRA	Yamaha	Forward Racing	1m 30.173s	Q1
20	Hayden	USA	Honda	Aspar MotoGP Team	1m 30.376s	Q1
21	Bradl	GER	Aprilia	Aprilia Racing Team Gresini	1m 30.634s	Q1
22	Di Meglio	FRA	Ducati	Avintia Racing	1m 30.959s	Q1
23	West	AUS	Honda	AB Motoracing	1m 31.205s	Q1
24	Elias	SPA	Yamaha	Forward Racing	1m 31.837s	Q1
25	Cudlin	AUS	ART	E-Motion IodaRacing Team	1m 33.884s	Q1

1 MARC MARQUEZ
Took his 50th GP victory in one of the best races you'll ever see with one of the best last laps you'll ever see. Massively quicker than the rest in qualifying but overheated his front tyre in the race and had to give it a rest. Risked all on the final lap to set the fastest lap of the race and win.

2 JORGE LORENZO
Twice looked like he was breaking away from the group but was worried about his front tyre in the slower corners – which is where Marquez took advantage. Led 23 of the 27 laps but couldn't hold off Marquez's stunning last-lap charge.

3 ANDREA IANNONE
His best-ever race in any class. With the leaders from start to finish, used the impressive top speed of the GP15 well and made some superb overtakes, including an astonishing two-in-one move on Rossi and Marquez.

4 VALENTINO ROSSI
Quickly made up for his distinctly average qualifying. The situation looked to be tailor-made for him, but Valentino failed to get a rostrum place for only the second time this season after he was unable to pass Iannone on the last lap. Lost seven points of his 18-point championship lead.

5 DANI PEDROSA
Started well but couldn't put the power down coming out of the last corner, so couldn't join the escape. Then got tangled in a fierce dice with Crutchlow and Viñales. When he got away from them, his lap times were as good as those of the leaders.

6 MAVERICK VIÑALES
His best result of the season, equalling the Suzuki team's best. Great race pace after a bad start, right there with the leading group, and the fourth best lap of the day. Finished only a little over six seconds behind the winner.

7 CAL CRUTCHLOW
A story of wheelspin everywhere, without which, said Cal, he would have been with the leading group.

8 POL ESPARGARO
Beat his team-mate for only the third time this season with a solid ride. But perplexed again by the difference in grip between warm-up and the race.

9 ALEIX ESPARGARO
Started well and stayed in touch with the leaders for half-a-dozen laps but ran into serious rear tyre degradation and consequent wheelspin.

10 BRADLEY SMITH
His worst finish of the season but still managed to increase his points lead over Dovizioso.

11 SCOTT REDDING
Made a terrible start but recovered four places. That effort used more of his front tyre than was ideal so he couldn't attack the group in front.

12 DANILO PETRUCCI
A hard race for not many points. Tried to race with the Espargaros and Smith off the start, then later with Redding, but was able to deal with the factory bike of Dovizioso.

LAP CHART

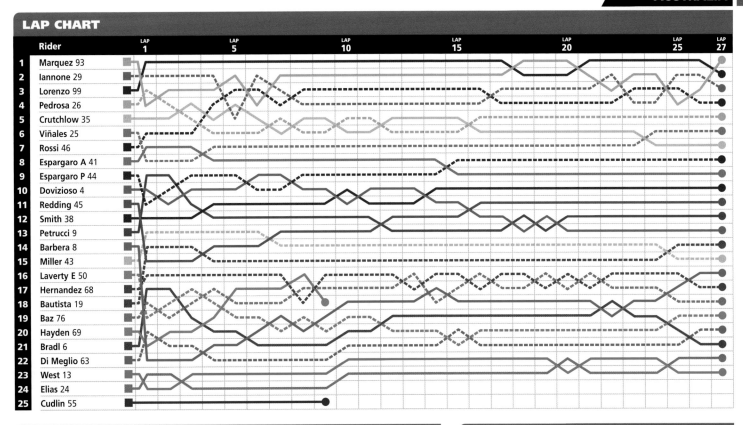

	Rider	LAP 1	LAP 5	LAP 10	LAP 15	LAP 20	LAP 25	LAP 27
1	Marquez 93							
2	Iannone 29							
3	Lorenzo 99							
4	Pedrosa 26							
5	Crutchlow 35							
6	Viñales 25							
7	Rossi 46							
8	Espargaro A 41							
9	Espargaro P 44							
10	Dovizioso 4							
11	Redding 45							
12	Smith 38							
13	Petrucci 9							
14	Barbera 8							
15	Miller 43							
16	Laverty E 50							
17	Hernandez 68							
18	Bautista 19							
19	Baz 76							
20	Hayden 69							
21	Bradl 6							
22	Di Meglio 63							
23	West 13							
24	Elias 24							
25	Cudlin 55							

RACE

	Rider	Motorcycle	Race time	Time +	Fastest lap	Avg. speed	🄱
1	Marquez	Honda	40m 33.849s		1m 29.280s	110.4mph	A/M
2	Lorenzo	Yamaha	40m 34.098s	0.249s	1m 29.711s	110.4mph	A/M
3	Iannone	Ducati	40m 34.779s	0.930s	1m 29.509s	110.3mph	A/M
4	Rossi	Yamaha	40m 34.907s	1.058s	1m 29.369s	110.3mph	A/M
5	Pedrosa	Honda	40m 38.911s	5.062s	1m 29.796s	110.1mph	A/M
6	Viñales	Suzuki	40m 40.649s	6.800s	1m 29.622s	110.0mph	A/M
7	Crutchlow	Honda	40m 43.224s	9.375s	1m 29.875s	109.9mph	A/M
8	Espargaro P	Yamaha	40m 52.250s	18.401s	1m 30.170s	109.5mph	A/M
9	Espargaro A	Suzuki	40m 53.888s	20.039s	1m 30.078s	109.4mph	A/M
10	Smith	Yamaha	40m 54.506s	20.657s	1m 30.207s	109.4mph	A/M
11	Redding	Honda	40m 55.695s	21.846s	1m 30.169s	109.4mph	A/M
12	Petrucci	Ducati	40m 56.689s	22.840s	1m 30.319s	109.3mph	A/M
13	Dovizioso	Ducati	41m 03.017s	29.168s	1m 30.067s	109.1mph	A/M
14	Bautista	Aprilia	41m 11.093s	37.244s	1m 30.319s	108.7mph	A/S
15	Miller	Honda	41m 14.041s	40.192s	1m 30.480s	108.6mph	A/S
16	Barbera	Honda	41m 22.112s	48.263s	1m 31.042s	108.2mph	A/M
17	Hernandez	Ducati	41m 22.421s	48.572s	1m 30.791s	108.2mph	A/M
18	Baz	Yamaha	41m 22.526s	48.677s	1m 30.816s	108.2mph	A/S
19	Laverty E	Honda	41m 24.050s	50.201s	1m 30.838s	108.1mph	A/S
20	Di Meglio	Ducati	41m 24.111s	50.262s	1m 31.070s	108.1mph	A/M
21	Bradl	Aprilia	41m 24.126s	50.277s	1m 31.214s	108.1mph	A/S
22	Elias	Yamaha	41m 54.791s	1m 20.942s	1m 32.008s	106.8mph	A/S
23	West	Honda	41m 57.303s	1m 23.454s	1m 31.927s	106.7mph	A/S
NC	Hayden	Honda	13m 50.295s	18 laps	1m 30.837s	107.8mph	A/S
NC	Cudlin	ART	22m 15.874s	18 laps	1m 33.323s	67.0mph	A/S

CHAMPIONSHIP

	Rider	Nation	Team	Points
1	Rossi	SPA	Movistar Yamaha MotoGP	296
2	Lorenzo	ITA	Movistar Yamaha MotoGP	285
3	Marquez	SPA	Repsol Honda Team	222
4	Iannone	ITA	Ducati Team	188
5	Pedrosa	SPA	Repsol Honda Team	165
6	Smith	GBR	Monster Yamaha Tech 3	158
7	Dovizioso	ITA	Ducati Team	153
8	Crutchlow	GBR	LCR Honda	107
9	Petrucci	ITA	Octo Pramac Racing	97
10	Espargaro P	SPA	Monster Yamaha Tech 3	96
11	Espargaro A	SPA	Team Suzuki ECSTAR	88
12	Viñales	SPA	Team Suzuki ECSTAR	84
13	Redding	GBR	EG 0,0 Marc VDS	78
14	Hernandez	COL	Octo Pramac Racing	49
15	Barbera	SPA	Avintia Racing	30
16	Baz	FRA	Forward Racing	28
	Bautista	SPA	Aprilia Racing Team Gresini	28
18	Miller	AUS	LCR Honda	17
19	Hayden	USA	Aspar MotoGP Team	16
20	Bradl	GER	Forward Racing	11
21	Laverty E	IRL	Aspar MotoGP Team	9
22	Nakasuga	JPN	Yamaha Factory Racing Team	8
	Pirro	ITA	Ducati Team	8
	Di Meglio	FRA	Avintia Racing	8
25	Aoyama	JPN	Repsol Honda Team	5
26	Takahashi	JPN	Team HRC with Nissin	4
27	De Angelis	RSM	E-Motion IodaRacing Team	2

13 ANDREA DOVIZIOSO
Described his weekend as 'embarrassing'. He never solved a variety of small problems and then had his rear tyre performance drop off massively in the last three laps.

14 ALVARO BAUTISTA
Not his best finish of the year, but the closest he has been to the leaders. Tried not to stress the tyre too much early on to avoid the major drop-off experienced in practice.

15 JACK MILLER
Fast all weekend, adapted his style cleverly to conserve his tyre and won the Open Class for the second time.

16 HECTOR BARBERA
Very unhappy with his pace on race day as it was nowhere near what he managed in practice and warm-up.

17 YONNY HERNANDEZ
Anonymous all day. Never found a set-up that dealt with the wheelspin.

18 LORIS BAZ
Diced with Barbera and Hernandez but lost out, especially on top speed.

19 EUGENE LAVERTY
Set his tyre pressures too high and suffered for it after a good start.

20 MIKE DI MEGLIO
Like his team-mate, raced with the harder rear tyre; happy with his race pace.

21 STEFAN BRADL
Had a bad weekend. Changed everything but couldn't find any improvement.

22 TONI ELIAS
Struggled to find any sort of feeling right through practice, and things didn't improve on race day.

23 ANT WEST
Stood in for Karel Abraham. Raced with Elias at the start but lost the tow.

DID NOT FINISH

NICKY HAYDEN
Qualified badly but had made up four places when the bike stopped on lap ten.

DAMIAN CUDLIN
Replaced the injured de Angelis. The bike developed downshifting problems on lap three that eventually forced his retirement.

DID NOT RACE

KAREL ABRAHAM
Still recovering from his foot injury. Replaced by Ant West.

ALEX DE ANGELIS
Once the team was happy that Alex was recovering from his Motegi injuries, they decided to field a replacement in veteran Aussie Damian Cudlin.

SHELL MALAYSIAN MOTORCYCLE GRAND PRIX
SEPANG INTERNATIONAL CIRCUIT

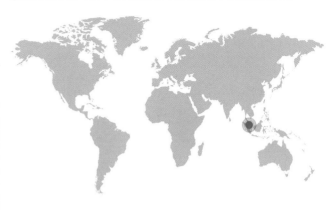

THE GAME OF THRONES

Dani Pedrosa won again but the feud between Valentino Rossi and Marc Marquez overshadowed everything

All the talk – in the paddock, the papers and on the TV – should have been about Dani Pedrosa's magnificent victory, which was proof, if it were needed, of his return to fitness and form. Instead, a chain reaction was initiated at the Thursday press conference that went on, as chain reactions do, to consume everything it touched.

The man who set it off was Valentino Rossi. He arrived at the press conference armed with a set of lap times from the previous race and a serious grievance. Having watched the race on TV, he considered that Marc Marquez had deliberately interfered with his race, played with him, in order to help Jorge Lorenzo's title ambitions. No, he wasn't joking. Of course he helped, said Jorge, 'especially on the last lap'. Marc's motivation for the alleged misdemeanours was said to be his belief that Valentino deliberately knocked him off in Argentina and shouldn't have been awarded the win at Assen because he cut the course.

In response Marc restricted himself to a straightforward description of his Australian race, but talked for considerably longer than he usually does and with a complete absence of his customary beaming smile. Not that Valentino looked like he was having fun: no grin, no jokes. In fact he looked pallid and drawn. The mood suddenly matched the local atmosphere, heavily polluted by smoke from illegal jungle clearances in Indonesia.

Undeterred, Valentino then set off on a round of TV interviews in which he once more spelt out his accusations, adding that he now doubted if Marc had really been a fan of his when he was a kid. Strong stuff. This was a planned campaign, an attack on all

'MARQUEZ KNOWS IT WASN'T RED MIST THAT CAUSED THE CRASH'
VALENTINO ROSSI

MALAYSIA MOTORCYCLE GRAND PRIX

fronts. What could Valentino possibly hope to gain from it? After all, his fight for the title was with Lorenzo. Was it an attempt to guarantee that Marquez would beat Lorenzo to show he wasn't favouring anyone? That would have the happy side effect of limiting the points gap between the Yamaha pair.

Maybe it was self-motivation. Valentino knocked Jorge off the front row in qualifying, his fourth front row in seven races, and it was the first time Jorge had been off the front row since the summer break.

Dani's pace shouldn't have been a shock, given his race simulation at the pre-season Sepang test, but it was. First he set his first pole position for over a year, atomising the record on the way, then he led from the first corner to the last for his second win in three races. It was a magnificent win.

Lorenzo had to get past Rossi and Marquez before giving chase – in vain. He took second place off Marquez at Turn Four when the Honda gave another one of those vicious, snapping head shakes that result when Marc pushes too hard in the early laps. It put him to the very edge of the track and he lost a lot of momentum – which put him back with Rossi. Given what Valentino had said on Thursday, he must have felt his prediction fulfilled as he saw Marc reversing towards him, not fighting Jorge. Valentino got into third place next time round as Marquez fought another big moment.

The serious stuff started on lap five with take and retake first through Turns One and Two, then through Four, Five and Six, and again through Nine, Ten and Eleven. Things were comparatively quiet next

ABOVE Australian Ant West had a second ride on the AB Cardion Honda and got it to the flag again

LEFT The Thursday press conference. Valentino Rossi is expounding his theory on what happened in Australia. His target audience doesn't look convinced

OPPOSITE Marc Marquez on the grid contemplating his race. Little did he know

Pictures from the TV helicopter showed there was no kick from Rossi but he did stick his knee out, as any rider does when bikes are about to touch, and his foot was pulled off its footrest by the impact. Valentino continued to a lonely third place, TV pictures now showing some very uncomfortable body language in his pit.

Race Direction decided to review the incident after the race rather than issue an instant penalty. Under the circumstances, that was an understandable and diplomatic decision. They found Rossi guilty of 'irresponsible riding causing another rider to crash' and put three points on his licence. As he already had one point from Misano, that took him to four points and an automatic start from the back of the grid at the next round – the championship decider. Valentino appealed to the FIM stewards, but it was rejected.

The bad feeling was taken to the rostrum by Lorenzo, who gave a thumbs-down as his team-mate received his trophy and then stalked off before the cava was sprayed. Lorenzo then took it further by telling interviewers the penalty was too lenient. Rossi, meanwhile, didn't turn up to the post-race press conference.

Both Rossi and Marquez later gave individual press conferences in their teams' hospitality units. Marc was coldly furious. Valentino was more defensive but still unapologetic, saying he was just trying to slow his opponent down. The battle lines were well and truly drawn, not just for Valencia but for the foreseeable future.

Just a small reminder: Dani Pedrosa won the race brilliantly.

ABOVE Smith and Crutchlow battled for top satellite bike and top Brit

BELOW Old rivals Pedrosa and Lorenzo – much more happy to see each other than they used to be

time round, apart from Marquez's pass at Fourteen. Rossi then spent half a lap catching the Honda again before another two quick exchanges of position found them at Thirteen almost side by side and heading into Fourteen. Rossi, on the inside, sat his bike up, slowed and moved to the outside, taking two big, long looks at his opponent as he did so. Marquez was still looking to turn in, the bikes touched and the Honda went down.

FALLOUT

The penalty as handed down by Race Direction would have had Valentino Rossi starting from the back row of the grid in Valencia.

To try to avoid that, Rossi appealed directly to the Court of Arbitration for Sport (CAS), asking for a Stay of Execution on the penalty before a full hearing. If that were to be successful, it wouldn't have been possible to enforce the grid penalty until after the hearing, several weeks after Valencia. If Rossi were eventually to be found guilty, then he would have to serve his penalty at the first race of 2016. A decision was expected by the Friday of the Valencia GP but arrived early. Rossi found out on the Thursday that he would indeed be starting from the ninth row of the grid.

Meanwhile, the frenzy escalated. Spanish and Italian media, with a couple of honourable exceptions, simply believed everything their men said. Repsol weighed in on Marquez's side; a crew from a satirical Italian TV show was involved in an altercation outside the Marquez family home; the President of the FIM published an open letter to both men; Honda offered to show anyone

Marquez's data then changed its mind; Yamaha cancelled its 60th anniversary champions dinner at Valencia, the long-planned centrepiece of the company's celebrations; social media and online forums went into meltdown.

The real problem was that two of MotoGP's top riders now believed things about the other that weren't true, and the people around them did nothing to dissuade them from those views. Inevitably, the atmosphere went from the usual level of competitiveness in elite sport to poisonous. Feuds of the past, like the Bill Ivy/Phil Read spat of the mid-1960s, had nothing on this.

RIGHT Marc Marquez and Valentino Rossi in the middle of their frantic fight

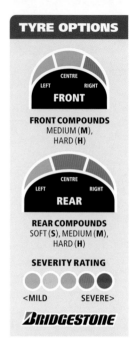

SHELL MALAYSIAN MOTORCYCLE GRAND PRIX
SEPANG INTERNATIONAL CIRCUIT

ROUND 17
OCTOBER 25

MotoGP — TISSOT
OFFICIAL TIMEKEEPER

CIRCUIT KEY
- **S** SPEED TRAP
- **1** CORNER NUMBER
- SECTOR 1
- SECTOR 2
- SECTOR 3
- SECTOR 4

TYRE OPTIONS

CENTRE
LEFT | RIGHT
FRONT

FRONT COMPOUNDS
MEDIUM (**M**),
HARD (**H**)

CENTRE
LEFT | RIGHT
REAR

REAR COMPOUNDS
SOFT (**S**), MEDIUM (**M**),
HARD (**H**)

SEVERITY RATING
<MILD   SEVERE>

BRIDGESTONE

RACE RESULTS

CIRCUIT LENGTH 3.447 miles
NO. OF LAPS 20
RACE DISTANCE 68.94 miles
WEATHER Dry, 35°C
TRACK TEMPERATURE 47°C
WINNER Dani Pedrosa
FASTEST LAP 2m 00.606s
102.775mph, Jorge Lorenzo (record)
PREVIOUS LAP RECORD 2m 01.150s,
102.340mph, Marc Marquez (2014)

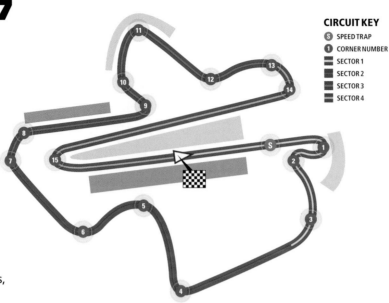

QUALIFYING

	Rider	Nation	Motorcycle	Team	Time	Pole +
1	Pedrosa	SPA	Honda	Repsol Honda Team	1m 59.053s	
2	Marquez	SPA	Honda	Repsol Honda Team	1m 59.462s	0.409s
3	Rossi	ITA	Yamaha	Movistar Yamaha MotoGP	1m 59.726s	0.673s
4	Lorenzo	SPA	Yamaha	Movistar Yamaha MotoGP	1m 59.737s	0.684s
5	Crutchlow	GBR	Honda	LCR Honda	2m 00.199s	1.146s
6	Iannone	ITA	Ducati	Ducati Team	2m 00.224s	1.171s
7	Dovizioso	ITA	Ducati	Ducati Team	2m 00.423s	1.370s
8	Viñales	SPA	Suzuki	Team Suzuki ECSTAR	2m 00.478s	1.425s
9	Smith	GBR	Yamaha	Monster Yamaha Tech 3	2m 00.652s	1.599s
10	Barbera	SPA	Ducati	Avintia Racing	2m 00.724s	1.671s
11	Espargaro A	SPA	Suzuki	Team Suzuki ECSTAR	2m 00.724s	1.671s
12	Espargaro P	SPA	Yamaha	Monster Yamaha Tech 3	2m 00.794s	1.741s
13	Petrucci	ITA	Ducati	Octo Pramac Racing	2m 01.223s	Q1
14	Bradl	GER	Aprilia	Aprilia Racing Team Gresini	2m 01.346s	Q1
15	Redding	GBR	Honda	EG 0,0 Marc VDS	2m 01.367s	Q1
16	Miller	AUS	Honda	LCR Honda	2m 01.725s	Q1
17	Bautista	SPA	Aprilia	Aprilia Racing Team Gresini	2m 01.727s	Q1
18	Hernandez	COL	Ducati	Octo Pramac Racing	2m 01.748s	Q1
19	Hayden	USA	Honda	Aspar MotoGP Team	2m 01.829s	Q1
20	Baz	FRA	Yamaha	Forward Racing	2m 01.862s	Q1
21	Elias	SPA	Yamaha	Forward Racing	2m 02.415s	Q1
22	Laverty E	IRL	Honda	Aspar MotoGP Team	2m 02.460s	Q1
23	Di Meglio	FRA	Ducati	Avintia Racing	2m 02.964s	Q1
24	West	AUS	Honda	AB Motoracing	2m 03.855s	Q1
25	Cudlin	AUS	ART	E-Motion IodaRacing Team	2m 06.051s	Q1

1 DANI PEDROSA
Started from pole and led from the first corner to the flag, but his second win in three races was unfairly overshadowed by the Marquez/Rossi incident.

2 JORGE LORENZO
Passed by the Ducatis down into Turn One, repassed them in one move, then caught his team-mate – couldn't close in on Pedrosa.

3 VALENTINO ROSSI
Found guilty of causing Marquez to crash by running deliberately wide on lap seven. The incident ended a frenzied dice and Valentino spent the rest of the race alone.

4 BRADLEY SMITH
A brilliant result to top a difficult weekend. Only 14th on Friday and had to go through QP1, but ran a near-perfect race and was able to maintain his pace on worn tyres to catch and pass Crutchlow.

5 CAL CRUTCHLOW
Inconsistency with the front brake lever feel spoiled Cal's race after he started it really well. It caused him to clip Dovizioso in the change of direction in Turns Five/Six, for which he apologised, and to lose out to Smith, whom Cal thought he should have dealt with easily.

6 DANILO PETRUCCI
A superb result underpinned by a great first lap, after which he fought his way past both Espargaro brothers. Described it as the hardest race of his career.

7 ALEIX ESPARGARO
Found himself jammed in the middle of the pack after the usual Suzuki start and unable to take his lines.

8 MAVERICK VIÑALES
Swamped off the start and ended the first lap in 16th place. After that, Mack mounted an impressive comeback but just failed to beat his team-mate to the line.

9 POL ESPARGARO
Knocked over by Barbera in warm-up, suffering nasty whiplash injury to his neck that nearly prevented him riding.

10 STEFAN BRADL
Delighted to lead the Aprilia team to its best result of the season so far. Equalled Bautista's best result but, impressively, was only a couple of seconds behind the Suzukis and the Tech 3 Yamaha.

11 SCOTT REDDING
Difficulties with the front all race, but happy to finish with no physical problems at a track that has troubled him in the past.

12 YONNY HERNANDEZ
Put to the back after some contact in the first corner, after which Yonny worked his way past the Open bikes. Always thinking about throttle use to conserve the rear tyre.

13 HECTOR BARBERA
Sent to the back of the grid for torpedoing Pol Espargaro in warm-up but still managed to win the Open Class.

14 TONI ELIAS
Delighted to score his first points for Forward Racing. Not quick at the start but was able to maintain good pace and pass the customer Hondas.

LAP CHART

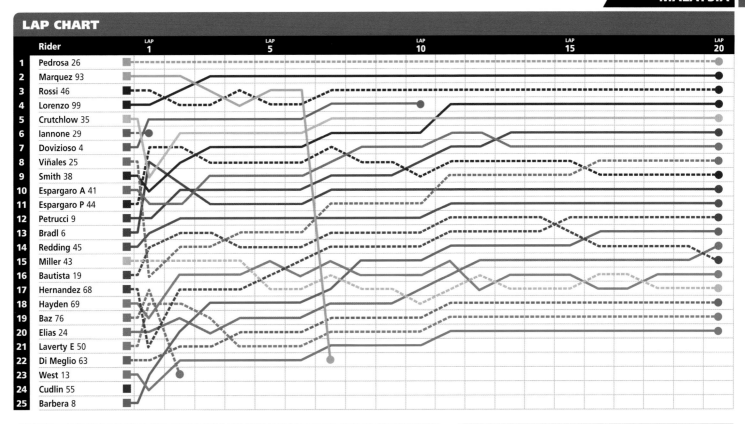

	Rider	LAP 1	LAP 5	LAP 10	LAP 15	LAP 20
1	Pedrosa 26					
2	Marquez 93					
3	Rossi 46					
4	Lorenzo 99					
5	Crutchlow 35					
6	Iannone 29					
7	Dovizioso 4					
8	Viñales 25					
9	Smith 38					
10	Espargaro A 41					
11	Espargaro P 44					
12	Petrucci 9					
13	Bradl 6					
14	Redding 45					
15	Miller 43					
16	Bautista 19					
17	Hernandez 68					
18	Hayden 69					
19	Baz 76					
20	Elias 24					
21	Laverty E 50					
22	Di Meglio 63					
23	West 13					
24	Cudlin 55					
25	Barbera 8					

RACE

	Rider	Motorcycle	Race time	Time +	Fastest lap	Avg. speed	🏍
1	Pedrosa	Honda	40m 37.691s		2m 00.795s	101.7mph	M/M
2	Lorenzo	Yamaha	40m 41.303s	3.612s	2m 00.606s	101.5mph	M/M
3	Rossi	Yamaha	40m 51.415s	13.724s	2m 01.127s	101.2mph	M/M
4	Smith	Yamaha	41m 01.686s	23.995s	2m 02.051s	100.7mph	M/M
5	Crutchlow	Honda	41m 06.412s	28.721s	2m 01.803s	100.5mph	M/M
6	Petrucci	Ducati	41m 14.063s	36.372s	2m 02.601s	100.2mph	M/M
7	Espargaro A	Suzuki	41m 16.981s	39.290s	2m 02.350s	100.1mph	M/M
8	Viñales	Suzuki	41m 17.127s	39.436s	2m 02.814s	100.1mph	M/M
9	Espargaro P	Yamaha	41m 20.153s	42.462s	2m 02.303s	100.0mph	M/M
10	Bradl	Aprilia	41m 22.292s	44.601s	2m 03.079s	99.9mph	M/S
11	Redding	Honda	41m 25.381s	47.690s	2m 02.860s	99.7mph	M/M
12	Hernandez	Ducati	41m 29.803s	52.112s	2m 03.038s	99.5mph	H/M
13	Barbera	Ducati	41m 30.051s	52.360s	2m 03.217s	99.5mph	M/S
14	Elias	Yamaha	41m 31.310s	53.619s	2m 03.493s	99.5mph	M/S
15	Bautista	Aprilia	41m 31.322s	53.631s	2m 03.080s	99.5mph	M/S
16	Hayden	Honda	41m 39.122s	1m 01.431s	2m 03.188s	99.2mph	M/M
17	Miller	Honda	41m 40.519s	1m 02.828s	2m 03.657s	99.2mph	M/S
18	Di Meglio	Ducati	41m 42.766s	1m 05.075s	2m 03.987s	99.0mph	M/S
19	Laverty E	Honda	41m 47.568s	1m 09.877s	2m 04.063s	98.9mph	M/M
20	West	Honda	42m 02.440s	1m 24.749s	2m 04.707s	98.3mph	M/S
NC	Dovizioso	Ducati	20m 30.937s	10 laps	2m 01.493s	100.7mph	M/M
NC	Marquez	Honda	14m 54.498s	13 laps	2m 00.818s	97.0mph	M/M
NC	Baz	Yamaha	5m 00.897s	18 laps	–	82.4mph	M/S
NC	Iannone	Ducati	2m 08.215s	19 laps	–	96.7mph	M/M
NC	Cudlin	ART	–	–	–	–	M/S

CHAMPIONSHIP

	Rider	Nation	Team	Points
1	Rossi	ITA	Movistar Yamaha MotoGP	312
2	Lorenzo	SPA	Movistar Yamaha MotoGP	305
3	Marquez	SPA	Repsol Honda Team	222
4	Pedrosa	SPA	Repsol Honda Team	190
5	Iannone	ITA	Ducati Team	188
6	Smith	GBR	Monster Yamaha Tech 3	171
7	Dovizioso	ITA	Ducati Team	153
8	Crutchlow	GBR	LCR Honda	118
9	Petrucci	ITA	Octo Pramac Racing	107
10	Espargaro P	SPA	Monster Yamaha Tech 3	103
11	Espargaro A	SPA	Team Suzuki ECSTAR	97
12	Viñales	SPA	Team Suzuki ECSTAR	92
13	Redding	GBR	EG 0,0 Marc VDS	83
14	Hernandez	COL	Octo Pramac Racing	53
15	Barbera	SPA	Avintia Racing	33
16	Bautista	SPA	Aprilia Racing Team Gresini	29
17	Baz	FRA	Forward Racing	28
18	Miller	AUS	LCR Honda	17
	Bradl	GER	Aprilia Racing Team Gresini	17
20	Hayden	USA	Aspar MotoGP Team	16
21	Laverty E	IRL	Aspar MotoGP Team	9
22	Nakasuga	JPN	Yamaha Factory Racing Team	8
	Pirro	ITA	Ducati Team	8
	Di Meglio	FRA	Avintia Racing	8
25	Aoyama	JPN	Repsol Honda Team	5
26	Takahashi	JPN	Team HRC with Nissin	4
27	De Angelis	RSM	E-Motion IodaRacing Team	2
	Elias	SPA	Forward Racing	2

---

15 ALVARO BAUTISTA
A bad weekend but still scored a point despite being beaten by his team-mate for the first time. The front tucked early in the race and then he ran out of rear grip.

16 NICKY HAYDEN
Thoroughly fed up with another 16th place. Slowed after a major moment with the front and was retaken by several riders. Got Miller back when the fuel load went down.

17 JACK MILLER
Had trouble with grip front and rear from the start and ended the race with precious little at the rear.

18 MIKE DI MEGLIO
Took a major gamble on set-up on race day, which turned out to be a good one. His dash went blank for seven laps, which hampered his pursuit of Hayden and Miller.

19 EUGENE LAVERTY
Felt like he was on ice, there was so little grip. Had been fast in hotter afternoon conditions but found the track surface in the race markedly different from practice.

20 ANT WEST
Ran into brake overheating in the race, a problem that hadn't surfaced on Friday or Saturday.

DID NOT FINISH

ANDREA DOVIZIOSO
Clipped by Crutchlow as the Honda man went past. Unlucky, but simply a racing incident for which Cal apologised.

MARC MARQUEZ
Fell on lap seven in the notorious incident for which Valentino Rossi was penalised.

LORIS BAZ
Crashed at the first corner of the second lap, probably ending his chances of beating Barbera in the Open championship.

ANDREA IANNONE
Retired after his radiator was holed by a stone kicked up early in the race. Lost fourth place in the table to Pedrosa.

DAMIAN CUDLIN
Got away well and was happy with the bike on a full tank, so pushed to stay with the Open Hondas only to lose the rear coming on to the back straight first time round.

DID NOT RACE

KAREL ABRAHAM
Still out with foot injury. Again replaced by Ant West.

ALEX DE ANGELIS
Recovered sufficiently from his Japan accident to be flown home on race day. Again replaced by Cudlin.

GRAN PREMIO MOTUL DE LA COMUNITAT VALENCIANA
CIRCUITO RICARDO TORMO

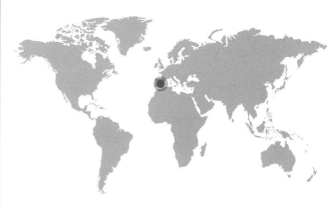

THE FINAL SHOWDOWN

Feelings ran high in the paddock and in the stands, but Jorge Lorenzo rose above it all to become champion for the third time

Jorge Lorenzo won again, for the seventh time this year, and he did it the way he won all the others. He was never headed from lights-out to chequered flag, starting the race with a run of 18 laps in the 1min 31sec bracket and finishing with a race pace that varied over every flying lap of the 30-lap race by less than one second. The Hondas chased him and closed down with a couple of laps to go, but then got in each other's way, allowing Jorge vital breathing space. Lorenzo won the race and the title.

Those are the bare facts, but it didn't stop the rancour. Valentino Rossi had to start from the back of the grid, the penalty for his offence in Malaysia. He carved through the field to fourth place, good enough to retain his championship lead and take his tenth title if – and it was a big if – both the Honda riders could relegate Lorenzo to third place. There was no way that Valentino, if practice and qualifying were any guide, was going to finish any higher than fourth no matter where he started. His fate was effectively out of his own hands.

Practice had also revealed that the Honda riders in general, and Marc Marquez and Cal Crutchlow in particular, were unhappy with the front tyre allocation. Too soft, they said. It wasn't a safety issue, said Bridgestone: 'If we give you a harder option there'll be a pile of motorcycles at Turn 4.' There was hope, particularly in the Honda pit, that race-day temperatures would be slightly lower than on Friday and Saturday and the tyre issue would be less critical. Come Sunday, there was hardly any change; everyone had tyre conservation on their minds, some more than others.

Under normal circumstances, a Valencia race in which the top three circulated in the same order for the

'I'VE RIDDEN WITH VALENTINO, MARC, CASEY AND DANI ON THE TRACK. FOR ME THESE ARE THE BEST RIDERS IN THE 21ST CENTURY'
JORGE LORENZO

duration wouldn't attract any comment; it has happened a lot. Not this time. Lorenzo led with Marquez at a respectable distance and, once Andrea Iannone had crashed, Dani Pedrosa was a lonely third. Lorenzo was in his finest metronomic form, Marquez followed a third-to-half-a-second behind. It was looking like a replay of Indianapolis. When would Marc attack? At Indy it was three laps from the end, at Assen the very last corner.

Two laps from home Marquez closed right up on the leader. It looked as if one Honda would go past Lorenzo – not enough to make Rossi champion. But Pedrosa flew across the last couple of seconds of the gap and arrived just as Marquez was shaping to attack. Now it looked as if both Hondas would pass Lorenzo – and make Rossi champion. Dani went past and for a moment it looked as if they were going to collide – both Hondas on the floor would have been another way of making Rossi champion. Dani couldn't hold his line on the next corner and ran wide, allowing Marc an easy repass. That exchange gave Lorenzo a few tenths of a second. It was enough.

Nothing remarkable there – but the events of the previous two weeks ensured that nothing was taken at face value.

The accusation was that Marquez hadn't attacked because he didn't want to hand Rossi the title. But why shouldn't Marquez have been re-enacting Indianapolis? Given the nature of the Ricardo Tormo circuit, you'd be deluded to have expected a repeat of Phillip Island. Also, his body language as seen from the on-board camera after the flag hardly suggested that Marc was happy with the result. That didn't stop a lot of people who

ABOVE Valentino Rossi rolls out of his pit as championship leader on his way to the back of the grid

OPPOSITE Nicky Hayden contemplates his final MotoGP. And maybe thinks of the 2006 Valencian GP

LEFT The story of the race in one picture: Jorge leads, Marc menaces, Dani hangs on

had clearly said they saw nothing wrong at Phillip Island wondering about what they'd seen at Valencia.

Rossi was in no doubt whatsoever. Marquez, he said, had 'finished the work he started in Australia'. It was a repeat of the accusations of Malaysia, backed up, said Valentino, by the events of the day. He then decided not to turn up to the FIM prize-giving ceremony. It wasn't pretty and it was in stark contrast to Valencia 2006, where Rossi and Nicky Hayden had decided the championship in the most sporting fashion. Valencia 2015 was Hayden's farewell to MotoGP and he'll be missed in more than one way.

The arguments and accusations overshadowed everything else. There was a fantastic ride by Cal Crutchlow from even further back on the grid than Rossi, and Maverick Viñales became Rookie of the Year.

But the main achievement that was overshadowed was Jorge Lorenzo's. He won more races in 2015 than anyone else and at various times of the year his opponents all admitted that he was the fastest man out there. This was his third MotoGP title, to add to his two 250cc crowns, and he was only the third man in history to overturn a points deficit at the last round of the year to win the title. The others were Nicky Hayden in 2006 and Wayne Rainey in 1992 (when he finally overhauled Mick Doohan's total after the Aussie missed four rounds after breaking his leg at Assen).

That last statistic alone speaks vividly of the level of concentration that Jorge maintained under the sort of stress levels only top sports people understand. His championship title may not have been the outcome the romantics wanted, but it was a just conclusion nonetheless.

ABOVE Machinery problems sent Cal Crutchlow to the back of the grid – note the Movember 'tache on the front of his helmet

BELOW Pol Espargaro got the better of his Tech 3 team-mate Bradley Smith for the third time

HAPPY BIRTHDAY

One of the casualties of the Sepang incident was Yamaha's grand celebration of its 60th anniversary, which was due to take place at Valencia with Yamaha champions from all over the world in attendance. Its cancellation somewhat diverted attention from Yamaha's achievements in 2015, mainly, it must be said, at the expense of Honda.

Yamaha not only took first and second places in the riders' championship but also won the triple crown of team and constructors' championships. A total of ten double-podium finishes for the factory squad ensured that the team title was won as early as Aragón, and the constructors' championship was sealed at Phillip Island. This was the fifth time that Yamaha had won the triple crown since these three championships were formalised in 2002.

Yamaha's satellite team, Tech 3, also provided the year's best satellite rider in Bradley Smith. He became only the fourth rider to score points in every race of an 18-race season and the only one apart from Valentino Rossi to do it this year. Along with his team-mate Pol

Espargaro and factory test rider Katsuyuki Nakasuga, Bradley put the cherry on top of Yamaha's cake by winning the Suzuka Eight Hours on the company's new R1.

The Eight Hours has always been of prime importance to the Japanese factories, but it has been a while since top Grand Prix riders were required to do the race as part of their contracts.

This was Yamaha's first full factory effort for years and the company faced Honda bringing in Casey Stoner to partner previous winners Michael van der Mark and Takumi Takahashi. For Yamaha to win under such circumstances was a special triumph, but it will only serve to ensure one thing, as will the MotoGP championships: that Honda will come roaring back on all fronts in 2016.

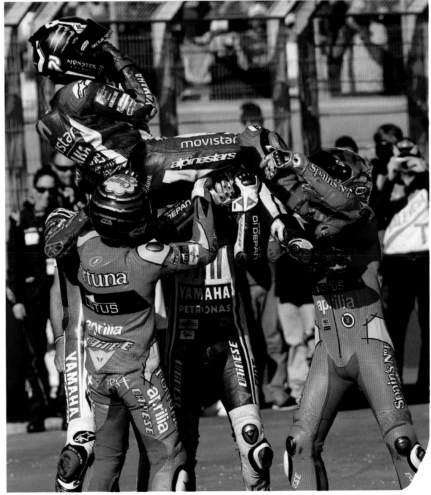

ABOVE AND RIGHT
Jorge Lorenzo admitted to getting quite emotional on the slowdown lap before celebrating with the four other championship-winning versions of himself

GRAN PREMIO MOTUL DE LA COMUNITAT VALENCIANA
CIRCUITO RICARDO TORMO

ROUND **18**
NOVEMBER 8

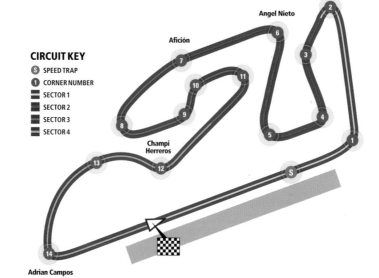
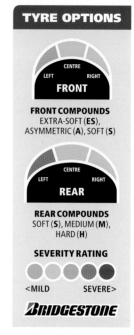

RACE RESULTS

CIRCUIT LENGTH 2.489 miles

NO. OF LAPS 30

RACE DISTANCE 74.658 miles

WEATHER Dry, 23°C

TRACK TEMPERATURE 29°C

WINNER Jorge Lorenzo

FASTEST LAP 1m 31.367s, 98.052mph, Jorge Lorenzo (record)

PREVIOUS LAP RECORD 1m 31.515s, 97.866mph, Marc Marquez (2014)

CIRCUIT KEY
- **S** SPEED TRAP
- **1** CORNER NUMBER
- SECTOR 1
- SECTOR 2
- SECTOR 3
- SECTOR 4

QUALIFYING

	Rider	Nation	Motorcycle	Team	Time	Pole +
1	Lorenzo	SPA	Yamaha	Movistar Yamaha MotoGP	1m 30.011s	
2	Marquez	SPA	Honda	Repsol Honda Team	1m 30.499s	0.488s
3	Pedrosa	SPA	Honda	Repsol Honda Team	1m 30.516s	0.505s
4	Espargaro A	SPA	Suzuki	Team Suzuki ECSTAR	1m 30.917s	0.906s
5	Crutchlow	GBR	Honda	LCR Honda	1m 30.948s	0.937s
6	Smith	GBR	Yamaha	Monster Yamaha Tech 3	1m 31.012s	1.001s
7	Iannone	ITA	Ducati	Ducati Team	1m 31.056s	1.045s
8	Espargaro P	SPA	Yamaha	Monster Yamaha Tech 3	1m 31.080s	1.069s
9	Dovizioso	ITA	Ducati	Ducati Team	1m 31.245s	1.234s
10	Petrucci	ITA	Ducati	Octo Pramac Racing	1m 31.292s	1.281s
11	Viñales	SPA	Suzuki	Team Suzuki ECSTAR	1m 31.340s	1.329s
12	Rossi	ITA	Yamaha	Movistar Yamaha MotoGP	1m 31.471s	1.460s
13	Pirro	ITA	Ducati	Ducati Team	1m 31.780s	Q1
14	Bradl	GER	Aprilia	Aprilia Racing Team Gresini	1m 31.824s	Q1
15	Barbera	SPA	Ducati	Avintia Racing	1m 31.851s	Q1
16	Baz	FRA	Yamaha	Forward Racing	1m 31.856s	Q1
17	Hayden	USA	Honda	Aspar MotoGP Team	1m 32.083s	Q1
18	Hernandez	COL	Ducati	Octo Pramac Racing	1m 32.142s	Q1
19	Bautista	SPA	Aprilia	Aprilia Racing Team Gresini	1m 32.282s	Q1
20	Redding	GBR	Honda	EG 0,0 Marc VDS	1m 32.448s	Q1
21	Miller	AUS	Honda	LCR Honda	1m 32.564s	Q1
22	Di Meglio	FRA	Ducati	Avintia Racing	1m 32.716s	Q1
23	West	AUS	Honda	AB Motoracing	1m 33.049s	Q1
24	Laverty E	IRL	Honda	Aspar MotoGP Team	1m 33.066s	Q1
25	Elias	SPA	Yamaha	Forward Racing	1m 33.092s	Q1
26	Parkes	AUS	ART	E-Motion IodaRacing Team	1m 33.577s	Q1

1 JORGE LORENZO
His seventh win of the year and again it was without being headed, like all the others. His consistency was remarkable; 18 consecutive laps in the 1min 31sec bracket, every flying lap within 0.964sec of each other. Add in his miraculous pole position and you have racing perfection.

2 MARC MARQUEZ
Shadowed Lorenzo the whole race, initially struggling to match his lap times. Worried about his front tyre overheating but was shaping up for a last-lap pass when Pedrosa arrived and their scuffle gave the Yamaha a vital half-second.

3 DANI PEDROSA
Had his usual problems with the bike at the start but closed rapidly towards the end of the race. He caught Marquez just as he was sizing up the leader, got past but ran wide allowing the repass. It was Dani's 100th rostrum in GPs.

4 VALENTINO ROSSI
Paid the penalty for his Sepang infringement by starting from the back of the grid. Ripped past 11 bikes on the first lap, most of them before he'd crossed the start line. Up to fourth by lap 13, but that was as far as he was going to get.

5 POL ESPARGARO
An impressive final race despite the effects of his Malaysia crash, beating his team-mate for only the third time in the season. Had a great fight with Dovizioso before pulling away from the Ducati.

6 BRADLEY SMITH
Finished in the points again. Only the fourth man to score points in every race of an 18-race season and the only one other than Rossi to do it this year.

7 ANDREA DOVIZIOSO
Again unhappy with his finishing position and inability to 'make the difference'.

8 ALEIX ESPARGARO
Combative at the start, fighting for fourth place with Rossi, but suffered from an extreme drop in tyre performance.

9 CAL CRUTCHLOW
But for Rossi, we'd have been raving about this ride from the back of the grid on his second bike. Cold tyres meant that Cal didn't do much for three laps, but then he made an astonishing number of passes.

10 DANILO PETRUCCI
Had a good dice with the Tech 3 Yamahas before his tyres' performance dropped off dramatically.

11 MAVERICK VIÑALES
Pushed out at the second corner and spent the rest of the race trying to recover.

12 MICHELE PIRRO
This was the third wild-card ride of the year for the Ducati factory's test rider and also the third time he scored points. Got a good start but couldn't hang on to the second group, or hold off Crutchlow and Viñales.

13 YONNY HERNANDEZ
His last race with the Pramac team after two seasons. Had a great start, gaining four places, then caught Bradl but was in turn passed by Crutchlow.

LAP CHART

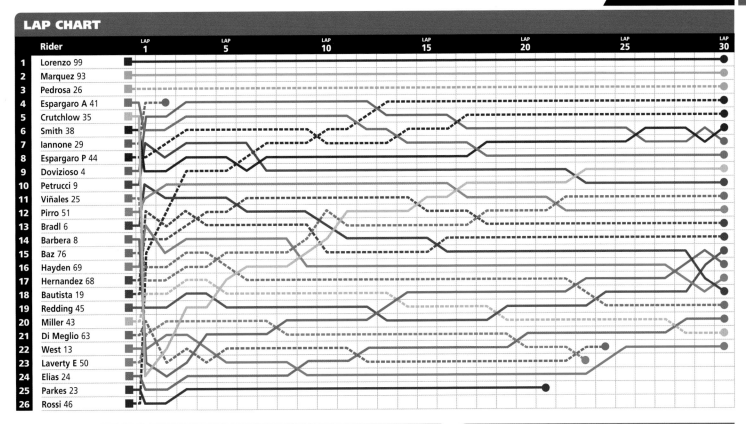

	Rider	LAP 1	LAP 5	LAP 10	LAP 15	LAP 20	LAP 25	LAP 30
1	Lorenzo 99							
2	Marquez 93							
3	Pedrosa 26							
4	Espargaro A 41							
5	Crutchlow 35							
6	Smith 38							
7	Iannone 29							
8	Espargaro P 44							
9	Dovizioso 4							
10	Petrucci 9							
11	Viñales 25							
12	Pirro 51							
13	Bradl 6							
14	Barbera 8							
15	Baz 76							
16	Hayden 69							
17	Hernandez 68							
18	Bautista 19							
19	Redding 45							
20	Miller 43							
21	Di Meglio 63							
22	West 13							
23	Laverty E 50							
24	Elias 24							
25	Parkes 23							
26	Rossi 46							

RACE

	Rider	Motorcycle	Race time	Time +	Fastest lap	Avg. speed	
1	Lorenzo	Yamaha	45m 59.364s		1m 31.367s	97.4mph	S/M
2	Marquez	Honda	45m 59.627s	0.263s	1m 31.455s	97.4mph	S/M
3	Pedrosa	Honda	46m 00.018s	0.654s	1m 31.478s	97.4mph	S/M
4	Rossi	Yamaha	46m 19.153s	19.789s	1m 31.820s	96.7mph	S/M
5	Espargaro P	Yamaha	46m 25.368s	26.004s	1m 32.236s	96.4mph	A/M
6	Smith	Yamaha	46m 28.199s	28.835s	1m 32.338s	96.4mph	S/M
7	Dovizioso	Ducati	46m 28.250s	28.886s	1m 32.041s	96.4mph	S/M
8	Espargaro A	Suzuki	46m 33.586s	34.222s	1m 32.121s	96.2mph	S/M
9	Crutchlow	Honda	46m 35.288s	35.924s	1m 32.240s	96.1mph	S/M
10	Petrucci	Ducati	46m 38.943s	39.579s	1m 32.385s	96.0mph	S/M
11	Viñales	Suzuki	46m 39.110s	39.746s	1m 32.381s	96.0mph	S/M
12	Pirro	Ducati	46m 46.417s	47.053s	1m 32.884s	95.8mph	S/M
13	Hernandez	Ducati	46m 53.445s	54.081s	1m 32.776s	95.5mph	S/M
14	Bautista	Aprilia	46m 56.010s	56.646s	1m 33.312s	95.4mph	S/S
15	Redding	Honda	46m 56.642s	57.728s	1m 32.942s	95.4mph	S/M
16	Barbera	Ducati	46m 56.727s	57.363s	1m 32.944s	95.4mph	S/M
17	Hayden	Honda	46m 58.106s	58.742s	1m 33.105s	95.3mph	S/S
18	Bradl	Aprilia	46m 58.450s	59.086s	1m 33.263s	95.3mph	S/S
19	Baz	Yamaha	47m 03.703s	1m 04.339s	1m 33.265s	95.1mph	S/S
20	Elias	Yamaha	47m 03.777s	1m 04.413s	1m 32.435s	95.1mph	A/S
21	Miller	Honda	47m 04.576s	1m 05.212s	1m 33.427s	95.1mph	S/S
22	West	Honda	47m 26.645s	1m 27.281s	1m 33.722s	94.4mph	S/S
NC	Di Meglio	Ducati	37m 47.565s	6 laps	1m 33.567s	94.8mph	S/M
NC	Laverty E	Honda	36m 17.895s	7 laps	1m 33.500s	94.6mph	S/S
NC	Parkes	ART	33m 26.310s	9 laps	1m 34.359s	93.8mph	S/S
NC	Iannone	Ducati	3m 09.398s	28 laps	1m 31.491s	94.6mph	A/M

CHAMPIONSHIP

	Rider	Nation	Team	Points
1	Lorenzo	SPA	Movistar Yamaha MotoGP	330
2	Rossi	ITA	Movistar Yamaha MotoGP	325
3	Marquez	SPA	Repsol Honda Team	242
4	Pedrosa	SPA	Repsol Honda Team	206
5	Iannone	ITA	Ducati Team	188
6	Smith	GBR	Monster Yamaha Tech 3	181
7	Dovizioso	ITA	Ducati Team	162
8	Crutchlow	GBR	LCR Honda	125
9	Espargaro P	SPA	Monster Yamaha Tech 3	114
10	Petrucci	ITA	Octo Pramac Racing	113
11	Espargaro A	SPA	Team Suzuki ECSTAR	105
12	Viñales	SPA	Team Suzuki ECSTAR	97
13	Redding	GBR	EG 0,0 Marc VDS	84
14	Hernandez	COL	Octo Pramac Racing	56
15	Barbera	SPA	Avintia Racing	33
16	Bautista	SPA	Aprilia Racing Team Gresini	31
17	Baz	FRA	Forward Racing	28
18	Bradl	GER	Aprilia Racing Team Gresini	17
	Miller	AUS	LCR Honda	17
20	Hayden	USA	Aspar MotoGP Team	16
21	Pirro	ITA	Ducati Team	12
22	Laverty E	IRL	Aspar MotoGP Team	9
23	Nakasuga	JPN	Yamaha Factory Racing Team	8
	Di Meglio	FRA	Avintia Racing	8
25	Aoyama	JPN	Repsol Honda Team	5
26	Takahashi	JPN	Team HRC with Nissin	4
27	Elias	SPA	Forward Racing	2
	De Angelis	RSM	E-Motion IodaRacing Team	2

14 ALVARO BAUTISTA
Struggled with the front end when the tank was full but picked up pace and places in the second half.

15 SCOTT REDDING
Salvaged a point from what looked like a weekend of torture. After no grip or traction, the bike came to him in the second half of the race.

16 HECTOR BARBERA
Clinched the Open championship in front of his home-town crowd, and also finished as top Open bike for the eighth time this season.

17 NICKY HAYDEN
Was top Open bike for 27 of the 30 laps but asked a lot of his front tyre. The problem came from a big performance drop from the right side of the rear tyre.

18 STEFAN BRADL
Excellent qualifying and a good start, but front-brake problems led to Stefan using a lot of rear brake and over-stressing the rear tyre.

19 LORIS BAZ
Never had confidence with rear grip, or lack of it, and the bike didn't improve as the race went on.

20 TONI ELIAS
No confidence with the full tank, but then found himself dicing with di Meglio, Laverty and West, and was able to close up to his team-mate Baz before the flag.

21 JACK MILLER
Not a good race, but Jack was happy to point to the progress made in his rookie year since his first test at the Valencia track.

22 ANT WEST
Replaced Karel Abraham again but still used too much lean angle, as on a Moto2 bike (not surprisingly), and got through the tyres quickly.

DID NOT FINISH

MIKE DI MEGLIO
Crashed in Turn 5 when he had a problem with the throttle.

EUGENE LAVERTY
Right footrest burned his foot.

BROC PARKES
Didn't want to risk a crash when the bike started sliding, so retired.

ANDREA IANNONE
Crashed on lap three while pushing hard.

DID NOT RACE

KAREL ABRAHAM
Missed his final GP due to the effects of his foot injury from Catalunya.

ALEX DE ANGELIS
Recovering from his massive crash in Japan, but – amazingly – present and walking around the paddock.

I LIVE MY LIFE AT A 45-DEGREE ANGLE.

Dunlop tires are dedicated to real riders. Those who never give up and most of all, who enjoy the sheer passion and excitement of riding their bikes.
The Dunlop SportSmart^2 is made for them.
The Performance and confidence they'd expect on a racetrack, perfectly adapted for the road.

SPORTSMART^2

dunlopmotorcycle.eu

DUNLOP
FOREVER FORWARD

WORLD CHAMPIONSHIP CLASSIFICATION

MotoGP

#	Rider	Nation	Motorcycle	QAT	AME	ARG	SPA	FRA	ITA	CAT	NED	GER	INP	CZE	GBR	RSM	ARA	JPN	AUS	MAL	VAL	Points
1	Lorenzo	SPA	Yamaha	13	13	11	25	25	25	25	16	13	20	25	13	–	25	16	20	20	25	330
2	Rossi	ITA	Yamaha	25	16	25	16	20	16	20	25	16	16	16	25	11	16	20	13	16	13	325
3	Marquez	SPA	Honda	11	25	–	20	13	–	–	20	25	25	20	–	25	–	13	25	–	20	242
4	Pedrosa	SPA	Honda	10	–	–	–	–	13	16	8	20	13	11	11	7	20	25	11	25	16	206
5	Iannone	ITA	Ducati	16	11	13	10	11	20	13	13	11	11	13	8	9	13	–	16	–	–	188
6	Smith	GBR	Yamaha	8	10	10	8	10	11	11	9	10	10	9	9	20	8	9	6	13	10	181
7	Dovizioso	ITA	Ducati	20	20	20	7	16	–	–	4	–	7	10	16	8	11	11	3	–	9	162
8	Crutchlow	GBR	Honda	9	9	16	13	–	–	–	10	9	8	–	–	5	9	10	9	11	7	125
9	Espargaro P	SPA	Yamaha	7	–	8	11	9	10	–	11	8	9	8	–	–	7	–	8	7	11	114
10	Petrucci	ITA	Ducati	4	6	5	4	6	7	7	5	7	6	6	20	10	–	–	4	10	6	113
11	Espargaro A	SPA	Suzuki	5	8	9	9	–	–	–	7	6	2	7	7	6	10	5	7	9	8	105
12	Viñales	SPA	Suzuki	2	7	6	5	7	9	10	6	5	5	–	5	2	5	–	10	8	5	97
13	Redding	GBR	Honda	3	–	7	3	–	5	9	3	–	3	4	10	16	4	6	5	5	1	84
14	Hernandez	COL	Ducati	6	–	–	6	8	6	–	2	4	4	5	–	–	6	2	–	4	3	56
15	Barbera	SPA	Ducati	1	4	3	2	3	3	–	–	3	1	–	3	–	–	7	–	3	–	33
16	Bautista	SPA	Aprilia	–	1	–	1	1	2	6	–	2	–	3	6	1	3	–	2	1	2	31
17	Baz	FRA	Yamaha	–	–	2	–	4	4	3	1	–	–	1	–	13	–	–	–	–	–	28
18	Bradl	GER	Aprilia	–	–	1	–	–	–	8	–	–	–	2	–	–	–	–	6	–	–	17
	Miller	AUS	Honda	–	2	4	–	–	–	5	–	1	–	–	–	–	4	–	1	–	–	17
20	Hayden	USA	Honda	–	3	–	–	5	–	–	–	–	–	–	4	–	–	1	3	–	–	16
21	Pirro	ITA	Ducati	–	–	–	–	–	8	–	–	–	–	–	–	–	–	–	–	–	4	12
22	Laverty E	IRL	Honda	–	–	–	–	2	1	4	–	–	–	–	–	–	2	–	–	–	–	9
23	Nakasuga	JPN	Yamaha	–	–	–	–	–	–	–	–	–	–	–	–	–	–	8	–	–	–	8
	Di Meglio	FRA	Ducati	–	–	–	–	–	–	2	–	–	–	–	–	3	3	–	–	–	–	8
25	Aoyama	JPN	Honda	–	5	–	–	–	–	–	–	–	–	–	–	–	–	–	–	–	–	5
26	Takahashi	JPN	Honda	–	–	–	–	–	–	–	–	–	–	–	–	–	–	4	–	–	–	4
27	Elias	SPA	Yamaha	–	–	–	–	–	–	–	–	–	–	–	–	–	–	–	–	2	–	2
	De Angelis	RSM	ART	–	–	–	–	–	–	1	–	–	–	–	–	–	1	–	–	–	–	2

CONSTRUCTOR

#	Motorcycle	QAT	AME	ARG	SPA	FRA	ITA	CAT	NED	GER	INP	CZE	GBR	RSM	ARA	JPN	AUS	MAL	VAL	Points
1	Yamaha	25	16	25	25	25	25	25	25	16	20	25	25	20	25	20	20	20	25	407
2	Honda	11	25	16	20	13	13	16	20	25	25	20	11	25	20	25	25	25	20	355
3	Ducati	20	20	20	10	16	20	13	13	11	11	13	20	10	13	11	16	10	9	256
4	Suzuki	5	8	9	9	7	9	10	7	6	5	7	7	66	10	5	10	9	8	137
5	Aprilia	–	1	–	1	1	2	6	–	2	–	3	6	1	3	–	2	6	2	36
6	Yamaha Forward	–	–	2	–	4	4	8	1	–	–	1	–	13	–	–	–	2	–	35
7	ART	–	–	–	–	–	–	1	–	–	–	–	–	–	1	–	–	–	–	2

TEAM

#	Team name	QAT	AME	ARG	SPA	FRA	ITA	CAT	NED	GER	INP	CZE	GBR	RSM	ARA	JPN	AUS	MAL	VAL	Points
1	Movistar Yamaha MotoGP	38	29	36	41	45	41	45	41	29	36	41	38	11	41	36	33	36	38	655
2	Repsol Honda Team	21	30	–	20	13	13	16	28	45	38	31	11	32	20	38	36	25	36	453
3	Ducati Team	36	31	33	17	27	20	13	17	11	18	23	24	17	24	11	19	–	9	350
4	Monster Yamaha Tech 3	15	10	18	19	19	21	11	20	18	19	17	9	20	15	9	14	20	21	295
5	Team Suzuki ECSTAR	7	15	15	14	7	9	10	13	11	7	7	12	8	15	5	17	17	13	202
6	Octo Pramac Racing	10	6	5	10	14	13	7	7	11	10	11	20	10	6	2	4	14	9	169
7	LCR Honda	9	11	20	13	–	–	5	10	10	8	–	–	9	9	10	10	11	7	142
8	EG 0,0 Marc VDS	3	–	7	3	–	5	9	3	–	3	4	10	16	4	6	5	5	1	84
9	Avintia Racing	1	4	3	2	3	3	2	–	3	–	–	5	3	–	8	–	3	–	41
10	Forward Racing	–	–	3	–	4	4	11	1	–	–	1	–	13	–	–	–	2	–	39
	Aprilia Racing Team Gresini	–	1	–	1	1	2	6	–	2	–	5	6	1	3	–	2	7	2	39
12	Aspar MotoGP Team	–	3	–	–	7	1	4	–	–	–	–	–	4	–	3	3	–	–	25
13	E-Motion IodaRacing Team	–	–	–	–	–	–	1	–	–	–	–	–	–	1	–	–	–	–	2

Moto2-Worldchampion 2015

Thanks to all our riders, teams, partners, suppliers, employees and fans

Moto2™
CHAMPIONSHIP

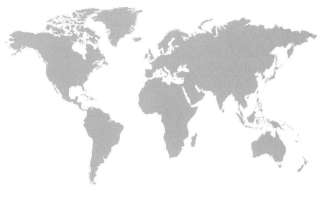

FLIPPING FRENCHMAN

Johann Zarco dominated the season in a way that shouldn't be possible

The point about a tightly regulated class is that it will produce close racing. If every rider has near-identical resources then it shouldn't be possible for any one rider to dominate the championship.

Frenchman Johann Zarco blew that theory out of the water this season. Riding an Ajo Motorsport Kalex, he won the title with three races to spare, having only twice failed to stand on the podium – and one of those occasions was due to getting stuck in gear at the first race of the year.

Zarco, now 25 years old, has always been fast but lacking in consistency, and given to the odd bit of flaky behaviour. He was the first-ever Red Bull Rookies champion back in 2007 and he came near to winning the last-ever 125cc championship in 2011, when he stood on the podium 11 times but won only once. It should have been more, but he contrived to throw away more victories, notably when sitting up before the line in Catalunya.

Three years in Moto2 followed, with half-a-dozen rostrum finishes on the increasingly uncompetitive Suter chassis before his old 125 team manager came calling. Aki Ajo wanted to add a Moto2 team to his other interests – as a Moto3 team manager and also the personal manager of several riders in other classes – and went back to his old employee. Bring in the ubiquitous Kalex chassis and you had the perfect set-up.

Zarco realised very quickly that Ajo was the missing piece in his jigsaw. He started the season with new-found confidence and the strength of that belief didn't waver until Aragón, when the championship was all but his.

For the first time Moto2 had a defending champion sporting the number-one plate, but Tito Rabat, who had

been nearly as dominant in 2014 as Zarco was in 2015, was one of several riders who had trouble coming to terms with the new Kalex chassis and Dunlop's new front tyre. Rabat's title defence got off to a stuttering start and he didn't win a race until Mugello, six rounds into the season. That took him to second place in the championship but injuries from training accidents ruined the second half of Tito's year.

With the help of WP suspension rather than the usual Ohlins, Zarco adapted his riding style to the new front tyre and was fast from the start of the season. Jonas Folger, on the other hand, won two of the first four races and then went AWOL.

The only non-Kalex rider to make any impact was Sam Lowes. In his second season in GPs on an Italian Speed Up machine, he lit up the year with his seriously

1 – QATARI GP

Practice and qualifying form suggested the smart money was on the top three qualifiers: Sam Lowes, Johann Zarco and Tito Rabat.

But then all three suffered misdemeanours in the race. Lowes' eagerness to stay with Zarco from the off was all too apparent as he hit a false neutral and tucked the front on lap three with the chasing Jonas Folger and Xavier Simeon already some 2.5 seconds in arrears.

Rabat was enduring his own kind of nightmare. Having dropped to eighth on lap one through a rare mistake, he was then shunted by Simone Corsi at Turn One, seconds after Lowes crashed. All this left Zarco four seconds clear for his first Moto2 win, until he suffered his own grim fate four laps from the end.

Exiting the final turn his gearshift lever broke, forcing the Frenchman to finish the race eighth while stuck in third gear.

All this left Folger free to collect his first GP win since the summer of 2012 by five seconds from Simeon. Thomas Lüthi narrowly fended off a late attack from class rookie Alex Rins to claim the final podium spot.

2 – AMERICAS GP

Sam Lowes went to the Moto2 grid from the Clinica Mobile following a huge FP2 highside crash that left him battered and bruised, but not so bad that it stopped him winning his first Moto2 race.

The Briton spent most of the race trying to get the better of Frenchman Johann Zarco and finally made it through with five laps to go. He eased away to win while Zarco fought hard with pole-starter Xavier Simeon; so hard that the pair collided, Zarco staying on while Simeon fell.

That gave rookie Alex Rins his first podium ahead of reigning champ Tito Rabat, who paid dearly for an early mistake.

'We had done a lot of work on old tyres during practice,' explained Lowes. 'On the slowdown lap I was in tears – this has been a long time coming.'

3 – ARGENTINIAN GP

Having already come so close in 2015, Johann Zarco made his pole position count and comfortably claimed his maiden Moto2 win. Continuing the form that saw him come within five laps of glory in Qatar, Zarco barged past second-place starter Tito Rabat to command the lead until the flag.

The move, at Turn Three, pushed Moto2 champ Rabat off track and to the back of the field in his third first-lap incident in as many races. A chasing group of Sam Lowes, Xavier Simeon, Mika Kallio and impressive rookie Alex Rins tried in vain to hunt down the Frenchman.

With Zarco maintaining around two seconds between himself and Lowes, the Englishman's focus shifted towards the advancing Rins behind him. The class rookie breezed by when Lowes mistakenly let him through, expecting to watch, learn and counter-attack. In fact he found himself unable to go with Rins.

Simeon crashed out of fourth, leaving Kallio to take the position ahead of impressive team-mate Franco Morbidelli.

4 – SPANISH GP

This was a tale of testosterone and tyres. The testosterone came from dynamic rookie Alex Rins, who was keen to continue his trend of bettering his last result by one, after taking fourth in Qatar, third in Texas and second in Argentina.

Tyres were the other factor as Rins and pole-man Tito Rabat chose the medium rear, while the rest of the top men chose soft, due to Sunday's cooler temperatures.

While Jonas Folger dominated the race after a Rabat error gifted him the lead, the real excitement came as the three men fighting over second approached the final hairpin for the last time. Rabat was fading, Rins had performed another late-race charge and Johann Zarco was right with them after coming through from 11th on lap one.

As Rabat swept into the corner he clipped Rins' front wheel and the Pons rider tumbled. That pushed Rabat wide, allowing Zarco to steal second place, just reward for his impressive comeback.

'When the tyre dropped it was difficult to adapt,' Folger said after his win, 'but in the end I was able to make a really constant race.'

5 – FRENCH GP

Ten years and two days after scoring his very first GP victory at the same track, Thomas Lüthi announced himself as a Moto2 championship hopeful with a commanding victory.

One second covered the first 18 riders in qualifying and the race was separated by equally fine margins. The huge crowd rose to its feet as local hero Johann Zarco stretched the field out in the first four laps from the front.

But, thanks to a post-Jerez test at Aragón, Lüthi had found a setting that allowed him to push from the start. He silenced the crowd by easing past Zarco on lap five, having pushed through to second from sixth on the grid three laps before.

Tito Rabat demoted the local hero to third with eight laps remaining, while Sam Lowes (the only front-runner to opt for Dunlop's softer rear tyre) closed on Zarco but the Frenchman held on for a podium finish. Pole-sitter Alex Rins crashed out of a six-rider scrap for fifth.

'At Aragón we found a good set-up,' said Lüthi. 'In the race I could push very aggressively from the start. I caught Johann and realised I could go faster.'

sideways style, taking pole position at the first race, then winning the second with the fastest lap. He also took pole at his team's home race and at the British GP. His year was impressive enough to secure a three-year contract with the Gresini team, for Moto2 in 2016 and then two years in MotoGP on the factory Aprilia.

Also in his second season, Franco Morbidelli looked another star for the future and took his first top-three finish at Indianapolis only to break his leg – training again – two races later. He'll be with the Marc VDS team in 2016 as Rabat moves up to MotoGP. Another young man who caught the eye was Italian teenager Lorenzo Baldassari, who, despite Forward Racing's problems, also took a maiden rostrum finish.

The other star of the season was Alex Rins, who was an even more impressive rookie than Maverick Viñales

ABOVE LEFT Takaaki Nakagami found some form in the second half of the season, making the rostrum at Misano

ABOVE Thomas Lüthi won once, at Le Mans; he took time to adapt to the Kalex after years on Suter chassis

LEFT Xavier Simeon took his first win in Germany but his only other top-three finish came in Qatar

6 – ITALIAN GP	7 – CATALAN GP	8 – DUTCH TT	9 – GERMAN GP	10 – INDIANAPOLIS GP
With the Renaissance city of Florence just a few miles away it was appropriate that Tito Rabat chose Mugello as the location of his championship renaissance. Few of his previous 149 GP starts carried as much importance after a title defence that had barely stuttered into life. Finally, in his 150th GP start he produced a performance worthy of his number 1 plate. Having seen Thomas Lüthi fall out of the lead on lap two, Rabat quickly disposed with surprise front-row starter Dominique Aegerter to hold a narrow lead. Meanwhile championship leader Johann Zarco muscled his way through to second and set about eradicating Rabat's 1.5-second lead. It was now that the reigning champion's experience came to the fore. Never showing signs of pressure, Rabat held his lap times as Zarco homed in. Even a personal best lap on the last lap from the Frenchman wasn't enough to stop the reigning champion claiming his first victory since Misano 2014. 'It was a tough race as I was having a few problems with the front in the last laps,' said Rabat	Moto2 had its best race in ages with three riders battling it out for the lead. In the end championship leader Johann Zarco won after steadily working his way through from fifth to bravely snatch the lead from reigning champion Tito Rabat on the last lap. Zarco held on for his second win of the year by 0.4 seconds from Alex Rins. Rins lost his chance of attacking Rabat when he ran wide on the penultimate lap and inherited second when Rabat also went wide with three corners to go. Rabat, winner in 2014, led most of the race after taking over from Sam Lowes. Lowes succumbed to Rabat and Rins to finish fourth, just 3.9 seconds down on the winner.	If the old adage of a championship being determined by the four races preceding the summer break rings true, another measured charge from Johann Zarco suggested that the Frenchman would end the nation's 15-year wait for an intermediate category champion. Qualifying set the precedent as the championship top three – Zarco, Tito Rabat and Sam Lowes – monopolised the front row. The race was shortened to 16 laps after the red flags came out following a fiery crash at Turn One. Jonas Folger was the surprise early leader as Rabat and Zarco scrapped for second. A close moment at Strubben on lap five forced the Frenchman wide and back to fourth. Initially this appeared to be decisive as Rabat caught and passed Folger but Zarco was forever homing in with Lowes close behind, slashing the one-second advantage to hover behind with three laps remaining. Four corners later and he pushed through and forged clear. 'In the final stretch I saw I had a stronger pace, so taking the lead and trying to escape was the best solution to get victory,' Zarco said.	The last Belgian to win a GP was Didier de Radigues – in the 1983 Belgian 250cc GP – so there were Belgian smiles all round when Xavier Simeon outfoxed runaway championship leader Johann Zarco to take the Moto2 race. Zarco led much of the way but couldn't resist Simeon's determined attack with four laps to go. 'It got hotter and hotter today so we decided to change the rear tyre at the last minute and that was the key,' said 25-year-old Simeon. 'At the end of the race I could push as hard as at the beginning.' Zarco finished less than a tenth behind Simeon but increased his points lead when reigning world champion Tito Rabat was scuttled by Franco Morbidelli at the final corner. That double tumble promoted rookie Alex Rins to third place ahead of Simone Corsi. Top non-Kalex was fifth-placed Speed Up rider Sam Lowes.	Rain peppered the grid before the intermediate race but the track dried sufficiently to ensure everyone started on slicks. Early leaders Hafizh Syahrin and Sam Lowes eventually fell by the wayside but this time Alex Rins made his pole position count, rising from fourth with five laps remaining to fend off points leader Johann Zarco for his début win in the class. Unfazed by his late error in Germany, Franco Morbidelli fought off Dominique Aegerter and Tito Rabat for his first GP podium, by a fraction of a second. 'When Zarco, Tito and Morbidelli passed me they were going strong,' said Rins. 'I changed my mentality and I went to the front and held it for the victory.'

RIGHT Alex Rins chases Aegerter at Misano before they came together and the Swiss rider crashed

OPPOSITE TOP Outgoing champion Tito Rabat produced a fitting finale with victory at Valencia to add to two wins earlier in the year

OPPOSITE BOTTOM Zarco was champion at Motegi before the race, but he won it anyway

BELOW The unmistakable style of Sam Lowes on his way to second place at Phillip Island

had been in 2014. Riding Sito Pons' Kalex, he was on the rostrum at the second race, pole at the fourth and won the tenth. Apart from one inexplicable piece of behaviour at Misano, Alex did everything in a calm, controlled way that marked him out as a MotoGP rider of the very near future.

It may not have been a closely fought year, but 2015 still delivered some great racing. The only real negative was the dominance of one make of chassis, but that was obscured by the willingness of Sam Lowes to go closer to the edge for longer than anyone else. Hopefully, Speed Up will have a few more bikes on the grid in 2016 on the strength of those performances. Johann Zarco will be staying with Aki Ajo to defend his title in 2016 (and the pair will probably be together in 2017 with KTM's new MotoGP team) so there will be more of those celebratory back-flips to admire.

11 – CZECH REPUBLIC GP

It's not often you see someone disappear into the distance during a Moto2 race – the rules were expressly written to stop that kind of thing from happening. But that's just what Johann Zarco did at Brno – he charged through from third at the start to grab the lead on lap two and never put a wheel wrong.

All the while he had reigning champ Tito Rabat and Alex Rins breathing down his neck, but he kept his nerve to cross the line 1.4 seconds ahead.

Alex Marquez, Marc's younger brother, had his best Moto2 ride in fourth, just 4.3 seconds behind the winner and well ahead of Sam Lowes, who was the first non-Kalex rider and charged through from 13th on the grid.

'I felt so good on the bike, so I could enjoy every corner and when Tito got close I could push some more,' said Zarco, who was now getting increasing interest from MotoGP teams.

12 – BRITISH GP

Johann Zarco put on an exhibition that equalled any performance of the day as he dominated Moto2.

The reworked race order had the intermediate class in action first, but as the track dried after the morning showers, the pack – on wet rubber – had to contend with a growing dry line. Zarco sat behind Alex Rins until lap seven to break clear of a six-rider dice that included Marc VDS Kalex team-mates Tito Rabat and Alex Marquez.

At times two seconds a lap faster than his pursuers, Zarco strolled to his fifth triumph of the year ahead of Rins and Rabat.

'When it got dry this was my chance and I was more comfortable than my rivals,' he said. 'With ten laps to go I tried to go away and I did it.'

13 – SAN MARINO GP

Johann Zarco's stroll to his first world title was robbing the intermediate category of drama. Such was the Frenchman's dominance that his 85-point pre-Misano advantage was the largest enjoyed by a rider in this class after 12 races, going all the way back to 1949.

While qualifying suggested that fellow front-row starters Alex Rins and reigning world champion Tito Rabat could provide stiff opposition, pole-man Zarco was never headed once Rins took out early leader Dominque Aegerter on lap six.

As Zarco built up a four-second advantage, slow-starting Rabat closed in on Takaaki Nakagami and Simone Corsi to claim second, three laps from the finish. Nakagami held on for his first podium finish in two years and later dedicated the result to his fallen friend Shoya Tomizawa, who died at Misano in 2010.

That could take nothing away from Zarco, whose celebratory back-flip was a regular fixture of the season.

'Rins' crash allowed me to take the lead,' Zarco said. 'I was able to relax and extend it, which was the perfect situation.'

14 – ARAGÓN GP

Shortened following an earlier pile-up, the Moto2 race turned into a straight duel between local heroes Tito Rabat and Alex Rins.

Rabat took the risk of using a soft rear for the restart, but Rins seized the initial advantage, leading the first half until Rabat sneaked ahead. From there Rins stayed put, saving his energy for a last-lap assault that nearly went his way. He got ahead on the downhill run, only for Rabat to counter-attack. The result was in doubt until the final turn, Rabat ahead by 0.096 seconds.

The reigning champ's second win of the year made the crown his for another few weeks because runaway title leader Johann Zarco could only manage sixth, at the front of a busy pack of four riders.

Austin winner Sam Lowes, the only non-Kalex rider in the championship top 12, took third on his Speed Up. It was his first podium since Assen.

15 – JAPANESE GP

Two days after being crowned Moto2 champion following Tito Rabat's withdrawal from the Motegi weekend due to a training accident, Johann Zarco underlined his dominance with a seventh victory in tricky damp conditions.

Zarco was incomparable in the 15-lap race (shortened from 23 laps due to a late start to the day caused by poor weather), taking the lead on the fifth lap from Jonas Folger. The German gave chase but could never match the pace of the newly crowned champ and crossed the line 4.5 seconds down.

With Zarco and Folger well ahead, interest centred on a thrilling duel for the final podium place between former Moto3 champion Sandro Cortese and Azlan Shah. Eleventh on the first lap, Cortese aggressively chased down his Malaysian rival, passing him on the penultimate lap for his first podium of 2015.

The pair were closely followed over the line by Hafizh Syahrin, Ricky Cardus, Simone Corsi, Sam Lowes, Marcel Schrotter and Randy Krummenacher.

CHAMPIONSHIP STANDINGS

	Rider	Nat	Team	Motorcycle	Points
1	Johann Zarco	FRA	Ajo Motorsport	Kalex	352
2	Alex Rins	SPA	Paginas Amarillas HP 40	Kalex	234
3	Tito Rabat	SPA	EG 0,0 Marc VDS	Kalex	231
4	Sam Lowes	GBR	Speed Up Racing	Speed Up	186
5	Thomas Lüthi	SWI	Derendinger Racing Interwetten	Kalex	179
6	Jonas Folger	GER	AGR Team	Kalex	163
7	Xavier Simeon	BEL	Federal Oil Gresini Moto2	Kalex	113
8	Takaaki Nakagami	JPN	IDEMITSU Honda Team Asia	Kalex	100
9	Lorenzo Baldassarri	ITA	Forward Racing	Kalex	96
10	Franco Morbidelli	ITA	Italtrans Racing Team	Kalex	90
11	Sandro Cortese	GER	Dynavolt Intact GP	Kalex	90
12	Simone Corsi	ITA	Forward Racing	Kalex	86
13	Luis Salom	SPA	Paginas Amarillas HP 40	Kalex	80
14	Alex Marquez	SPA	EG 0,0 Marc VDS	Kalex	73
15	Mika Kallio	FIN	QMMF Racing Team	Speed Up	72
16	Hafizh Syahrin	MAL	Petronas Raceline Malaysia	Kalex	64
17	Dominique Aegerter	SWI	Technomag Racing Interwetten	Kalex	62
18	Julian Simon	SPA	QMMF Racing Team	Speed Up	58
19	Axel Pons	SPA	AGR Team	Kalex	41
20	Marcel Schrotter	GER	Tech 3	Tech 3	32
21	Randy Krummenacher	SWI	JIR Racing Team	Kalex	31
22	Ant West	AUS	QMMF Racing Team	Speed Up	30
23	Azlan Shah	MAL	IDEMITSU Honda Team Asia	Kalex	24
24	Ricard Cardus	SPA	JPMoto Malaysia	Suter	20
25	Louis Rossi	FRA	Tasca Racing Scuderia Moto2	Tech 3	7
26	Tomoyoshi Koyama	JPN	NTS T.Pro Project	NTS	3
27	Yuki Takahashi	JPN	Moriwaki Racing	Moriwaki	2
28	Robin Mulhauser	SWI	Technomag Racing Interwetten	Kalex	1

16 – AUSTRALIAN GP

While the first and third races of the day had you chewing your fingernails down to the bone, the Moto2 was more drawn out. Tito Rabat was partly to blame, after crashing heavily on Friday and deciding to rest his injured arm until Valencia, but newly crowned champion Johann Zarco was also responsible because he never found feeling from his front tyre.

But mostly it was the fault of pole-man Alex Rins, who put tyre concerns to one side to dominate. Could this be a sign of things to come in 2016? Once past early leader Sam Lowes, Rins steadily built up a six-second lead to cruise to his second win in the class.

Lowes then had to deal with the advancing Thomas Lüthi, who had superior speed but was using more of his Dunlop rubber in the process. The pace soon told as Lüthi ran off track at MG hairpin, falling on the grass, giving Lorenzo Baldassarri his maiden top-three finish.

'It wasn't easy to keep the focus but I'm so happy,' said Rins. 'I want to try and keep this same mentality, because now I have more experience than earlier in the year.'

17 – MALAYSIAN GP

Johann Zarco called upon reserves of strength he hadn't previously known existed. Twice he appeared beaten in the punishing heat, as race-long leader Thomas Lüthi only occasionally showed signs of wilting.

The lead hovered between 0.6s and 1.0s for the majority of the race, until Zarco made his final push with three laps to go. By then Lüthi had used up all his edge grip and was powerless as Zarco shot beneath him for his eighth win of the year.

'I figured that if I stuck to him it would be the two of us fighting for first and second place and that was how it ended up,' said Zarco.

Phillip Island winner Alex Rins couldn't keep up in the early stages, then lost the front on lap ten. Having pressured Rins from the start, Jonas Folger inherited the final podium slot.

18 – VALENCIAN GP

Outgoing Moto2 champ Tito Rabat made a heroic return from a broken arm with his 13th win in the class, just days before embarking on his MotoGP career.

The Spaniard dominated the race – restarted after an earlier multiple crash – and fought off some serious pressure from top rookie Alex Rins. Finally Rins relented, aware that third place would be good enough to give him second overall in the championship ahead of Rabat, who had missed the previous three races due to injury.

Rabat crossed the finish line three tenths of a second ahead, with Thomas Lüthi a further three seconds back. Lüthi had been second in the early stages but didn't have the pace to resist Rins, then had his hands full dealing with the very real threat of the up-and-coming Lorenzo Baldassarri, who he bettered by less than three tenths.

Sam Lowes was a comfortable fifth to secure fourth overall in the championship behind champ Johann Zarco, who lacked the feeling to find his usual speed.

An unmissable line up on BT Sport

Free for our BT TV Customers

To check availability visit bt.com/sport
or call 0800 201 2201

BT Sport

BT Sport on BT TV requires min. line speed - check bt.com

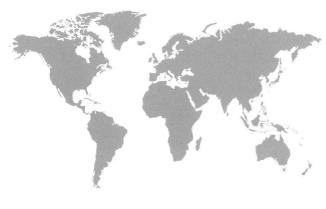

AT LONG LAST

Danny Kent became the first British world champion for 38 years, but he stretched his fans' nerves to breaking point

It was the proverbial game of two halves. Danny Kent and his Leopard Honda dominated the first half of the season but, once the KTM factory brought its revised chassis into play at Misano, Miguel Oliveira didn't finish lower than second.

Kent won six of the first 12 races, with Silverstone his final victory of the season, in front of home fans. Until that point he had looked nigh-on unbeatable. Even when the weather conspired to put him on the back of the French grid, he managed to ghost his way at will through some intense Moto3 group lunacy to finish fourth. He displayed that magic knack of all champions, being in the right place on track at the right time, and he made it look effortless.

After Silverstone, Kent appeared to have a crisis of confidence and his 70-point championship lead was whittled away. Danny's lowest point came at Aragón when a last-lap highside out of a certain rostrum position made it look as if he was feeling the strain. Then the mathematics started to look decidedly dodgy after he also crashed out of the Australian GP, this time thanks to a racing incident.

Meanwhile, Oliveira, who had already become the first Portuguese rider to win a Grand Prix, had been overhauling fast young Italian Enea 'The Beast' Bastianini to take up the role of title challenger. When both Kent and Bastianini appeared to become distracted by off-track issues around their futures, Oliveira took full advantage.

On the new, less rigid KTM chassis, Oliveira won three out of four races from Aragón to Malaysia and went to the final round still in with a chance of the championship. He now looked as infallible as Kent

RIGHT Danny Kent leads Fabio Quartararo, Miguel Oliveira and Brad Binder early in the season

BELOW Alexis Masbou won the first race but, like team-mate John McPhee, then suffered a variety of problems and didn't get back on the rostrum again

had done in the first half of the season and British fans were getting nervous; you can understand why when you consider that Miguel had been 110 points behind Danny after Silverstone. Oliveira rounded off the season with three consecutive wins to equal Danny's total of six wins and his similar feat of three wins on the trot (from Texas to Jerez).

At the Valencia finale, Danny needed two points to secure the title while Miguel needed to win with Danny 15th or lower. Both men did what they had to. Danny stayed out of trouble and came home safely in the points. Miguel won superbly. The gap was only six points in the end, perhaps reflecting accurately the performance of both the main players, who will be team-mates in Moto2 in 2016.

Behind Kent and Oliveira, who are both already in their 20s, some quick teenagers emerged from the pack. Spaniard Jorge Navarro was rookie of

1 – QATARI GP

Gone were 2014's leading trio of Alex Marquez, Jack Miller and Alex Rins but the class of 2015 ensured they wouldn't be missed. Class veteran Alexis Masbou took only his second GP win with a perfectly timed last-lap attack, a day after claiming his first pole in his 141st GP.

Early favourite Miguel Oliveira crashed out on the first lap but that did little to dull the spectacle. Halfway through the 18 laps a freight train of 17 contested the podium places. Chief among them were rookie extraordinaire Fabio Quartararo and Italian starlet Enea Bastianini, recovering from a dismal seventh start.

As Efren Vazquez began the final lap in front, Quartararo's inexperience showed, the Frenchman running himself and Francesco Bagnaia wide at Turn Five. That left Bastianini free to scythe under Vazquez before Masbou, who started the lap eighth, out-dragged him to the line to win by 0.027 seconds. Danny Kent's last-corner move sealed the final podium spot and demoted Vazquez to fourth.

2 – AMERICAS GP

There's no rule that says you can't win a Moto3 race by almost nine seconds, but there may as well be because it never usually happens. But on a track that was still damp in parts from earlier rain, Leopard Honda's Danny Kent took off, leaving the pack to scrap over the crumbs.

After several of his pursuers had slid off – most notably Niccolò Antonelli and Miguel Oliveira – the battle for the final podium places came down to six men: Alexis Masbou, Fabio Quartararo, Enea Bastianini, Efren Vazquez (Kent's team-mate), Brad Binder and John McPhee. In the end it was Quartararo and Vazquez who made the box, but only just, while Masbou slid off at the final turn.

'My plan was to follow the others for the first few laps to see where the damp patches were, then I made my move,' said Kent.

3 – ARGENTINA GP

In 2014 there were 13 Moto3 podiums settled by half a second or less. Three races into 2015, however, Danny Kent seemed intent on making a mockery of his opposition. For the second race in a week he destroyed the 34-rider field, his winning margin of 10.3 seconds the biggest dry-weather advantage in Moto3 history.

While main opponents Niccolò Antonelli and Jorge Navarro collided and crashed on lap five, Kent set about putting one second a lap into the chasing pack of 17. Pole-sitter Miguel Oliveira continued his flaky start to life as a factory KTM rider by fading and only later regaining his pace to contest runner-up spot.

Joining him was Efren Vazquez, Isaac Viñales and a stream of 11 others as the latter's devilish late-braking prowess at Turn Five was repeatedly outdone by Vazquez at Turns 12 and 13. In the end Vazquez made it stick, nudging Viñales into third by 0.06s.

'I've never felt a feeling like that before in my whole career,' said Kent. 'This weekend has been a replica of how it was in Austin, maybe even stronger.'

4 – SPANISH GP

The first race of the day was billed as a straight shoot-out between pole sitter and class rookie Fabio Quartararo and Danny Kent, winner of the previous two races. In fact both had Red Bull KTM Ajo runners Miguel Oliveira and Brad Binder, and later Kent's team-mate Efren Vazquez, to contend with as they treated the crowd to an absorbing five-way fight.

In the final laps Vazquez, still suffering the after-effects of a virus, dropped back, leaving the front four to jostle for position. Exiting the penultimate turn Oliveira held the advantage, but not for long. Kent braked late on his inside, but not as late as Quartararo. With both wheels out of line, the 16-year-old looked like he would take down all three riders until he miraculously found the space to stand his bike up and run off track. That left Kent clear to take his third successive win by 0.09s from Oliveira with Binder third.

'Fabio went to pass me and Oliveira and we were quite lucky to stay on the bike,' said Kent. 'It was a good fight because in the last few races I've been able to pull away.'

5 – FRENCH GP

Saturday's lunchtime deluge caused chaos in Moto3 qualifying. Rain began falling minutes into the session, just as Danny Kent went out to set a time. He qualified 31st.

Kent's charge enlivened the race as he made dazzling progress through the pack while French pole-sitter Fabio Quartararo took on an all-Italian leading gaggle that included a rejuvenated Romano Fenati, Francesco Bagnaia and Enea Bastianini.

A leading group of eight grew by one as Kent caught them on lap 15. Three laps later the group split into two when Quartararo's youthful exuberance saw him highside out.

Now four fought for the win. Fenati, emboldened by set-up changes that allowed him to get on the gas earlier, drafted past Bagnaia on the run to Turn One for the final time. From there he held on for KTM's first win of 2015 as Bastianini, a lowly qualifier in 18th, outbraked both Bagnaia and Kent to take second on an all-Italian podium.

'The start of the season was difficult because the bike's performance was less but today it was perfect,' grinned Fenati.

FAR LEFT For the strangest race of the year, at Indianapolis, Livio Loi was the only man to start on slicks – and he won

LEFT The nearly-men of 2015: Enea Bastianini, Niccolò Antonelli and Brad Binder share the rostrum at Brno

BELOW Romano Fenati, who was a model of inconsistency, leads in France from Bastianini, a crashing Quartararo and Bagnaia on his way to Mahindra's only rostrum of the year

the year with a pole position and four rostrums in the last five races. Italian Niccolò Antonelli stopped crashing and took two wins, two poles and two fastest laps after the summer break. Frenchman Fabio Quartararo got two rostrums in the first half of the year but the rest of his rookie season was littered with too many crashes.

If there was a disappointment, it was that the Mahindras couldn't quite match the Hondas and KTMs. Francesco Bagnaia's single rostrum, front-row start and fastest lap are all the factory has to show for its season. Hopefully, they will find the fractional improvement necessary to be competitive in 2016. Britain's other representative, John McPhee, had a difficult season with a team that exhibited signs of corner cutting, but the Scot nevertheless scored a rostrum and a pole position, and will be back for 2016.

6 – ITALIAN GP	**7 – CATALAN GP**	**8 – DUTCH TT**	**9 – GERMAN GP**	**10 – INDIANAPOLIS GP**
This Moto3 encounter posed the question: who needs outright speed when you have the slipstream? Pole sitter Danny Kent was a full 0.2s fastest in qualifying and 0.7s in morning warm-up. But that came when lapping alone.	This was another group brawl, like Mugello, with nine riders at it until some fell off the pace and others just fell off. By the final few laps the battle was between five men, chopping and changing places every other corner.	This was a race-long game of Russian roulette, but with seven barrels in the chamber instead of six. The battle skirted the fine line of disaster as the leading group switched back and forth through the sixth-gear Ramshoek left-hander, four or five abreast.	Series leader Danny Kent once again performed his magic disappearing trick to take the biggest win of the day in the closest GP class. The Briton took the first few laps to get into the groove on his Leopard Honda and then quickly left his pursuers way behind to score his fifth win from nine races and extend his series lead to 66 points.	Sunday's rain hit Indy before the first race of the day, so all but one of the Moto3 grid completed the sighting lap on wets, the exception being Belgian Livio Loi in a distant 26th on the grid.
History didn't serve him well when he spoke of intending to break clear as he had done in Texas and Argentina – since 2004 the biggest small-class winning margin at Mugello had been just 0.21s!	With two laps to go championship leader Danny Kent was at the back of the group but once again he proved himself master of mêlée. The Briton stayed out of trouble, used the draft, saved his tyres and let his rivals do the work until it was time to use his tactical nous to be in the right place at the right time. You only need to lean on one lap.	As at Mugello, Red Bull KTM's Miguel Oliveira led most of the laps but he was never given a moment's rest as the Estrella Galicia Hondas of Fabio Quartararo and Jorge Navarro joined Danny Kent, Enea Bastianini, Romano Fenati and Brad Binder in giving chase.	'I didn't make a great start, then I struggled a bit with the tyres, having one moment with a big slide in Turn 12,' said Kent. 'Anyway, from that point the tyres got better so everything went according to plan.'	Front-row men Danny Kent and Miguel Oliveira told their crews they would pit for slicks after lap one because the track was drying rapidly.
And so it proved. Kent, Romano Fenati and Miguel Oliveira regularly sat at the front of a train – at times 16 riders deep – that refused to let anyone escape. Oliveira jumped eight places to lead on lap nine and from there he led all but one lap, his KTM's improved agility catapulting him out of the crucial final corner, giving him enough of a margin to lead across the line.	So Kent took the lead on the last lap to cross the line 0.035s ahead of Enea Bastianini, Efren Vazquez, Niccolò Antonelli, Miguel Oliveira and Jorge Navarro.	Oliveira blinked latest through Ramshoek on the final lap as the gaggle behind aimed and fired this way and that. Kent sought to challenge the Portuguese rider as the chicane approached, only for Quartararo to put the gun to his own head with a do-or-die move. Just 0.06s ahead at flag, Oliveira headed the Frenchman and Kent to claim his second victory in three races.	Team-mate Efren Vazquez took second, chased hard by a wild gang of seven riders fighting for the final spot on the podium. On the final lap it was Enea Bastianini who muscled past Romano Fenati to claim third place, with just six tenths of a second covering the group down to ninth place.	Efren Vazquez and impressive first-timer Lorenzo Dalla Porta led the early laps but soon Loi's slicks came to the fore, as those around him pitted for dry tyres. By lap six John McPhee was second, with Philipp Oettl, who had started from pitlane with slicks, 10 seconds behind in a topsy-turvy top ten that at one point had only six riders on the same lap as the leader.
That looked in jeopardy the final time around, however, as Fenati, Francesco Bagnaia and Kent barged past, but Oliveira wasn't going to let his first GP win go easily and he picked off the men in front to beat Kent by 0.071s and become Portugal's first-ever GP winner.		'After warm-up I didn't know if I could win but I tried to believe in myself,' Miguel said. 'I had a good strategy and in the final braking move I defended my position.'		So Loi ran out the winner while McPhee and Oettl completed the podium positions. 'My team manager told me on the grid, "You're the only one on slicks, the first laps will be difficult",' said Loi. 'But I didn't listen to him – I just went for it.'

RIGHT It's Australia, and Miguel Oliveira leads from Fenati and Vazquez, with Kent behind

OPPOSITE TOP John McPhee had a tough season but rallied at the end of the year, setting pole at Valencia

OPPOSITE BOTTOM He made us wait, but Danny Kent got there at the final round

BELOW Enea Bastianini was fast until contractual squabbles distracted him from the job in hand

For his Moto2 season in 2016, Danny Kent will be staying with the same team, which means that, vitally, he will continue to work with his Dutch race engineer Peter Bom, who played such an important part in Danny's season. That continuity gives Danny the best chance possible as a rookie in a class that will have talent in great depth, including the defending champion Johann Zarco.

Yes, it was close, but Britain has a Grand Prix champion for the first time in nearly 40 years. The last British champion was Barry Sheene in the 500cc class in 1977, and to find the last British winner in the lightweight class you have to go all the way back to 1969 and Dave Simmonds, Kawasaki's first world champion, in the old 125cc class. Despite the nerves that affected the second half of his season, Danny shows every sign of being able to wear his crown lightly. Barry – and Dave – would approve.

11 – CZECH REPUBLIC GP

Rossi protégé Niccolò Antonelli won a typically manic Moto3 race, which had the first eight riders cross the line covered by just 1.1 seconds. Not only was it the 17-year-old's first win, it was also his first podium.

The race – shortened to 12 laps after a first corner pile-up and restart – turned into a ten-man brawl at the front, riders trading places at every corner. Antonelli made his move with two laps to go and stayed just far enough ahead to prevent fellow podium men Enea Bastianini and Brad Binder from attempting a last-lap lunge.

Championship leader Danny Kent had his second bad race in a row. After failing to score at Indy – following a lengthy pit stop to change tyres – he found himself near the back of the lead group in seventh. In two races his series advantage over Bastianini had shrunk from 66 to 45 points.

12 – BRITISH GP

In the last race of the day held in worsening conditions, Britain's Danny Kent chased early leader Isaac Viñales until the Catalan fell at the treacherous Turn Three, a corner that also claimed pole-sitter Jorge Navarro on the first lap.

From there, the championship leader eased clear of Jakub Kornfeil. Apart from one out-of-the-seat moment three laps from the flag, Kent cruised home eight seconds clear of Kornfeil, who took his first GP podium.

Niccolò Antonelli took advantage of Aspar Mahindra's Francesco Bagnaia's late spill to collect a second consecutive podium while Kent's principal title challenger Enea Bastianini fell while dicing for sixth on the penultimate lap, handing Kent a near-unassailable 70-point championship lead.

'You're never safe in conditions like that,' said Kent. 'It was the longest race of my career, but it was probably my best. If there's one race on the calendar that you want to win, it's your home Grand Prix.'

13 – SAN MARINO GP

The first victory for Enea Bastianini, one GP racing's brightest talents, will live long in the memory.

The race was no easy affair, the 17-year-old having to work throughout the 23 laps to hold on to and then overtake long-time leader Miguel Oliveira and then, in a nail-biting last lap, resist the Portuguese rider's advances.

In the early laps the lead group was seven-men strong, but later only Brad Binder, Romano Fenati and Niccolò Antonelli stayed with the leader.

By then Leopard Honda's Efren Vazquez had crashed out, while team-mate Danny Kent was told to drop a position and thus out of contention after repeatedly running wide and exceeding the track limit beyond the kerbs.

Bastianini made the decisive move at Curvone six corners from the flag, while Antonelli held off Fenati for his third consecutive podium finish.

'It was the greatest thrill of my life,' beamed Bastianini. 'After having missed the win so many times, to get it here in Misano is a great feeling.'

14 – ARAGÓN GP

The Aragón Moto3 race was proof that you never knows what's going to happen in a motorcycle race until it happens. This was a typical madcap Moto3 encounter, with ten leaders chopping and changing at every other turn, with all eyes on title leader Danny Kent and main rival Enea Bastianini, who were both in the thick of it.

Every podium position was in doubt until the final chicane, where Bastianini rammed second-placed Brad Binder, taking them both out and leaving race leader Miguel Oliveira a clear run to victory.

But the drama wasn't over. The double tumble promoted Kent to third, behind Jorge Navarro, to increase his already comfortable points advantage over Bastianini. However, riding through the fast, final curve, Kent had a nasty highside – and so his title lead remained unchanged at 55 points.

15 – JAPANESE GP

The first race of the day got underway on a soaking track, 19-year-old Italian Niccolò Antonelli immediately seizing the initiative and working hard in the early laps to build an unbeatable advantage.

As the shortened race went on, Miguel Oliveira piled on the pressure to reduce the gap to just 1.053 seconds at the flag. Third-placed Jorge Navarro came from 13th to finish 8.5 seconds down on the winner.

After falling at the last corner at Aragón, championship leader Danny Kent rode an intelligent race. Swamped in the early stages, he was 16th for the first couple of laps, but kept a cool head to work his way through the pack, eventually passing title rival Enea Bastianini on the last lap for sixth place.

CHAMPIONSHIP STANDINGS

	Rider	Nat	Team	Motorcycle	Points
1	Danny Kent	GBR	Leopard Racing	Honda	260
2	Miguel Oliveira	POR	Red Bull KTM Ajo	KTM	254
3	Enea Bastianini	ITA	Gresini Racing Team Moto3	Honda	207
4	Romano Fenati	ITA	SKY Racing Team VR46	KTM	176
5	Niccolò Antonelli	ITA	Ongetta-Rivacold	Honda	174
6	Brad Binder	RSA	Red Bull KTM Ajo	KTM	159
7	Jorge Navarro	SPA	Estrella Galicia 0,0	Honda	157
8	Efren Vazquez	SPA	Leopard Racing	Honda	155
9	Isaac Viñales	SPA	RBA Racing Team	KTM	115
10	Fabio Quartararo	FRA	Estrella Galicia 0,0	Honda	92
11	John McPhee	GBR	SAXOPRINT RTG	Honda	92
12	Jakub Kornfeil	CZE	Drive M7 SIC	KTM	89
13	Alexis Masbou	FRA	SAXOPRINT RTG	Honda	78
14	Francesco Bagnaia	ITA	MAPFRE Team MAHINDRA	Mahindra	76
15	Philipp Oettl	GER	Schedl GP Racing	KTM	73
16	Livio Loi	BEL	RW Racing GP	Honda	56
17	Jorge Martin	SPA	MAPFRE Team MAHINDRA	Mahindra	45
18	Karel Hanika	CZE	Red Bull KTM Ajo	KTM	43
19	Andrea Migno	ITA	SKY Racing Team VR46	KTM	35
20	Andrea Locatelli	ITA	Gresini Racing Team Moto3	Honda	33
21	Hiroki Ono	JPN	Leopard Racing	Honda	29
22	Niklas Ajo	FIN	RBA Racing Team	KTM	21
23	Zulfahmi Khairuddin	MAL	Drive M7 SIC	KTM	19
24	Juanfran Guevara	SPA	MAPFRE Team MAHINDRA	Mahindra	15
25	Lorenzo Dalla Porta	ITA	Husqvarna Factory Laglisse	Husqvarna	13
26	Jules Danilo	FRA	Ongetta-Rivacold	Honda	12
27	Stefano Manzi	ITA	San Carlo Team Italia	Mahindra	10
28	Tatsuki Suzuki	JPN	CIP	Mahindra	9
29	Maria Herrera	SPA	Husqvarna Factory Laglisse	Husqvarna	9
30	Remy Gardner	AUS	CIP	Mahindra	6
31	Nicolò Bulega	ITA	SKY Racing Team VR46	KTM	4
32	Manuel Pagliani	ITA	San Carlo Team Italia	Mahindra	3
33	Matteo Ferrari	ITA	San Carlo Team Italia	Mahindra	1

16 – AUSTRALIAN GP

If Danny Kent felt that securing his first world title was a mere formality after his only serious challenger, Enea Bastianini, qualified 29th, he was very much mistaken. The year's most chaotic race saw Kent narrowly escape disaster when Francesco Bagnaia crashed behind him at Honda Hairpin on lap ten, the Mahindra pushing the Englishman off-track.

In a frantic rush to retrieve positions, Kent collided with Niccolò Antonelli on the exit of the Southern Loop. This time Kent crashed and brought down Bastianini.

That left a frantic six-way scrap for the win, Miguel Oliveira inching clear of Efren Vazquez on the final lap to win. Oliveira's team-mate, Brad Binder, was third in a top five covered by two tenths of a second. The Portuguese rider's fourth win of the season maintained his slim title hopes, 40 points behind Kent.

'I wanted to go into the last lap in second and I got good slipstream on the straight,' Oliveira said. 'That enabled me to start the last lap with a little gap which I was able to defend very well.'

17 – MALAYSIAN GP

Nearing the end of the Moto3 race, Danny Kent was moments from winning the world championship. Starting the last lap, he sat fifth in a seven-rider train, just behind Miguel Oliveira, the only man who could prolong Britain's 38-year wait for a GP title. Hold the position and the title would be his. Easy.

Not so. For this wasn't the Danny Kent who dominated the start of the year. Until the final exchanges, Kent had ridden like a man with the weight of the world on his shoulders. Sixteenth at the close of lap two, he gradually made his way towards the leading group.

By then, Oliveira was watching over the pack, plotting his final move with the kind of seasoned control you'd expect of a potential champion. His last-corner move on team-mate Brad Binder to win while Kent was shuffled back to seventh showed how one man's confidence had faded and the other's grown.

'I didn't see any info on my board about Danny so I forgot about him and went for the victory,' said Oliveira, who went to the final round 24 points in arrears with 25

18 – VALENCIAN GP

Danny Kent could hardly have made his last-gasp chance to take the Moto3 title any more nerve-wracking. The man who needed to finish 14th to take the crown if on-form Miguel Oliveira won the race qualified way down in 18th, leaving him with a mountain to climb.

In the early stages while Oliveira battled for the lead, Kent languished in the midst of Moto3's nest of vipers, trading 13th and 14th places. As Oliveira seemed to take control out in front, Kent moved up to 11th, but he was still far from safe.

In the final laps Oliveira was just ahead of local rider Jorge Navarro, Efren Vazquez and Romano Fenati, with Brno winner Niccolò Antonelli closing rapidly. At the final corner Antonelli got over-excited, his attack going awry: the Italian teenager fell, taking Vazquez and Fenati with him. That put Oliveira, Navarro and Jakub Kornfeil on the podium, while Hiroki Ono cheekily overtook team-mate Kent in the closing moments of the race.

But Kent's ninth place was good enough to make him Moto3 champion. He certainly did it the

RED BULL ROOKIES
PETER CLIFFORD

Winning five races in a row is a pretty good way to start any championship season. With the resulting huge points advantage, Bo Bendsneyder could have relaxed somewhat and taken the easy road to claim the 2015 Red Bull MotoGP Rookies Cup. But racers are racers.

Tall and good looking with an easy smile, the 16-year-old Dutchman has an easy nature but, as with all winners, that hides his fierce competitiveness. He was determined to take that sixth win in a row. It was Race 2 at the Sachsenring and he was going for his third double. Into the last corner Bendsneyder tailed 16-year-old Italian Fabio di Giannantonio and went outside for the drive up the hill, but the front tyre slid and he couldn't catch it. His victory run was over.

That didn't stop Bendsneyder taking the Rookies Cup but di Giannantonio mounted a great challenge. Bendsneyder secured the title with two races to spare when di Giannantonio slid off – his second fall of the season – as the pair battled for the win at Misano. Like Bendsneyder, di Giannantonio carried himself with a level of professionalism and sportsmanship that some of those in the MotoGP class would have been wise to emulate.

It was another fine year for the Rookies Cup, which has proved to be an excellent *entrée* into GP racing. Former Rookies won both the Moto3 and Moto2 titles in 2015, and they made up 40 per cent of the season's Moto3 entry (50 per cent if Spanish and Italian riders are excluded).

So with plenty to shoot for, the current Rookies fought through every corner as usual. If Bendsneyder and di Giannantonio were the 'old

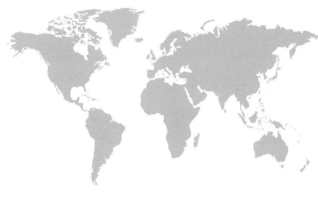

FAST AND FURIOUS

One young Red Bull Rookie dominated like never before – have the Netherlands found the star they've been looking for?

LEFT Bo Bendsneyder doing what he did all year in the Red Bull Rookies Cup – leading. This is San Marino

INSET Bendsneyder celebrates his title – the amount of orange on his crash helmet is a clue to his nationality

hands', both in their second Rookies Cup seasons, there were plenty of new guys who weren't just learning but were threatening too.

Ayumu Sasaki, the 14-year-old Japanese rider, was on the pace even at the pre-season test and almost made it to the podium the first weekend in Jerez. Sasaki was second in Race 1 at the Sachsenring, then won Race 2 at the soaking wet Silverstone. That was an atypical race in that Sasaki trailed 18-year-old Frenchman Enzo Boulom as the pair drew away from the field by almost half a minute. After 10 of the 12 laps, Sasaki knew everything necessary about the lack of grip and where he had the edge over Boulom, and he eased ahead for a great maiden win. Bendsneyder was a careful third while a good number slid off; di Giannantonio struggled home, 11th of only 13 finishers.

That left di Giannantonio a steep hill to climb with only three races remaining and a 52-point deficit as he headed to his home race at Misano, where he had to finish in front of Bendsneyder. He gave it everything. After struggling with bike settings in qualifying, he was ninth on the grid but soon hunted down Bendsneyder in the race, but it wasn't a fairytale home event as he slid off on lap 11. However, di Giannantonio had taken the fight to Bendsneyder again and was satisfied with that, at least publicly. On the podium again was Sasaki in third with another young star ahead of him, Raúl Fernández. The 14-year-old Spaniard was a further great find of the season and backed up his Misano result with another second in Race 1 at Aragòn.

The hero of the final round in Spain was yet another first-year Rookie. Rory Skinner, the 13-year-old Scot, struggled to get in the points early in

the season but put together a year of steady yet impressive progress to take pole at the final event by a quarter of a second over newly crowned champion Bendsneyder. He then led 11 of the 23 racing laps on Saturday and Sunday, picking up two third places. Fernández was sixth in the final race while di Giannantonio scored a great consolation win, robbing Sasaki on the line. Bendsneyder was ninth, limited by a wrist injury from a multi-bike crash on Saturday. The crash put Alex Viu in hospital with hip and foot injuries but the 14-year-old Spaniard soon stated his determination to join Fernández, Skinner and Sasaki in chasing the 2016 crown.

Viu's best result was fifth in Race 1 at Misano but he improved through the year and is very likely to feature in 2016, the tenth year of Rookies Cup. The competition will certainly be in good hands with Marc Garcia, the 15-year-old Spaniard who finally got his first win in Race 1 at Aragòn, going into his third season after finishing fourth overall in the 2015 Cup, 10 points behind Sasaki.

Obviously not everyone comes away from the Cup with what they wanted as there's only ever one winner and some very talented riders miss out. An example is Olly Simpson. This was his third Cup season and with two third places in Jerez his year started well. An early fall in Assen injured his shoulder and though he only missed that weekend the momentum was lost and his results didn't reflect his obvious talent.

For Bendsneyder, though, it was an almost perfect season. He left the Cup to join the Red Bull KTM Ajo factory team in Moto3 for 2016 with a record number of eight wins from 13 Cup races in 2015.

MOTORRAD GRAND PRIX VON ÖSTERREICH 2016

12.08.2016 – 14.08.2016

projekt-spielberg.com

RIDERS FOR HEALTH
BARRY COLEMAN

THE BEST MEDICINE

Barry Coleman, co-founder of Riders for Health, reports on the MotoGP charity's invaluable work during the Ebola crisis

By the time of Day of Champions this year (and the related event, the British Grand Prix) you had more or less stopped hearing about Ebola. Just as well. The disease – a virus that causes the internal organs to disintegrate extremely rapidly and painfully and takes you swiftly and biblically to the point of no return – is nasty in every imaginable way. Not least because it spreads quickly and efficiently and takes out whole communities before they can prepare themselves to do anything about it.

Or it used to. There is now a whole handbook of 'things we learned about Ebola this time around'. And among the things learned was that no country can afford to have any areas that are too remote or too isolated to be reached by health-care professionals – but that's something Riders for Health have always known. It's 25 years since we set up our first programme with a ministry of health in Africa. That was in Lesotho, before it was ravaged by HIV-AIDS, and we and the MoH already knew about the health dangers of isolation. In those days we were helping to offset the impact of poor sanitation and the occasional outbreak of bubonic plague.

During the course of the 25 years, quite a few people in positions of authority in the global health industry have seen the point of Riders' enabling health professionals to reach communities with health care, especially health care of the preventive kind – the kind that stops outbreaks of things like Ebola in the first place. We are now operating in eight countries.

A couple of years ago we were summoned to Liberia to talk to its ministry of health about putting in place a fleet-management system for motorcycles and all other useful vehicles so that the whole country could be reached routinely and predictably. It was a good visit and the

AFTER EBOLA: RIDERS IN LIBERIA

In 2015 Riders officially opened a brand-new programme in Liberia – helping to rebuild the country's health system and put reliable transport at its heart. Already we are reaching over four million people. In less than a year we have:

- Set up a motorcycle courier system that covers the entire country. Now 70 motorcycle couriers are transporting around 3,500 specimens each month between health centres and laboratories.
- Trained 329 vehicle drivers and 70 motorcycle riders.
- Begun building six workshops across Liberia.
- Trained 32 mechanics to maintain motorcycles and four-wheel-drive vehicles.

outcome was positive. Riders would put in place a new system, to be run by Liberians. And a few months later Ebola hit.

The Riders replication team (experts from our programmes across Africa and the UK) went anyway. Their first task was to set up a system for transporting blood samples for analysis (and action). The system meant that the Ebola virus could be detected quickly and those affected could be isolated and treated. It was difficult but effective and Liberia was the first of the three affected countries to be declared (for now) Ebola-free.

This is a good time to repeat my yearly message, my annual mantra: no sport other than MotoGP has ever given rise to a humanitarian movement.

And this is indeed the Riders story – a story like no other.

If you were at Day of Champions this year (and if not, why not?) you won't have noticed anything at all about how it ran. But the fact was that we had lost our beloved Jeanette (Wragg), who, from the beginning, had made DoC happen. And what that meant was bringing about something that otherwise just couldn't happen. Just between us, our stars can be a little, well, self-important at times. But not with Jeanette they weren't. Her very heavily disguised wish was their command and they did things for Jeanette that their sponsors or even their factories wouldn't have dreamed of asking for. They were horrified when Jeanette died, especially Bradley, whom Jeanette had known from childhood, and especially Valentino. But they all were.

25 YEARS IN MotoGP

This year saw the 25th anniversary of one of the biggest and best events on the MotoGP calendar – Day of Champions at the British MotoGP. It's our chance to show MotoGP fans how motorcycles are saving lives across Africa and to raise funds for our life-saving work.

The very first Riders for Health Day of Champions took place in 1990 at Brands Hatch and was the brainchild of Riders co-founders Andrea and Barry Coleman, Jeanette Wragg and racing legend Kenny Roberts.

Roberts was able to persuade the great racers of the day, such as Eddie Lawson, Wayne Rainey and John Kocinski, to take part, and they were joined, of course, by Riders' co-founder Randy Mamola, who has played a crucial role in the event ever since.

Day of Champions was born in the MotoGP paddock, and thanks to support from Dorna and the various race circuits and teams over the years, it has stayed there ever since. It's now one of the largest charity-led outdoor fundraising events in the UK and attracts over 4,000 visitors every year.

The 2015 Day of Champions turned out to be a record-breaker. The stars and fans of MotoGP raised over £100,000 during the now-famous Riders for Health auction – the most we've ever achieved.

And we were breaking records elsewhere too. Nearly 400 fans attended our MotoGP Paddock Experience Days –

held before the Spanish and Dutch GPs – and our competition to meet Valentino Rossi at the Valencia race raised a record sum.

After 25 years, the teams, riders and fans of MotoGP haven't failed us. The people in the MotoGP paddock are still as important as ever to the work of Riders for Health – together we're keeping health care moving and changing lives across Africa.

Now we of little faith expected the worst – a DoC without Jeanette the Enforcer in the paddock. It could only be chaos. But we should have known. The riders were perfect. Out of respect and love for Jeanette and the work of Riders for Health, they behaved like choirboys. They were wonderful. The whole MotoGP paddock were wonderful – they rallied around to ensure that we put on a good show in honour of Jeanette.

Those two things: the grip on Ebola and the support and belief of our own unique and beloved sport. That day, before the gates opened, we said goodbye to Jeanette with a little ceremony in which balloons floated away into a blue sky. Well, we sort of said goodbye but we knew she was watching us, like a beady-eyed little hawk. As she always will.

What a day.

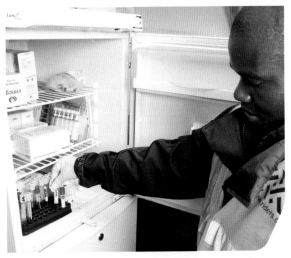

OPPOSITE Some of Riders' work is educational – this is an HIV support group meeting in Kenya

THIS PAGE The swift collection and analysis of samples is important at the best of times, but when dealing with something as virulent as Ebola it's utterly vital

OFFICIAL BEER

GO WHERE THE OTHERS
HAVE NEVER BEEN BEFORE

SINGHA - THE OFFICIAL SPONSOR OF MotoGP™ WORLD CHAMPIONSHIP

Drink sensibly